GREEK AND ROMAN MYTHOLOGY A TO Z

A Young Reader's Companion

Kathleen N. Daly

Facts On File
New York • Oxford

Greek and Roman Mythology A to Z: A Young Reader's Companion

Facts On File, Inc.
460 Park Avenue South
New York NY 10016

Library of Congress Cataloging-in-Publication Data
Daly, Kathleen N.
  Greek and Roman mythology A to Z : a young reader's
companion.
      p.   cm.—(Mythology A to Z)
  Includes bibliographical references and index.
  Summary: Presents the gods, goddesses, heroes, places, and
other aspects of Greek and Roman mythology in alphabetically
arranged entries.
  ISBN 0-8160-2151-1 (alk. paper)
1. Mythology, Classical—Encyclopedias, Juvenile. [1. Mythology,
Classical—Encyclopedias.] I. Title. II. Series: Daly, Kathleen
N. Mythology A to Z.
BL715.D26   1992
292.1'3'03—dc20   91-43037

A British CIP catalogue record for this book is available from the
British Library.

Facts On File books are available at special discounts when
purchased in bulk quantities for businesses, associations,
institutions or sales promotions. Please call our Special Sales
Department in New York at 212/683-2244 or 800/322-8755.

Text design by Ron Monteleone
Jacket design by Catherine Hyman
Photo research by Elyse Rieder
Composition and manufacturing by the Maple-Vail Book
  Manufacturing Group
Printed in the United States of America

10 9 8 7 6 5 4 3 2

This book is printed on acid-free paper.

CONTENTS

INTRODUCTION

WHAT IS MYTHOLOGY?

From earliest times man has had a need to explain to himself the origins and wonders of the world around him: the mountains and the oceans, the changing seasons, the earthquakes and storms, volcanoes, floods, the existence of animals, including mankind. Early man, in every culture on earth, made up stories about these phenomena and invented gods and supernatural beings to comfort and instruct himself. And sometimes, people such as the Greeks made up stories just for the fun of it; for example, the story of PYGMALION and Galatea explains nothing in nature or science, but it's a good story, still told today in George Bernard Shaw's play *Pygmalion* (1913) and later adaptations of the play such as the musical and the movie *My Fair Lady.*

As the ages passed, and tribes shifted from place to place, broke up, regrouped, increased in size and migrated to different climes, they brought their stories with them. As the stories, or myths, were passed on they changed with the language, climate and local folklore of the people. Eventually men erected shrines and temples to their gods and heroes. They prayed to them for help, made sacrifices to them and celebrated them with festivals. In some countries, such as early Egypt, current rulers took on the status of divinities. The early pharaohs (kings) who built the pyramids and temples of Egypt that still stand today were looked upon as gods. Thus was religion born of myth, and religions and rulers became part of history. That is why, in Greece, we find temples built in honor of ZEUS, ATHENE, APHRODITE and other gods and goddesses. Their names live on in place names, in people's names and in history, for the people who worshiped the divinities firmly believed that they had once lived upon earth.

In the early mythologies of most cultures, women were the supreme gods. The Earth Mother was the creator of new life. She was also the moon or sun goddess who ruled the skies, the seasons and the harvests. As eons went by, it was discovered that the male, as well as the female, was necessary for the procreation of the species. The Earth Mother and moon goddess were gradually replaced by male sky- and sun-gods, often typified by bulls or rams. The queen-mother's decline is typified in Greek mythology by the attitude of Zeus toward his sister-wife, HERA. He was a mischievous, unfaithful and disrespectful husband. His indiscretions and Hera's anger may reflect the conservative religious feeling (personified by Hera) against marriages or other liaisons (those of Zeus) between the new Hellenic chieftains and the local moon-priestesses and nymphs.

Other stories were invented to explain new developments such as the introduction of grain cultivation, the making of bread and of wine (see under DIONYSUS), and the breeding of domestic goats, pigs, and cattle.

THE GREEKS: WHERE DID THEY COME FROM?

Greek mythology is extremely old: The Great Mother was worshiped in 2000 B.C., in the land that we now call Greece. Early invaders from Aeolia and Ionia (Asia Minor) brought with them an early form of Indo-European language and the worship of Aryan sky-gods. They settled peacefully in Thessaly and central Greece and intermarried with the natives.

Next came the more destructive and aggressive waves of what Homer called the Achaeans and Dorians, tribes from the north. These people who arrived on the scene were not peace-loving: for example, in Sparta (the southern Peloponnesus) they enslaved the entire native population, using them to perform menial tasks. The Achaeans called these slaves Helots. The Achaeans spoke a dialect of ancient Greek and used a simple type of picture-writing scholars now call Linear B.

While savages and barbarians inhabited what we now call Greece, there was already a flourishing civilization on the island of Crete, which lies to the south of Greece. Crete had long been trading with the even more ancient civilizations of Egypt and the East. It had reached its height in about 1600 B.C., and was known as the Minoan culture when it reached Greece, and later, as the Mycenaean culture, named after Mycenae, the town in Argolis that was its center. In 1400 B.C. the Minoan civilization collapsed, probably due to a natural phenomenon such as an earthquake, whereupon the Greeks took over Crete and adopted Cretan mythology.

We find many instances of Cretan myths in Greek stories, such as those of the upbringing of the god Zeus in Crete, the story of EUROPA and the bull and the MINOTAUR who was vanquished by THESEUS. However, the ancient divinities gradually took on the aspect of the invaders of Greece, so that what we know about the ancient Aegeans is really very little.

The Greek myths, as we know them, came from all over ancient Hellas: Thrace, Boeotia, Attica, the Peloponnesus, Argos and Mycenae, and many of the islands, including, of course, Crete, and also from Asia Minor and places farther afield, such as Babylon and Sumeria. HOMER, whose work may be that of several poets writing between about 1000 and 800 B.C., is considered the "supreme source," and the "triple fountain" (the best sources of mythology), was thought to be Troy, Thebes and Mycenae.

GREEK MYTHOLOGY

Greeks were the first people to create gods and goddesses that looked like real human beings: beautiful men and women, old people with humor and dignity, splendidly natural animals (as well as a few monsters). Not for the Greeks were the mysterious sphinxes or frightening images of human bodies with heads of animals. All the art and all the thought of Greece centered on human beings and human feelings.

Further, the Greek gods and goddesses usually had their homes and birthplaces in towns and countries that are still familiar: Mount Ida,

on the island of Crete, where the god ZEUS was brought up, exists to this day; the hero HERACLES had his home in the city of Thebes; the exact spot where the goddess APHRODITE emerged from the sea can be pointed out near the island of Cythera; the winged horse Pegasus had a stable in Corinth; and Mount Olympus, the home of the gods, still stands in Thessaly, as does Mount Parnassus, in Phocis, where DEUCALION's ark came to rest after the Flood.

Greek mythology was peopled by heroes who vanquished their enemies by superior wit. Odysseus, for example, was said to have thought of the wooden Trojan horse, inside which were hidden invading Greek soldiers. (See under ODYSSEUS.) Greek intelligence went much further than clever strategy. The Greeks had a clear-eyed curiosity about themselves and all creation. The playwright SOPHOCLES (496–406 B.C.) said, "Wonders are many and none is more wonderful than man." And Herodotus (c. 480–425 B.C., the Greek historian) said, "Of old, the Hellenic (Greek) race was marked off from the barbarians as more keen-witted and more free from nonsense."

THE GREEK CREATION MYTH

All creation myths the world over have a certain similarity to each other, in that they explored the efforts of early man trying to explain to himself the origin of the earth, the sun, the moon and the stars, and the creatures of earth, including men and women.

The best-known Greek creation myth is the one told by the renowned poet HESIOD (some time in 800 B.C., after HOMER). It tells of the original CHAOS, a swirling, formless mass, from which came GAIA, Mother Earth, and her son-consort, URANUS, the heavens. These two created all the animals and vegetation that covered the earth. They also created the TITANS, the one-eyed CYCLOPES and other monsters that Uranus banished underground.

Uranus was eventually ousted by his son, CRONUS. From Cronus and RHEA were born the 12 who would become the Olympians, the great Greek pantheon of gods and goddesses.

HOW TO USE THIS BOOK

The entries in this book are in alphabetical order and may be looked up as you would use a dictionary. A list of the chief characters of Greek mythology follows just below. If you search out the entries concerning these characters, you will get a general overview of Greek (and therefore of Roman) mythology. Cross-references to other entries are printed in SMALL CAPITAL LETTERS. The Index at the rear will also help you to find your way around this book.

THE OLYMPIANS The gods and goddesses who lived atop Mount Olympus, in Greece, were called the Olympians. The king and queen of the gods were ZEUS and HERA.

ZEUS Zeus was the son of TITANS: He was primarily a sky- and weather-god, with the thunderbolt as his emblem, but his presence was inescapable throughout Greek mythology. Zeus shared the world with his brothers POSEIDON and HADES. Although HERA, his sister, was also his wife, Zeus had many other loves and sired many children, including APOLLO and ARTEMIS, HERMES, ARGOS, PERSEUS, DIONYSUS and others.

HERA An ancient goddess, existing long before the time of the migrations and the new gods, including Zeus. She was the protector of women, children and marriage. Her cult was so strong that the newcomers had to acknowledge it and absorb it into their own mythology by making Hera the consort of Zeus.

POSEIDON The god of seas and of horses, and the cause of earthquakes ("The Earthshaker"). In ancient times, long before the appearance of Zeus, Poseidon was worshiped as a god of fertility and of herdsmen. His symbol, the three-tined trident, was a symbol for the thunderbolt.

DEMETER The goddess of fertility and the mother of PERSEPHONE, who was carried off to the UNDERWORLD by HADES. The winter months were dark and unfruitful, for that was when Persephone went underground. (See *Demeter and Persephone*, under DEMETER.)

HADES The ruler of the dead and of the Underworld. Since he didn't live in Olympus, his qualifications as an Olympian are in dispute but as a brother of Zeus and Poseidon, he was a powerful force among the Olympians.

ATHENE A goddess of war, but also a patroness of the arts and crafts; she was the goddess of wisdom, and the patron goddess of the city of Athens. (See *Athene and Poseidon*, under ATHENE.)

APOLLO The only god to have the same name in both Greek and Roman mythology. He had many functions: he was the god of poetry, music, archery, prophecy and the art of healing. He was a sun-god of great antiquity, just and wise and of great beauty.

ARTEMIS The sister of APOLLO, goddess of the hunt and of beasts, of childbirth and of chastity. She is usually depicted with a bow and arrows.

HEPHAESTUS The god of fire and of craftsmen, especially the smiths who worked in metal. He was known as "the divine artificer." Hephaestus was lame and not as handsome as the other gods. Nevertheless, he was married to the beautiful APHRODITE, goddess of love, and was able to punish her for her unfaithfulness in a most subtle way. (See *Ares and Aphrodite*, under ARES.)

APHRODITE The goddess of love, Aphrodite was born of the sea foam that swirled around the flesh of URANUS, that had been cast into the sea. She was married to the smith-god, HEPHAESTUS, but had many other loves. She is often depicted with the infant EROS.

DIONYSUS A Greek fertility god of very ancient origin. Attended by the SATYRS (half-man, half-beast, the spirits of wild life) and MAENADS (mad women), he was famous for his frenzied festivities.

HERMES The winged messenger of the gods, Hermes was also the god of merchants and thieves, of roads, of flocks and of luck.

HESTIA The goddess of the hearth and the fire within it. There are few myths about this gentle goddess, though she was much loved.

Other gods and spirits of land and sea included HELIOS, a sun-god. Four winged horses drew his chariot across the sky each day. He was identified with APOLLO and also with SOL, a Roman god. His consort was Rhodos, after whom the island of Rhodes is named. SELENE was an ancient goddess of the moon. She too was drawn across the sky in a chariot pulled by white horses. She loved a youth named EN-DYMION.

ASCLEPIUS A god of medicine and healing. His emblem was the caduceus (a wand with a snake wound about it). According to legend, he learned the art of healing from the gentle CEN-TAUR, CHIRON.

PAN A very ancient deity from the mountains of Arcadia. He was a god of herds and flocks, fertility and wildlife. He is usually depicted as half-man, half-goat and playing the SYRINX (or Pipes of Pan) with magical effect on those that heard him.

CENTAURS Wild creatures, half-man, half-horse. They were begotten by the mortal IXION and the goddess HERA, who produced a son, CENTAURUS. Centaurus then mated with the wild mares of Thessaly and the Centaurs were born. They were wild, lusty and drunken, except for the gentle CHIRON. Chiron was the teacher and guardian of ACHILLES, JASON, HER-ACLES and other Greek heroes.

EROS A god of love, Eros was often depicted as an infant in the company of the love-goddess, APHRODITE.

The NYMPHS were young and beautiful spirits of nature. Generally kind to men, they could also be mischievous.

The HARPIES were birdlike creatures with the faces of women. They embodied violent winds, strong enough to snatch people away, and were greatly feared. They appear in the story of the ARGONAUTS.

GREEK TRAGEDIES
Apart from the epic hero-stories of Homer's ILIAD and ODYSSEY and Virgil's AENEID, and the various stories about the gods and goddesses, there are many other stories memorable in Greek mythology. Some are love stories. Some are fertility stories. Many are tragic stories about men and women who could not escape their fate. The Greeks believed in destiny. They knew that man could not escape his fate, no matter what: No matter that THETIS, the mother of ACHILLES, dipped her baby in the magical waters of the river STYX to protect him from danger; she held the baby by the heel, and it was in that unprotected heel that Achilles received a fatal wound.

OEDIPUS Even though he didn't know his real parents, Oedipus managed to kill his father and marry his mother, just as prophesied, in spite of a lifetime spent trying to avoid this destiny.

ORPHEUS A fine musician and poet, he sailed with the ARGONAUTS, and later married EURYD-ICE, who died of a serpent bite. Orpheus tried to rescue her from the UNDERWORLD but disobeyed the orders of HADES (by looking back to see that Eurydice was following him) and so lost her forever.

PELOPS His story involves one tragedy after another for several generations, thanks to the curse of the charioteer MYRTILUS (see *Pelops and the Charioteer*, under PELOPS). It includes the tragedies of King AGAMEMNON and all his family.

AGAMEMNON The king of Mycenae and the leader of the Greek armies that went to Troy to avenge the capture of HELEN, his sister-in-law. The story of Agamemnon's family relates one tragedy after another. When Agamemnon came back from the war he was murdered by his jealous wife, CLYTEMNESTRA, as was CAS-SANDRA, a princess of Troy taken by Agamemnon as one of his spoils of war.

IPHIGENIA The daughter of AGAMEMNON and CLYTEMNESTRA. The king sacrificed his daughter to the wind-god, Aulis, to gain a favorable wind to Troy. Her death incurred the wrath of Clytemnestra.

ELECTRA and ORESTES The surviving daughter and son of AGAMEMNON and CLYTEMNESTRA avenged their father's death by killing their mother and her lover, AEGISTHUS.

FERTILITY STORIES

Other Greek stories concern the changing of the seasons and the death and resurrection of vegetation, a theme common to all mythologies the world over. The abundance of animals, including birds, insects and fish, was and is of utmost importance to all people, but especially to our ancestors who relied on the bounties of nature for their day-to-day survival. Fertility stories include those of DEMETER and PERSEPHONE (see *Demeter and Persephone*, under DEMETER). Demeter was one of the OLYMPIAN GODS. Her daughter Persephone was carried off to the UNDERWORLD by HADES. She was forced to stay underground for four months of the year. She personified the months of flowering and fruitfulness that disappeared in the winter months.

In the story of ADONIS and APHRODITE, the handsome Adonis was the beloved of the love-goddess. Adonis had been reared by Persephone, queen of the Underworld, who also loved him. Adonis spent half his time with Persephone (this period represents the dark winter months) and half above ground with Aphrodite (the time of warmth and fruitfulness).

In yet another fertility story, ATTIS was a vegetation-god, beloved of the great Earth-Mother, CYBELE. Cybele turned him into a pine tree and his spirit went to the UNDERWORLD. After a period of mourning, Attis returned from the Underworld, only to be killed again at the end of the fruitful season, thus personifying the corn that grows anew each year, is harvested (killed) and then reappears again the next year.

THE HEROES

Finally, but most important, are the heroes. A recurring pattern in the hero stories is that of a young man who goes on a journey or quest; he is set a number of tasks and in the end wins the hand of a princess or inherits a kingdom or both.

HERACLES The hero of heroes, Heracles was portrayed as a muscular he-man, using brawn rather than brain. The goddess HERA afflicted the youth with madness that brought on murderous rages, for which he was punished by having to perform the Twelve Labors (see *The Twelve Labors of Heracles*, under HERACLES), seemingly impossible tasks that he executed bravely.

JASON Most famous for his quest for the GOLDEN FLEECE (see *Jason and the Argonauts*, under JASON), Jason built the ship ARGO and recruited 50 extraordinary people (the ARGONAUTS) to sail with him on his search. With the help of the witch MEDEA, he succeeded in his mission.

THESEUS The hero of Athens, Theseus was most famous for slaying the MINOTAUR, a creature half-bull and half-man, that lived in the LABYRINTH of King Minos of Crete.

PERSEUS This hero slew the GORGON, MEDUSA, who turned men into stone, and rescued ANDROMEDA from a sea-monster.

Other heroic tales concern ASCLEPIUS, ODYSSEUS, AENEAS and the heroine ATALANTA, who killed the Calydonian Boar.

Homer's epic poem the ILIAD tells of the siege and capitulation of Troy; the ODYSSEY tells of the homeward voyage of one of the heroes, Odysseus.

THE ROMANS

Rome, which became one of the world's largest and most successful empires, famous for law-giving, material and cultural achievements, was a small, pastoral community when Greece was at its height.

The Romans' forbears, called Latiums, were simple folk, living in close-knit clans, but trading and intermarrying with other clans. For centuries they had been overrun by tribes from the north: first were the Ligurians, who originally came from North Africa and settled around the land still called Liguria, near Genoa. In the third millennium B.C. came the *terramara*, people who lived in stilt-houses and brought with them the art of making bronze artifacts and also weapons, which ensured them military supremacy. In the 11th century B.C. came the Villanovans (named after a small town, Villanova, near Bologna, in northern Italy).

The next wave of invaders were more civilized than the earlier ones: They were the Etruscans, who arrived early in the first millennium B.C. They could not only write (a skill hitherto unknown in Italy), but they were also skilled in metalwork, sculpture, painting and good living. Nobody knows exactly where the Etruscans came from (possibly from Asia Minor), but it seems certain that they had had close contact with Greek culture and had helped spread it abroad.

Historians note with interest that the Romans were already sophisticated and discerning enough to adopt only those Etruscan mores that they thought would be useful to them. For instance, they eagerly embraced the idea of building temples to the deities (for an increasingly urban population, a temple was the logical place to worship, much better than the rocks and turf traditionally set up in a field). They also accepted the idea of divination (that is, the art of foretelling the future, often by means of animal sacrifice). The Romans were already a superstitious but cynical people; the idea that the future could be influenced by magic rituals, including sacrifices, and the casting of spells, fit in very well with their native shrewdness and practicality.

From the point of view of mythology, perhaps the most important factor was the introduction of the Etruscan pantheon—a collection of 12 deities, whom the Romans came to identify with the 12 Olympians of Greece.

The Romans, like all peoples, already had their gods: three chief gods (JUPITER, MARS, QUIRINUS) and lots of "household gods," such as TERMINUS and Cloacina. The Romans were practical people, not given to fantasizing about the family lives of their gods. Indeed, they seldom gave them names, let alone lifelike representations such as the later statues and paintings. The Romans paid homage to their gods, in return for which they expected protection, prosperity, fertility, good health and so on.

Jupiter was of humble origin. In fact he started out his mythological life as a lump of stone, Jupiter Lapis. The worship of stones goes back to neolithic times (the Stone Age) or before, when knives and ax-heads were made from flint stones. Even in the Bronze Age, Jupiter continued to be worshiped as a terrifying flint figure.

Mars, who became assimilated with the Greek god of war, ARES, was at first worshiped as a god of fields and crops as well as a god of war. In early societies, agriculture went hand-in-hand with war: the time for war was when the crops had been harvested and next year's growth did not need tending; the men were free to go to war between autumn and spring. In the temperate northern hemisphere, March (named after Mars) was the ideal month for war.

Quirinus, the third god of the Roman triad, was also a war-god, probably of Sabine origin. He has almost no mythology, and later became assimilated with Mars.

As for the minor Roman gods and goddesses (numina), there was one for almost every situation, including Cloacina, who presided over sewers; Febris brought fever; Robigus was the god of rust and mildew. There were household gods (lares and penates) who presided over the hearth and pantry. But these godlings didn't enter into mythology, any more than did the elves and goblins of other folklore.

However, as time went by, and Rome developed from being a pastoral community to a great imperial empire, the Romans felt a need to have a pantheon as grand and as human as that of the Greeks. And, being practical, they shrewdly assimilated their gods with those of the Greeks. As mythologist Stewart Perowne says, "It was Julius Caesar (? 102–44 B.C.) who realized that what the fledgling Roman nation needed was a pedigree. The Romans had plenty of gods but no mythology. Their godlings, for example, VENUS, were nobodies. But once assimilated with the divine APHRODITE, Venus became a goddess worth having."

Greek gods were different from Roman gods. Greek gods were like human beings, only bigger and better and more beautiful. Roman gods were often inhuman creatures, such as VULCAN, who was feared and placated as the god of fire. There was no mythology for Vulcan—he was a tough Roman craftsman and that's all we know. When he became assimilated with the Greek god HEPHAESTUS (known affectionately as "the divine artificer"), Vulcan was endowed with a wife and various attributes culled from Greek mythology.

Jupiter took on the glory of Greek ZEUS, and was worshiped in Rome as Optimus Maximus (the Best and Greatest). Temples and statues were erected to Jupiter and his consorts, JUNO and MINERVA. Juno, originally a very ancient moon-goddess, became assimilated with HERA. Minerva became assimilated with the Greek ATHENE. No Roman counterpart was found for APOLLO, so he retained the same name in both Greek and Roman mythologies.

ROMAN NAMES	GREEK NAMES
Gods:	
Jupiter	Zeus
Neptune	Poseidon
Mars	Ares
Apollo	Apollo
Vulcan	Hephaestus
Mercury	Hermes
Goddesses:	
Juno	Hera
Minerva	Athene
Diana	Artemis
Venus	Aphrodite
Vesta	Hestia
Ceres	Demeter

THE CULTURAL IMPACT OF GREEK AND ROMAN MYTHOLOGY

Authors and artists through the centuries have eagerly looked to the Greek and Roman mythologies for inspiration for countless works of art, from the early Greek classicists such as Euripides, Aeschylus and Sophocles (all born between 525 and 480 B.C.), to later artists such as Botticelli (A.D. 1444–1510) (painter of *The Birth of Venus*), the builders of the Parthenon, in Athens, the sculptors of renowned works of art such as the Venus de Milo and the Winged Victory (the Greek goddess of Victory, Nike) to be seen in the great museums of the world. Today's science-fiction movies, such as *Star Trek* and *Star Wars*, also have their heroes and heroines and villains who go on seemingly impossible quests, just like the Argonauts of old, and come back triumphant. And, like the an-

cient Greeks and Romans, today's writers and creators tend to think of the gods of the universe as being akin to human beings rather than supernatural and mysterious beings.

Indeed, the most remarkable facet of the Greek (and later, Roman) characters who populate the myths is that they are so human, so much like us, that reading about them helps us to explore and try to understand the world around us. For example, we can look at the role of destiny in our lives (see ACHILLES and his heel and OEDIPUS and his unfortunate relationships with his parents); the benefits of using intellect rather than brute force (see under ODYSSEUS and the TROJAN HORSE); the tangled and often tragic relationships that exist among families (see under PELOPS); the power of learning (see CHIRON); the inescapable forces of nature, embodied in mythological characters such as DEMETER and PERSEPHONE, ADONIS and APHRODITE, ATTIS and CYBELE.

From the marvelous epic poems of HOMER (in the ILIAD and the ODYSSEY) came the flowering of Greek drama, an art whose roots went back to the Bronze Age and beyond. The content of Greek drama was mythology, found in the vast collection of epics and poems of Homer, his contemporaries and successors. Homer's works were engraved on the heart and mind of every Greek, it is said. The adventures and dilemmas of the characters in the myths mirror every kind of human situation and force people to face the fact that the world we live in is full of ambiguities: there is good and bad, kind and cruel, tragic and amusing.

All over Greece, the poetry was sung to an audience (it was not yet written down for the solitary reader). Gradually, the art of acting (with one, then several people playing various roles) developed into the sophisticated theater that we know today.

Another effect of Homer's poems was profound: They served to unify the Greeks, who were widely scattered over the Aegean and Asia Minor, and to preserve and affirm the tales of vigorous action along with heroic sacrifice. In fact the Homeric works played a role in the ultimate emergence of Ionian as the universal language of the Greek world, the language we now call Greek.

Through the networks of trade the Greeks learned from other cultures how to enrich their own artistry. In Egypt they saw how monumental figures could be hewn out of hard stone, instead of wood and limestone. From other cultures they learned how to cast bronze, which allowed the artist greater flexibility than carving marble. Potters developed new ways of decorating vases and other vessels that differed from city to city. These decorations depicted vivid scenes of contemporary life that give us insight into the day-to-day life of the Greeks of the period.

Apart from drama, poetry, art and architecture, our legacy from the Greeks and Romans includes thousands of words that we use every day (*uranium*, from URANUS; *Saturday*, from SATURN; *January*, from JANUS; *typhoon* from Typhoeus; *martial* and *March* from MARS; *volcano* from VULCAN; *panic*, from PAN; and thousands of others). These words go back directly to the myths. In such ways do the lively ghosts of the ancient Greeks and Romans still walk among us, a part of our cultural heritage.

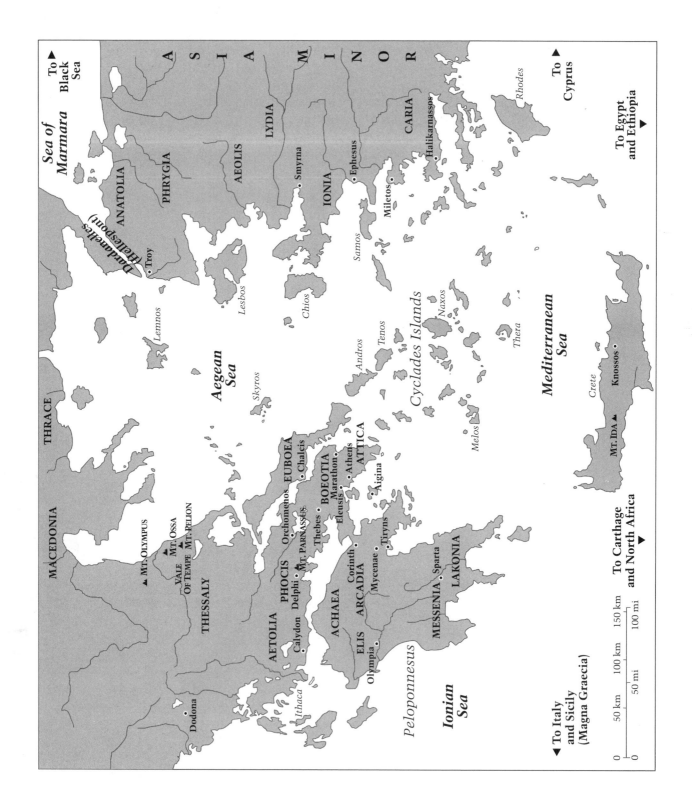

A

ACHELOUS In Greek mythology, river-god who turned himself into a serpent to overcome his rival, HERACLES, for the hand of DEIANIRA. The hero Heracles finally subdued Achelous and won the maiden. Rivers and their gods were worshiped by the Greeks, who believed them to be the offspring of the gods OCEANUS and TETHYS.

ALCMAEON, one of the SEVEN AGAINST THEBES, cursed by his mother, finally finds refuge on a island newly formed from silt carried down by the river Achelous.

ACHERON (River of Sadness) In Greek mythology, the "woeful river" of the UNDERWORLD into which flow the Phlegethon and the Coctyus. Acheron was the son of GAIA. He had quenched the thirst of the TITANS during their war with ZEUS, who then changed Acheron into a river. To cross the river Acheron, it was necessary to seek the help of CHARON, the ancient ferryman of the Underworld.

Acheron is sometimes used as a synonym for HADES, the Underworld.

ACHILLES (Greek) In Greek mythology, son of PELEUS and THETIS; married to Deidamia; father of NEOPTOLEMUS. Achilles is the central figure of HOMER'S ILIAD, the story of the TROJAN WAR, a 20-year battle between the Greeks and the Trojans after the abduction of HELEN by PARIS. It had been prophesied that without the aid of Achilles the Greeks would never defeat the Trojans. Achilles went bravely into battle and indeed the war was won by the Greeks. Achilles was a hero in battle, and he has become a symbol of the fighting man who appears in all cultures throughout all the ages, doomed to die in war but glorying in the fulfillment of heroism and achievement. He is a vivid character, given to rages and revenge, such as his barbarous treatment of the body of the slain Trojan

hero HECTOR. (See *The Childhood of Achilles* and *Achilles at War,* below.)

ACHILLES, THE GREAT HERO OF THE TROJAN WAR.
(NEW YORK PUBLIC LIBRARY PICTURE COLLECTION)

1

The Childhood of Achilles THETIS, the mother of Achilles, was a sea-nymph who had been wooed by ZEUS and POSEIDON. She reluctantly married PELEUS and left him soon after the birth of Achilles. Knowing that Achilles was destined to be a hero who would win glory but also die in battle, she bathed the infant in the river STYX, trying to make him invulnerable to wounds. But the heel by which she held the child remained dry, and it was from a wound in the heel that Achilles eventually died; the arrow was shot by either APOLLO or PARIS, toward the end of the Trojan War.

As the child Achilles grew, Thetis put him in the care of CHIRON, the gentle and wise CENTAUR. Chiron fed the lad with the entrails of lions and the marrows of bears to make him brave, and taught him the arts of riding and hunting as well as of music and healing.

When the Greek leaders began to prepare for war with TROY, Thetis, knowing that Achilles faced certain death in Troy, took her son away from Chiron to the court of Lycomedes, king of Scyros, and disguised him as a girl. However, since the seer CALCHAS had prophesied that without Achilles the Trojans would never be defeated in the war, the Greeks were determined to seek out the young man. ODYSSEUS, another Greek hero, sent presents to the "girl," among them a superb spear and shield. When Achilles promptly and expertly took up these objects in a battle alarm, the Greeks recognized him for the man that he was and they led him off to the battlefield. (See *Achilles at War*, below.)

Achilles at War Achilles had had early training in the arts of war (as well as of music and healing) from CHIRON, the wise CENTAUR (see *The Childhood of Achilles*, above). When he went to war against the Trojans, Achilles led his own army, unlike the rest of the Greeks, who acknowledged AGAMEMNON as their leader. It had been prophesied that without Achilles the Trojans would triumph over the Greeks. Therefore there was much dismay when Agamemnon and Achilles quarreled over the beautiful captive BRISEIS, who had been stolen away from Achilles by Agamemnon. In a fury, Achilles withdrew his army from the war, with disastrous results for the Greeks. This is the quarrel from which the events described in the ILIAD commence.

When the Greeks began to lose ground in the battle against the Trojans, Achilles finally sent his troops back into war under the leadership of PATROCLUS, his dearest friend. Patroclus was killed by the Trojan hero HECTOR. Achilles then went back into the war and routed the Trojans. He slew Hector. Despite the anguished pleas of PRIAM (king of the Trojans and father of Hector), Achilles dragged the body around the walls of Troy and the tomb of Patroclus. Achilles finally gave the mutilated body of Hector back to Priam in return for the warrior's weight in gold.

ACTEON In Greek mythology, son of Aristaeus and Autonoi, a hunter. He aroused the anger of the goddess ARTEMIS when he saw her bathing naked in a river. Artemis changed Acteon into a stag. His own dogs set upon him and tore him to pieces.

ADMETUS In Greek mythology, king of Pherae in THESSALY; one of the ARGONAUTS. Admetus was a kind master to APOLLO, who had been his slave as a punishment for killing the CYCLOPES. When Apollo heard that Admetus was soon to die, Apollo went to the FATES and persuaded them to prolong Admetus's life. They agreed, on condition that someone else should be sent in his stead. Not even the parents of Admetus would give up their lives. But his faithful wife, ALCESTIS, agreed to do so. She took a draught of poison and went down to HADES. But PERSEPHONE refused to let her stay. She sent her back to her husband and children. Another version of the story says that HERACLES went to the UNDERWORLD and wrestled with Hades for the life of Alcestis. The story is the subject of a play, *Alcestis*, by EURIPIDES and of an opera, *Alceste*, by the German composer Christoph Willibald Gluck (1714–1787).

ADONIS In Greek mythology, the beloved of APHRODITE and the personification of masculine beauty. His mother was the beautiful Myrrha (or Smyrna); his father, King Cinyrus of Cyprus, who was the father of Myrrha. The

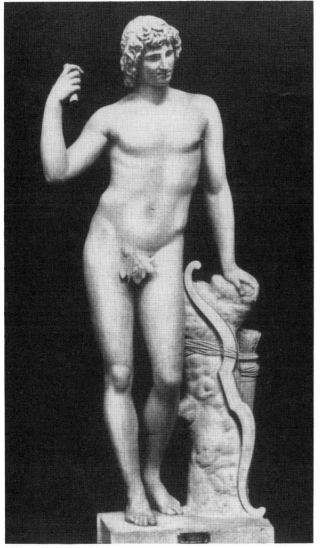

ADONIS, THE PERSONIFICATION OF MASCULINE BEAUTY, WAS LOVED BY THE GODDESS APHRODITE. (THE BETTMANN ARCHIVE)

strange parentage of Adonis came about because Aphrodite was jealous of Myrrha's beauty and caused the girl to unite with her own father. When Cinyrus found out that he had been tricked, he chased Myrrha with a sword, intending to kill her and her unborn child. Aphrodite, repenting of her deed, quickly turned the girl into a myrrh tree. The king's sword split the tree and out stepped the beautiful child, Adonis. Aphrodite hid the baby in a box and gave it to PERSEPHONE, queen of death, to look after. Persephone reared Adonis in the UNDERWORLD; he grew to be a handsome young man, whereupon Aphrodite claimed him back.

Persephone refused to give him up. Appealed to by the two goddesses, ZEUS decreed that each should have him for half of the year. When he stayed in the Underworld it was winter. When he returned the earth blossomed into spring and summer.

In some versions of the story, when ARES hears that Aphrodite loves the youth Adonis, he changes himself into a wild boar and gores the boy to death. Anemones spring from the blood of Adonis and his spirit returns to the Underworld. In response to the two tearful goddesses, Zeus determines that Adonis should stay with each of them in turn for half the year.

According to scholars, the death and resurrection of Adonis represents the decay and revival of the plant year. He was worshiped as a corn-god (that is, a god of grain crops, which were much more important to the ancient inhabitants of the Mediterranean lands than the berries and roots of the wilderness that nourished their primitive, pre-agrarian ancestors).

ADRASTIA (Inescapable One) In Greek mythology, daughter of Melisseus, king of CRETE; sister of IDA (1). With Ida and the goat-nymph AMALTHEA, Adrastia tended the infant god ZEUS on Mount IDA (2), in Crete. Later mythology identified Adrastia with NEMESIS, the goddess of vengeance.

ADRASTUS In Greek mythology, king of ARGOS; the leader of the warriors known as the SEVEN AGAINST THEBES. The attack on THEBES was a disaster. Of the seven champions, only Adrastus lived, escaping on his winged horse, ARION. Later, Adrastus made another attempt to gain Thebes, when the children of the Seven, called the EPIGONI, were old enough to become warriors. This time the battle was a success, but it was a sad victory for Adrastus because his only son, Aegialeus, was killed in the conflict.

AEGEUS In Greek mythology, king of ATHENS and father of the hero THESEUS, with Aethra, daughter of King Pittheus of Troezen. (Some say that the sea-god, POSEIDON, was the father of Theseus, and that possibly Aegeus and Poseidon were one and the same.)

When Aegeus left Troezen, Aegeus told Aethra that if a child should be born of their union, it was to be reared quietly in Troezen, with King Pittheus as guardian. Aegeus then hid his sword and sandals under a rock, telling Aethra that she was to lead the child, when it became old enough, to the hiding place so that he or she could recover the tokens of its identity. (See *Theseus and Aegeus* and *Theseus and Medea*, under THESEUS.)

When Aegeus thought that his son, Theseus, had been killed, he threw himself into the sea that today bears his name—the Aegean Sea.

AEGINA An island in the Saronic Gulf, south of ATHENS; in Greek legend, named after Aegina, a lover of the god ZEUS. When plague struck the island, Zeus repeopled it by turning the ants of the island into people, who were known as MYRMIDONS. The ancient Cretan deity BRITOMARTIS took refuge here from the attentions of King MINOS. The Aegeans called her DICTYNNA. Aegina was the birthplace of PELEUS, son of King Aecus.

AEGIS (Goat Skin) In Greek mythology, the shield of ZEUS made by the smith-god HEPHAESTUS and covered with the skin of the goat-nymph AMALTHEA. The shield had the power to terrify and disperse the enemy. When Zeus shook it, it produced tremendous thunder-and-lightning storms. It also had the power to protect friends. The aegis was also worn by ATHENE, when it bore the head of the GORGON, MEDUSA, in its center. The aegis is a symbol of divine protection.

AEGISTHUS In Greek mythology, son of Pelopia and THYESTES. Aegisthus became the lover of CLYTEMNESTRA, the wife of King AGAMEMNON, after the king had gone off to the TROJAN WAR. Aegisthus and Clytemnestra killed Agamemnon when he returned from the war, and were in turn murdered by ORESTES and ELECTRA, Agamemnon's children.

Aegisthus was one of the descendants of PELOPS and a victim of the curse laid upon the family by the murdered charioteer, MYRTILUS (see under PELOPS).

When his mother Pelopia realized that Aegisthus was the son not of her husband Atreus but of her own father, Thyestes, she placed the infant on a mountainside to die. But the baby survived, suckled by a she-goat, and grew up to play his part in the tragic story of the house of Pelops. (See ATREUS AND THYESTES.)

Eventually Aegisthus killed his supposed father, Atreus, and acknowledged Thyestes as his real father.

It was only at the death of Aegisthus and Clytemnestra that the FURIES were satisfied and put an end to the tragedies and atrocities that had stained the house of Atreus (the Atreids) and the descendants of Pelops with generations of bloodshed.

There are several versions of the geneology of this accursed family, involving further incest, murder and intrigue.

AENEAS Trojan hero of both Greece and Rome. Aeneas appears in the Latin epic poem, *The Aeneid*, by VIRGIL. He was the son of ANCHISES and the goddess VENUS (APHRODITE); the nephew of King PRIAM of TROY. In HOMER'S ILIAD, Aeneas is an ally of Troy during the TROJAN WAR and a gallant warrior, frequently aided by the gods.

After the fall of Troy and many travels, Aeneas eventually established himself on the banks of the river TIBER, in western Italy, married LAVINIA (daughter of LATINUS) and built the town of Lavinium. (See AENEID, THE, for a fuller account of the life of Aeneas.)

Aeneas was worshiped by the Romans as the founder of their race.

AENEID, THE The epic poem composed by Latin poet VIRGIL between 30 and 19 B.C. It is divided into 12 books and was considered unfinished by Virgil when he died. Nevertheless, *The Aeneid* is one of the cornerstones of world literature. It had enormous influence on Roman thought, for here at last was a genuinely Roman myth, glorifying Rome and foretelling its future glory. It became the bible of Rome. People of all classes knew it by heart; it was quoted constantly.

Unlike most poets, authors and artists, Virgil was greatly admired in his own lifetime, for his contemporaries at once understood his greatness and the relevance of his epic to their own culture.

Like the ODYSSEY, written by Greek poet HOMER between the 8th and the 9th centuries B.C., *The Aeneid* is the tale of a hero who fought in the TROJAN WAR. Aeneas fought on the Trojan side. He fled the burning city with his father, ANCHISES, on his back. Part of his story is told in flashback form to Queen DIDO of CARTHAGE, who falls in love with him. Ever the favorite of the gods, Aeneas is told by JUPITER (via his messenger, MERCURY) that he must leave Dido, for his destiny is to found an empire on the west coast of Italy. When he deserts her, the lovelorn Dido kills herself with his sword. When he reaches the kingdom of LATIUM, at the mouth of the river Tiber, King LATINUS gives him the hand of his daughter LAVINIA in marriage. Aeneas founds the city of Lavinium in her honor. However, Lavinia has already been promised to Turnus, king of the RUTULI. War is declared between the rivals. Helped by Evander, leader of the Arcadians, and the goddess VENUS (who brings Aeneas a shield crafted by VULCAN), the troops of Turnus are routed. Turnus and Aeneas agree to end the war in single combat. Despite the aid of the warrior maiden CAMILLA, Turnus is defeated and the Trojans are victorious.

AEOLUS Greek god of the winds. In HOMER'S ODYSSEY Aeolus helped the hero ODYSSEUS by imprisoning the winds in a huge leather bag, leaving only the west wind free to blow the ships of Odysseus homeward to ITHACA. When the ships were near home, Odysseus fell asleep from exhaustion. The restless, curious crew of the ship opened the bag. The winds escaped and blew all the ships away from Ithaca and back toward the island of Lipara, where Aeolus, their master, lived. Aeolus was angry and refused to help Odysseus further.

AEROPE In Greek mythology, wife of Atreus, mother of AGAMEMNON and MENELAUS, and possibly of Anaxibia and Pleisthenes. Aerope was thrown into the sea by her husband for her adultery with his brother, THYESTES. (See *The Golden Fleece*, under ATREUS AND THYESTES.)

AESCHYLUS Greek poet (525–456 B.C.), held by many to be the founder of Greek tragedy. He was the first dramatist to introduce a second actor onto the stage; before him, drama had only one actor appearing at a time. The innovative use of dialogue between the actors brought a hitherto unknown vividness to the stage. He also developed the use of costumes and of special effects. Only seven of his many plays survive, among them *The Seven Against Thebes*, *Prometheus Bound* and *The Oresteia*, a trilogy that tells the epic drama of King AGAMEMNON and how his murder was arranged by his son ORESTES.

AESON King of IOLCUS (in THESSALY); with Queen Alcimede, father of JASON; half-brother of PELIAS, who usurped the throne of Iolcus.

AETES In Greek mythology, king of Colchis; father of the witch MEDEA and of her brother APSYRTUS. Aetes was the guardian of the GOLDEN FLEECE, which was sought by JASON. (See *Jason and the Argonauts*, under JASON.)

AETOLIA District of the southern Greek mainland. One of its chief towns was CALYDON, site of the CALYDONIAN BOAR HUNT. It was named after Aetolus, son of ENDYMION.

AGAMEMNON In Greek mythology, king of ARGOS and MYCENAE, regions in the northern Peloponnesus; son of Atreus and Aerope. He was the grandson of PELOPS and the last of that line that was doomed to one tragedy after another. He was the brother of MENELAUS and Anaxibia; and the husband of CLYTEMNESTRA, with whom he fathered Chrysothemis, ELECTRA, IPHIGINIA and ORESTES. King Agamemnon was the leader of the Achaean (Greek) forces in the TROJAN WAR. He was eventually killed by Clytemnestra and AEGISTHUS (see below).

Driven from Mycenae after the murder of their father, Atreus, Agamemnon and Menelaus fled to SPARTA. There Agamemnon wed Clytemnestra, and Menelaus wed HELEN. Agamemnon was chosen to lead the Greeks in the expedition to rescue his sister-in-law, Helen, who had been abducted by PARIS. The expedition was stalled when Agamemnon offended the goddess ARTEMIS. A soothsayer, CALCHAS, said that only the sacrifice of Agamemnon's daughter Iphiginia would appease ARTEMIS and AEOLUS, the wind-god. Agamemnon tricked his wife into sending their daughter to her death.

In another act of treachery, Agamemnon stole BRISEIS, the beloved of the hero ACHILLES, who then laid down his arms and withdrew from the Trojan War (though he later rejoined it).

When Agamemnon returned in triumph from the war, 10 years later, accompanied by the Princess CASSANDRA as booty, both he and she were murdered by Clytemnestra and her lover, Aegisthus. Agamemnon was trapped in a net and drowned in a bathtub, an ignoble end for a hero.

Agamemnon was one of the principal characters in HOMER's ILIAD. He was a brave and successful warrior but a selfish and treacherous man.

Historians believe that there was a real King Agamemnon in Argos or Mycenae, since Agamemnon appears often in Greek mythology and there were many cults of Agamemnon in various places in ancient Greece.

AGDISTIS In Greek mythology, a Phrygian mother-goddess, sometimes known as CYBELE, goddess of fertility, and associated with RHEA, Greek earth mother and mother of the OLYMPIAN GODS.

AGENOR In Greek mythology, king of Tyre (in PHOENICIA); son of sea-god POSEIDON and LIBYA; father of EUROPA, CADMUS, PHOENIX and CILIX; husband of Telephassa. When Europa was carried off by the god ZEUS, Agenor sent his three sons in search of their sister. The sons didn't find her, and settled down elsewhere to found new nations. Phoenix was the ancestor of the Phoenicians; Cilix of the Cilicians; and the celebrated Cadmus, who settled in Boeotia and built the Cadmea (a fortress), was the founder of the city of THEBES.

The dispersal of Agenor's sons seems to refer to the westward flight of the Canaanite tribes (early Phoenicians) in the second millennium B.C., under pressure from Aryan and Semitic invaders.

AJAX (1) Son of Telamon, king of Salamis. He was one of the heroes who sailed with the Greeks to the TROJAN WAR. He is represented in HOMER's ILIAD as second only to ACHILLES in bravery. Ajax is described as tall and strong though perhaps slow-witted, prone to rages and madness. He lost the contest for the armor of Achilles and in a fit of despair took his own life.

AJAX (2) (**"The Lesser"**) Son of Oileus; a Greek warrior in the TROJAN WAR. Unlike AJAX (1) (see above), he was a small man, but swift-footed and a skilled spearman. Ajax the Lesser was drowned on his way home to Greece after the fall of Troy; some say he was the victim of the sea-god, POSEIDON; some claim that he was the victim of the goddess ATHENE.

AGAMEMNON, KING OF ARGOS AND MYCENAE, LED THE GREEK TROOPS AGAINST THE TROJANS. FOR MANY YEARS THIS BEAUTIFUL GOLD MASK WAS THOUGHT TO BE THE DEATH MASK OF AGAMEMNON. (SCALA/ART RESOURCE)

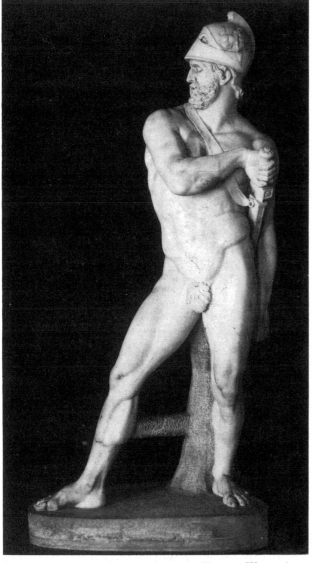

AJAX WAS ONE OF THE HEROES OF THE TROJAN WAR. (NEW YORK PUBLIC LIBRARY PICTURE COLLECTION)

ALBA LONGA A city of ancient LATIUM, southeast of Rome. It is the site of the modern Castel Gondolfo. According to Roman legend, it was founded by ASCANIUS, the son of AENEAS, one of the Trojan heroes. Tradition has it that ROMULUS AND REMUS were born in Alba Longa, thus making it the mother city of Rome.

ALCESTIS In Greek mythology, the daughter of PELIAS. Married to ADMETUS, she was the symbol of wifely devotion: She willingly gave up her life for Admetus so that he could live a little longer. But PERSEPHONE, queen of the UNDERWORLD, refused to admit her and sent her back to earth. In another version, HERACLES wrestles with HADES for her life, and wins the battle. Alcestis and Admetus are the subjects of a play by EURIPIDES, *Alcestis*, and an opera by the German operatic composer Christoph Willibald Gluck (1714–1787).

ALCINOUS King of the Phaecians on the island of Scheria. In HOMER'S ODYSSEY Alcinous and his daughter NAUSICAA entertain the Greek hero ODYSSEUS, who has been shipwrecked on his way home from the TROJAN WAR.

ALCIPPE In Greek mythology, daughter of the war-god ARES and the NYMPH Aglauros. Alcippe was ravished by Halirrhothius, a son of the sea-god POSEIDON. Halirrhothius was killed by Ares for this crime. (See *The Children of Ares*, under ARES.)

ALCMAEON In Greek mythology, the son of AMPHIARAUS (one of the SEVEN AGAINST THEBES) and of ERIPHYLE; brother of Amphilochus. The sons of the seven fallen champions who had fought at THEBES were called the EPIGONI (Descendants); they swore to avenge their fathers, and Alcmaeon rather reluctantly became their leader. He had been persuaded by his mother, Eriphyle, who in turn had been bribed with the coveted magic robe and amber necklace of HARMONIA.

When Alcmaeon learned that his mother had been similarly bribed to send his father off to war, he killed her. Her dying curse was that no land would ever shelter Alcmaeon. Alcmaeon wandered from place to place, pursued by the FURIES, who gave him no rest. Finally he found an island newly formed from silt brought down by the river ACHELOUS. Since the island hadn't existed when Eriphyle uttered her curse, Alcmaeon was able to find peace, at least for a while. He married CALLIRHOË, the daughter of OENEUS, king of CALYDON. Callirhoë heard about the fabulous robe and necklace that had been given to Eriphyle; as the wife of Alcmaeon, she demanded that the treasures be given to her. She didn't know that in his unhappy wanderings her husband had married Arsinoë, daughter of an Arcadian king, and given the treasures to her. Alcmaeon returned to ARCADIA and begged King Psophis to give him the treasure, as he wanted to place it in the shrine of APOLLO at DELPHI. The king couldn't refuse such a request; but when he heard the truth from one of the unfortunate Alcmaeon's servants, he had Alcmaeon killed.

Princess Arsinoë witnessed the death of her husband and, knowing nothing of his treachery, vowed vengeance on her father. The king sent the treasure to Delphi, in the hope that no further harm would come of it. But the treasure of Harmonia was accursed: eventually the king (Phegeus) and all his family were killed by the vengeful sons of Alcmaeon and Callirhoë.

This story of the folly of men and the greed and vanity of women has few mythic elements, but has been described (by scholar Robert Graves, 1895–1985), as "a popular minstrel tale . . . with a strong moral flavor" that stressed the inescapable curse visited on anyone who committed the dreadful crime of matricide.

ALCMENE In Greek mythology, daughter of Electryon; granddaughter of the hero PERSEUS; wife and cousin of AMPHITRYON; mother of HERACLES (by ZEUS) and of Iphicles (by her husband).

While her husband was at war the god Zeus, disguised as Amphitryon, visited Alcmene. According to HESIOD, Alcmene was a most virtuous woman and would not have entertained Zeus had he appeared as himself. Zeus realized this, and wanting to sire a champion for both gods and men, he wooed Alcmene as if he were her own husband. It is said that the experience was so enjoyable that Zeus, with his magic, made one night last the length of three. Alcmene bore the hero HERACLES, son of Zeus.

When Alcmene died many years later, Zeus had her taken to the ISLANDS OF THE BLESSED, where she married RHADAMANTHUS.

ALOEIDS (or ALOADAE) In Greek mythology, sons of Iphimedia by POSEIDON. Their names were Ephialtes and Otus; they were called the Aloeids after ALOEUS, the husband of Iphimedia. The brothers grew at an enormous rate; by the time they were nine years old they were 36 feet high. These giants declared war on OLYM-PUS, the home of the gods. Ephialtes determined to capture HERA, wife of the great god ZEUS; Otus swore he would capture ARTEMIS, goddess of the hunt. But first they seized ARES, god of war, and confined him in a bronze vessel, where he remained for 13 months until he was rescued by HERMES. Then their siege of Olympus began: The giants piled Mount PELION atop Mount OSSA (in THESSALY) to create a ladder to the heavens. They were not afraid of the gods, for it had been prophesied that neither gods nor men would kill them. Artemis tricked them by turning herself into a white doe and prancing before them. The brothers threw their spears at the doe, who skillfully darted away, and they accidentally killed each other with their spears. Thus the prophecy was fulfilled, for neither gods nor men had killed them; they had killed each other. The souls of the Aloeids went down to TARTARUS, where they were tied back-to-back on either side of a pillar, with cords that were living vipers.

The story of the Aloeids symbolizes the revolt of the GIANTS against the gods. The imprisonment of Ares may symbolize a 13-month truce between two warring tribes of ancient Greece, when warlike tokens of both nations were sealed into a bronze jar to ensure peace.

In another version of the myth (in HOMER's ODYSSEY), it is said that the twins would have successfully stormed Olympus if the god APOLLO hadn't slain them with his arrows.

The Aloeids were worshiped on the island of NAXOS (where Artemis had appeared to them as a doe) and in the city of Ascra, in BOEOTIA, where they were regarded as founders of the city.

Myths of the Aloeids also appear in Homer's ODYSSEY and in VIRGIL's AENEID.

ALOEUS In Greek mythology, son of POSEIDON; husband of Iphimedia. Iphimedia had two sons, Otus and Ephialtes, by Poseidon. When she married Aloeus the sons were known as the ALOEIDS (sons of Aloeus).

AMALTHEA (Tender) In Greek mythology, the goat-nymph that suckled the infant ZEUS on Mount IDA in CRETE (see *The Childhood of*

Zeus, under ZEUS). Zeus was grateful to the goat-nymph. When he became lord of the universe, he set Amalthea's image among the stars as CAPRICORN (The Goat). He also borrowed one of her horns, which were as large and full as a cow's, and gave it to ADRASTIA and IDA (1) (the ash-nymphs who, with Amalthea, had tended the infant Zeus) as the CORNUCOPIA (Horn of Plenty). The horn would always be filled with food and drink for its owners. The AEGIS, the shield worn by Zeus (and sometimes by ATHENE), was covered with the skin of Amalthea.

AMAZONS In Greek mythology, a legendary race of female warriors, supposed to live in ASIA MINOR or possibly Africa, or, as Greek navigators explored further, "at the edge of the world." The Amazons were sometimes associated with ARTEMIS, goddess of the hunt, but no close connection can be found except that the name of one Amazonian leader was Artemis. Some scholars say that the legend of the Amazon warriors may be connected with the invasion of the beardless nomads (Scythian and Mongolian) from the Russian steppes.

The Amazons appear in several legends, including those of the hero HERACLES (see *The Twelve Labors of Heracles*, 9; The Girdle of the Amazon, under HERACLES; and *Theseus and the Amazons*, under THESEUS). The most famous queen of the Amazons was HIPPOLYTA, whose girdle was stolen by Heracles, and who was vanquished by Theseus, to whom she bore a son, HIPPOLYTUS. PENTHESALIA, an Amazon queen, fought valiantly for the Trojans in the TROJAN WAR. She was slain by ACHILLES.

The Greeks cited the conquest of the Amazons as a triumph of civilization over barbarism. Others have cited it as a triumph of male dominance over female independence.

Early Spanish explorers in the Americas (about the 16th century) claimed to have seen tall female warriors on the banks of the great river that they named the Amazon, in memory of the Greek myths. Other sources say that the Amazon river was named after a tidal phenomenon, *amassona* ("destroyer of boats," a tidal bore).

It is said by some that the Amazon warriors cut off one breast in order to facilitate use of the bow. However, there are no known depictions of this phenomenon in ancient art.

AMMON Egyptian divinity, identified with ZEUS and JUPITER in later Greek and Roman mythology. Ammon was celebrated as a great ORACLE, whose shrine was in LIBYA (2), North Africa. In the myth of Perseus and Andromeda, (See *Perseus and Andromeda*, under PERSEUS), it was Ammon who said that ANDROMEDA must be sacrificed to the sea-monster sent by POSEIDON to ravage the land of ETHIOPIA.

AMPHIARAUS Known as the seer of ARGOS in Greek mythology, he was the brother-in-law of King ADRASTUS, leader of the SEVEN AGAINST THEBES. He foresaw that the war would be a disaster but was reluctantly persuaded to join the warriors by his wife, ERIPHYLE, the sister of Adrastus. Amphiaraus would have been killed by the Thebans but for the intervention of the god ZEUS. He vanished into a cleft in the earth made by Zeus. The spot became famous as an oracular shrine.

AMPHION In Greek mythology, son of ZEUS and Antiope; twin brother of Zethus; husband of NIOBE. The twin brothers captured THEBES and decided to build a wall around it. Zethus found the stones and Amphion, who had been given a lyre by the god HERMES, played so sweetly that the stones assembled themselves into a wall. Amphion married Niobe, with whom he had many children. Niobe made the mistake of boasting about her numerous offspring and was punished by another set of formidable twins, the gods APOLLO and ARTEMIS. (See NIOBE.)

AMPHITRITE An ancient Greek sea-goddess; daughter of NEREUS or OCEANUS; wife of POSEIDON; mother of TRITON, Rhode and Benthescyme. She was the female personification of the sea.

Amphitrite was not pleased when the sea-god, Poseidon, tried to woo her; she fled into the Atlas Mountains, in North Africa. Poseidon sent DELPHINUS to win her and eventually she consented to become Poseidon's wife. She bore him three children.

Amphitrite discovered that Poseidon was a faithless husband. One of his lovers was the beautiful nymph SCYLLA, whom Amphitrite changed into a terrible monster.

AMPHITRYON Grandson of the Greek hero PERSEUS; husband of ALCMENE; father of Iphicles and foster-father of the hero HERACLES, who was the son of Alcmene and the god ZEUS. His brother Electryon was the father of Alcmene, and king of MYCENAE. The brothers quarreled and Amphitryon accidentally killed Electryon. Amphitryon and Alcmene fled to THEBES and were given refuge by King Creon. In gratitude, Amphitryon helped to rid Thebes of a monster known as the Teumessian vixen, a fox that had terrorized the country by demanding the sacrifice of a child every month. With the help of the marvelous hound LAELAPS, who could catch anything it hunted, and the god Zeus, Amphitryon rid the country of the dreaded fox.

ANCHISES In Greek mythology, a Trojan prince or king loved by the goddess APHRODITE, who bore him a son, AENEAS. When Anchises boasted that he had been loved by the goddess, he was stricken with blindness or lameness (stories differ) and was rescued from the burning city of TROY by his son, Aeneas, who carried him away on his shoulders. This story is told in VIRGIL'S AENEID and is the subject of works of art by Italian artists Giovanni Bernini (1598–1680) and Raphael (1483–1520).

ANDROGEUS In Greek mythology, son of MINOS and PASIPHAË; brother of ARIADNE and PHAEDRA. Androgeus was a great athlete. He beat all his opponents at the OLYMPIC GAMES in Athens, whereupon the jealous King AEGEUS had him assassinated. Subsequently, King Minos of CRETE declared war on Athens (for the consequences of which see *Minos and the Minotaur*, under MINOS; and *Theseus, Ariadne and the Minotaur*, under THESEUS).

ANDROMACHE In Greek mythology, a touching, tragic figure in the TROJAN WAR. She was the daughter of King Thebe of Cilicia; wife of the Trojan hero HECTOR; mother of Astyanax. Andromache lost her father and brothers at the fall of Troy and was given as booty to NEOPTOLEMUS; her son Astyanax was murdered by the victorious Greek hero ODYSSEUS. Andromache was cruelly treated by Hermione, the wife of Neoptolemus, but finally found peace with her fellow Trojan captive, HELENUS. Her story is told in *Andromache,* a play by EURIPIDES, and in HOMER'S ILIAD.

ANDROMEDA (Ruler of Men) In Greek mythology, the daughter of CEPHEUS and CASSIOPEIA of ETHIOPIA, a country in northeast Africa; wife of the hero PERSEUS; mother of many sons, including Perses who is said to have founded the land of Persia.

According to Greek mythology, the fates of Andromeda and Perseus became entwined in the following way: Cassiopeia had boasted of her daughter's beauty (or possibly of her own), claiming that it was greater than that of the sea NYMPHS, daughters of the god POSEIDON. Greatly angered, Poseidon sent a sea-monster to ravage the country of Ethiopia. AMMON, the ORACLE, declared that only the sacrifice of Andromeda to the monster could appease Poseidon and save the Ethiopians from flood and plague. So Andromeda was chained to a rock in the sea to await death. She was rescued by the hero Perseus, who turned the monster into stone with the head of MEDUSA and claimed Andromeda in marriage. The wedding feast was interrupted by the arrival of PHINEUS, brother of Cepheus, to whom Andromeda had been promised in marriage. In the ensuing battle, Perseus again used the Medusa's head to turn Phineas and his soldiers into statues of stone. (See *Perseus and Andromeda*, under PERSEUS.)

The dramatic rescue of Andromeda by Perseus inspired many artists, among them Peter Paul Rubens (1577–1640), the foremost Flemish painter of the 17th century; Titian (c. 1490–1576), a Venetian and one of the greatest painters of the Renaissance; and Jean Auguste Dominique Ingres (1780–1867), a French painter. An ancient fresco still extant at Pompei (near Naples, Italy) also depicts the rescue.

After their deaths, Andromeda, Cassiopeia and Cepheus were set among the stars as constellations.

ANTICLEA In Greek mythology, daughter of AUTOLYCUS; wife of LAERTES; mother of ODYSSEUS. Autolycus was a son of the god HERMES. It is said that Odysseus inherited his shrewdness and cunning from his grandfather Autolycus and his great-grandfather Hermes. Anticlea died of grief when her son went off to the TROJAN WAR.

ANTIGONE In Greek mythology, the daughter of OEDIPUS and Jocasta; sister of Eteocles and Polynices. Antigone accompanied her blind father when he went into exile. Her two brothers killed each other in the war of the SEVEN AGAINST THEBES. King Creon of THEBES forbade the burial of the rebel Polynices. Antigone disobeyed the king's orders and performed the burial service herself. In one version of the myth, she finally hanged herself after Creon ordered her to be buried alive. In another version, Antigone was rescued by a son of Creon and sent to live among shepherds.

Antigone was one of SOPHOCLES' greatest plays. The striking tragic heroine appears also in Sophocles' *Oedipus at Colonus*, in AESCHYLUS' *Seven Against Thebes*, in EURIPIDES' *The Phoenician Women* and, in modern times, in *Antigone* by Jean Cocteau (1889–1963), which has a 20th-century setting.

It is not known whether Antigone was a real person or a purely poetic creation.

APHRODITE (Foam Born) Greek goddess of love, beauty and fertility. One of the 12 OLYMPIAN GODS; identified with the Roman VENUS and, much earlier, with the Near Eastern fertility goddesses Astarte and Ishtar. Aphrodite was a very ancient deity, an earth-mother whose domain embraced all creation, vegetable and animal as well as human. She represented sacred love and marriage as well as sensuality and desire. She was so beautiful that all men who saw her loved her.

The origins of Aphrodite are obscure. She is called "Foam Born" in an attempt to make her the offspring of GAIA (Earth) and URANUS (Heaven), who was cast into the sea after being mutilated by his son, CRONUS. She was supposed to have emerged from the sea foam that had formed around the remains of Uranus. She is depicted as riding on a scallop shell in many pieces of art, including the famous *Birth of Venus*, painted by the Florentine artist Sandro Botticelli in the late 15th century.

The myth of Aphrodite as a descendant of the Titans probably refers to a goddess who preceded the peoples later called Greeks. When the migrating tribes settled in Greece, they adopted Aphrodite into the Olympian family by making her the daughter of ZEUS and DIONE.

According to HOMER, Aphrodite was the daughter of Zeus and Dione (in the ILIAD). Also according to Homer, Aphrodite was married to the smith-god, HEPHAESTUS. But Aphrodite was faithless and had many lovers. See *The Loves of Aphrodite*, below.

The Loves of Aphrodite Aphrodite, goddess of love, was married to HEPHAESTUS, but she had many other loves, among them ARES, god of war. She bore him Phobos (Fear), Deimos (Terror), HARMONIA (Peace or Concord) and, in some accounts, EROS (Love) (see *Aphrodite and Eros*, below).

Although Hephaestus was a very gentle god, he proved himself capable of subtle revenge on Aphrodite and Ares by snaring them in a skillfully crafted golden net. (See *Ares and Aphrodite*, under ARES.)

POSEIDON, god of the sea, fell in love with Aphrodite when he saw her entrapped in the golden net. With Poseidon, the goddess had two sons, Rhodus and Herophilus, and some say, Eryx.

With HERMES, a son of ZEUS, Aphrodite bore HERMAPHRODITUS, and some say, EROS. With DIONYSUS, god of the vine, another son of Zeus, she bore PRIAPUS; with the Trojan mortal ANCHISES, she bore AENEAS. With another mortal, the beautiful ADONIS, Aphrodite spent the months of the year that symbolized fruitful spring and summer; some accounts say that she bore him a son (Golgos) and a daughter (Beroe). From the legend of Aphrodite and Adonis comes the word aphrodisiac, meaning a potion or other agent that induces love.

Aphrodite was also beloved by PYGMALION, who created a statue of her so beautiful that he fell in love with it. And there were many other lovers, for Aphrodite inspired love in all who saw her.

Aphrodite and Eros Aphrodite, Greek goddess of love and fertility, known to the Romans as VENUS, was often depicted with the infant god, EROS (Love), who some said was her son with HERMES. However, mythologists believe that Eros was a very ancient god, an adult rather than a child. He was to become the plump, babyish CUPID (his Roman name), companion or son of Aphrodite, only in later times.

Aphrodite and Paris The tale of the Greek goddess of love, Aphrodite, and the young hero PARIS is told in HOMER'S ILIAD. Paris was supposed to choose the fairest among three OLYMPIAN GODS: HERA, ATHENE and Aphrodite. (See *The Judgment of Paris*, under PARIS.) Each goddess offered Paris a bribe. Aphrodite offered him the love of the most beautiful woman in the world, and Paris awarded Aphrodite a golden apple as reward. The beautiful woman turned out to be HELEN of Troy. The love affair of Paris and Helen was the leading cause of the TROJAN WAR.

Aphrodite and Art Aphrodite, Greek goddess of love, was worshiped as a great beauty as well as a goddess of fertility. She is the subject of some of the world's greatest art masterpieces, in which she is usually known by her Roman name, VENUS. The most famous statue of her was by the Greek Praxiteles (c. 350 B.C.); the original has been lost but there is a Roman copy in Munich, Germany; and the Venus de Milo (to be seen at the Louvre, in Paris, France). *The Birth of Venus*, by Botticelli (see under APHRODITE, above) is world-renowned. She is often depicted with the infant EROS, supposed to have been her son and constant companion. (See *Aphrodite and Eros, above.*)

APOLLO One of the greatest OLYMPIAN GODS and the only one to appear with the same name in both Greek and Roman mythology. He was the son of ZEUS and LETO; brother of ARTEMIS; half-brother of HERMES; and father of many, including ARISTAEUS and ASCLEPIUS. Apollo had many functions: he was the god of poetry, music, archery, prophecy and the art of healing. Associated with the care of herds and crops, Apollo was a sun-god of great antiquity; yet he is represented as an ever-youthful god, just and wise and of great beauty. He has been the subject of many great paintings and statues throughout the ages; perhaps the most famous is the Apollo Belvedere, an ancient statue that now stands in the Belvedere Gallery in the independent papal state, the Vatican, in Rome.

Apollo was well loved among the gods. Only his half-brother, Hermes, dared to play a trick on him when he stole Apollo's cattle (see *The Childhood of Hermes*, under HERMES).

As well as physical beauty Apollo represented the moral excellence that we think of as civilization. His cult at DELPHI had enormous influence on matters of statecraft and religion, as well as on everyday law and order. The influence of Apollo at Delphi helped to spread tolerance in all social ranks. Apollo was, above all, a god of justice, law and order.

The many and varying functions of Apollo suggest that the god had many personalities

APOLLO, A GREAT GOD OF MUSIC AND HEALING, IS SHOWN HERE PLAYING A LYRE AND POURING A HEALING LIBATION UPON THE EARTH. (NEW YORK PUBLIC LIBRARY PICTURE COLLECTION)

derived from various origins. Some mythologists say that he was a sun-god from Asia who merged with a pastoral god from the countries north of Greece, known as Hyperborea, that is, "the Far North."

The Birth of Apollo

According to the poet HESIOD, the Greek god Apollo was the son of the great god Zeus and LETO, the gentle TITAN. HERA, the wife of Zeus, was jealous of her rival; familiar with the rages of Hera, no land would give Leto sanctuary in which to bear her child. At last Leto found refuge in the floating islands of Ortygia and DELOS, which became firmly anchored only after the birth of her first child, ARTEMIS. Artemis grew miraculously fast and was able to help her mother across to the island of Delos, where she assisted Leto in the birth of her twin brother, Apollo.

Apollo was fed on nectar and ambrosia and quickly grew to manhood.

Apollo and Python

Apollo, one of the greatest of the OLYMPIAN GODS, grew to manhood very soon after his birth (see *The Birth of Apollo*, above). Supplied with arms by the smith-god HEPHAESTUS, an expert metalworker, the young Apollo set off in search of the serpent PYTHON, who had tormented Apollo's mother, Leto, during her homeless wanderings. Apollo tracked down Python at DELPHI and killed her, thus defiling a sacred place with blood. Zeus sent his son Apollo to be purified at the Vale of TEMPE. After his purification Apollo returned to Delphi and took the shrine for himself. Python, or Pythia, was to be his oracle. The dramatic battle between Apollo and Python was later celebrated in the festival Septaria.

The Loves of Apollo

Apollo, god of music, poetry, healing and law, was one of the foremost gods of OLYMPUS and supremely handsome. Like all the gods and goddesses, Apollo had many loves, not all of them happy: The nymph DAPHNE fled from the god and turned herself into a laurel tree rather than submit to him. Apollo made the laurel tree his sacred tree and emblem.

With CORONIS Apollo begot ASCLEPIUS, god of healing and medicine; but Coronis deserted Apollo for love of Ischyus. Apollo's sister, AR-TEMIS, killed Coronis with her arrows. Apollo snatched the infant Asclepius from the funeral pyre and had him brought up by HERMES, or some say CHIRON, the gentle CENTAUR.

Apollo fell in love with CASSANDRA, daughter of King PRIAM. He conferred on her the gift of prophecy, but Cassandra was untrue to him. Apollo then breathed a kiss into her mouth that took away her powers of persuasion. From then on, no one would believe in the prophecies of Cassandra.

With the nymph CYRENE Apollo begot ARIS-TAEUS, who was worshiped as a protector of flocks and crops and especially of the art of beekeeping.

Among Apollo's male loves was HYACIN-THUS, a beautiful youth after whom the spring flower, hyacinth, is named.

APSYRTUS In Greek mythology, son of AETES; brother of the witch MEDEA. Medea slew her brother and scattered his remains along the way as she and JASON fled from Aetes with the GOLDEN FLEECE. (See *Jason and the Argonauts*, under JASON.)

ARACHNE (Spider) In Greek mythology, the daughter of Idmon of Colophon in LYDIA (ASIA MINOR). Arachne was a skillful weaver. Marveling at her work, people said that she must have been taught by ATHENE herself. Arachne denied this and rashly invited the goddess Athene to come and compete with her. Athene was annoyed but accepted the invitation. She became angry when she could find no fault in the maiden's clever weaving and amusing, if disrespectful, depictions of the antics of the gods and goddesses. Athene tore the work apart and destroyed the loom. Terrified, the maiden tried to hang herself. Athene turned Arachne into a spider, doomed to show off her artful weaving of cobwebs forever more.

This story was told by OVID in *Metamorphoses*. Some scholars think that the explanation of this myth lies in the commercial rivalry between the Athenians (represented by Athene) and the Lydians (represented by Arachne) for the export of textiles. The spider-emblem was frequently found on the seals of the sea-lords and the weavers. It would seem that the Ath-

ARACHNE, THE WEAVER, WAS TRANSFORMED INTO A SPIDER BY THE GODDESS ATHENE. (NEW YORK PUBLIC LIBRARY PICTURE COLLECTION)

enians (and especially Athene herself) had good reason to be jealous of the spider Arachne.

ARCADIA In ancient Greece, the central plateau of the Peloponnesus, surrounded by and dissected by mountains. It was inhabited mostly by shepherds and hunters who worshiped PAN and other nature-gods. In the myth of DEMETER, the corn-goddess turns herself into a mare and hides in a herd owned by King Oncus of Arcadia (she is nevertheless discovered by the amorous god POSEIDON).

ARCAS or ARCTOS (Greek *Arktos*, Bear) Son of CALLISTO and ZEUS, married to the dryad Erato, father of many. Arcas was king of ARCADIA, an isolated, mountainous area in the Peloponnesus peninsula. He had been taught his skills by TRIPTOLEMUS, a favorite of the goddess DEMETER. Arcas taught the Arcadians agriculture and attendant arts, such as those of spinning wool. Arcas was also a great hunter. In one story, he almost killed the she-bear Callisto, who was his mother in another guise. The god Zeus, to prevent Arcas from killing his own mother, turned Arcas into a bear and set him and his mother up in the stars as the Great Bear (Ursa Major) and Arcturus (Guardian of the Bear). (See ARCTURUS.)

ARCTURUS (Guardian of the Bear) The brightest star in the constellation Boötes. It is named after ARCAS (Bear), in Greek mythology the Little Bear, son of CALLISTO (the Great Bear).

ARES The Greek god of war; son of ZEUS and HERA. ERIS (Discord) was his sister and constant companion.

Ares has been depicted wearing a golden helmet and riding in a speedy chariot, brandishing his enormous spear; however, there are in fact few likenesses of him in the art of ancient Greece. He was not a popular god. A vicious crowd followed him, among them Pain, Panic, Famine and Oblivion; his sons, Phobos (Fear) and Deimos (Terror), prepared his chariot. Thus were the horrors of war symbolized.

Although usually identified with the Roman god of war, MARS, Ares bore little resemblance to the noble Mars.

The grisly followers of Ares, the hatred of Zeus toward him, and the humiliation and defeats that plagued him (see *Ares, the Unloved God*, and *Ares and Aphrodite*, below) all symbolized the horror that the Athenians felt toward Ares, the personification of senseless war and brutality. For them, war was to be waged only for a good and noble reason; for Ares, war didn't have to have any reason at all: He liked battle and violence for their own sake.

Ares, The Unloved God

Ares, god of war, was bloody and brutal. Even his father, ZEUS (in HOMER's ILIAD), declared that he hated his son for his perpetual violence and aggression.

Ares was not always successful in battle and was often thought of as cowardly and inept. Helped by the wisdom of the goddess ATHENE, DIOMEDES (1), one of the heroes at the siege of TROY, defeated Ares. Athene, although a goddess of war and half-sister of Ares, despised Ares's behavior. She wounded him enough so that he was forced to leave the field bellowing with rage and pain. On another occasion he was severely wounded by HERACLES, with whom he fought in defense of his son, CYNCUS.

The brother of Ares was HEPHAESTUS, the smith-god. Hephaestus defeated Ares not in violent battle, but by using his subtle cleverness. (See *Ares and Aphrodite*, below.)

Otus and Ephialtes, known as the ALOEIDS, also despised Ares. They managed to imprison him in a bronze jar, where he remained trapped for 13 months until the god HERMES found him and released him. This myth is thought to symbolize a historical 13-month truce between two warring tribes of ancient Greece, when warlike tokens of these nations were sealed in a bronze jar and kept inside a temple.

The Children of Ares

Ares, god of war, was often unlucky in battle (see *Ares, the Unloved God*, above). His children were equally ill-fated in their lives.

Ares was the father of ALCIPPE by the nymph Aglaurus. When Alcippe was violated by Halirrhothius, a son of POSEIDON, Ares killed the youth. He went on trial for murder, perhaps the first murder trial in historical legend. Ares was acquitted. The proceedings took place on a hill in Athens, which became known as the Areoipagus, "The Hill of Ares."

DIOMEDES (2), a son of Ares who fed his horses human flesh, was put to death by the hero HERACLES (see *The Twelve Labors of Heracles*, under HERACLES).

CYNCUS, a son by Pelopia or by Pyrene, was also killed by HERACLES, whom he challenged in battle; and another son, OENOMAUS (by Harpina), was defeated in a chariot race and subsequently died.

Ares and Aphrodite

Ares, god of war, was not a popular god. But APHRODITE, fickle goddess of love, perversely favored the warlike god over her gentle husband, HEPHAESTUS. HELIOS (the Sun), who saw everything, discovered that Ares and Aphrodite were lovers, and informed Hephaestus of this. Hephaestus was the smith-god, famous for his skills and artistry in metalworking. He created a golden net so fine that it was invisible. He placed it on the couch where he knew Aphrodite and Ares would lie; then he announced that he was going for a few days to Lemnos, one of his favorite retreats. As soon as he had gone, Aphrodite summoned Ares, and the two lay upon the couch. Then Hephaestus, with a crowd of the OLYMPIAN GODS and goddesses, burst in upon them. Ares and Aphrodite tried to leap up but became hopelessly entangled in the invisible golden net. The gods and goddesses delighted in this scene, laughing and pointing and making ribald remarks. Thus was Ares made to look ridiculous to all. It was a subtle revenge for Hephaestus, and another example of how disliked Ares was. This story is told in HOMER's ODYSSEY.

ARETHUSA In Greek mythology, a naiad or NYMPH of fountains and rivers. In one legend, told by OVID in *Metamorphoses*, the nymph is pursued by river-god Alpheus. Arethusa calls to the goddess ARTEMIS for help; Artemis turns Arethusa into a fountain on the island now called Sicily at Syracuse (where the Fontana Arethusa still exists).

ARGO In Greek mythology, the ship in which JASON and the ARGONAUTS sailed in quest of the GOLDEN FLEECE. (See *Jason and the Argonauts*, under JASON.) ARGUS, son of PHRIXUS, built the vessel, with the help of the goddess ATHENE. Within the ship was a beam cut from the divine tree (an oak or a beech) at DODONA, a shrine sacred to the god ZEUS and the Dodona ORACLE. It was said that the beam could help foretell the future.

ARGONAUTS (Sailors of the *Argo*) The crew gathered by Greek hero JASON to sail on his ship, the ARGO. There were 50 oars and 49 men and one woman, ATALANTA. (See *Names of the Argonauts*, below.) It is said that never before or since was so gallant a ship's company gathered together. Their quest was to capture the GOLDEN FLEECE, and this they did, after many adventures. (See *Jason and the Argonauts*, under JASON.)

Names of the Argonauts Many different names have been included in the muster roll of the ARGO, the ship sailed by JASON in his quest for the GOLDEN FLEECE. The following 50 names are those "given by the most trustworthy authorities," according to scholar Robert Graves (1895–1985).

Acastus, son of King PELIAS
Actor, son of Deion, the Phocian
ADMETUS, prince of Pherae
AMPHIARAUS, the Argive seer
Ancaeus of Samos
Ancaeus of Tegea, son of POSEIDON
ARGUS (2), the builder of the ARGO
Ascalaphus, son of ARES
Asterius, a Pelopian
ATALANTA of CALYDON, the great huntress
Augeias of ELIS
Butes of ATHENS

Caeneus the LAPITH
Calais, winged son of Boreas
Canthus the Euboean
Castor, one of the DIOSCURI
Cepheus, son of the Arcadian Aleus
Coronus the Lapith
Echion, son of HERMES
Erginus of Miletus
Euphemus of Taenarum
Euryalus, son of Mecisteus, one of the EPIGONI
Eurydamus the Dolopian
HERACLES of TIRYNS, the strongest man who ever lived
Hylas, companion to Heracles
Idas, son of Aphareus of Messene
Idmon, the Argive, son of APOLLO
Iphicles, son of Thestius
Iphitus, brother of King EURYSTHEUS of MYCENAE
JASON, the captain
LAERTES, son of Acrisius the Argive
Lynceus, brother to Idas
MELAMPUS, son of Poseidon
MELEAGER of Calydon
Mopsus, the Lapith
Naupilus the Argive, son of Poseidon, a noted navigator
Oileus, father of the hero AJAX
ORPHEUS, the poet
Palaemon, son of HEPHAESTUS
Peleus, the MYRMIDON
Peneleos of BOEOTIA
Periclymenus, son of Poseidon
Phalerus, the Athenian archer
Phanus, the Cretan son of DIONYSUS
Poeas, son of Thaumacus the Magnesian
Polydeuces, one of the DIOSCURI
Polyphemus, son of Elatus, the Arcadian
Staphylus, brother of Phanus
Tiphys, the helmsman of the *Argo*
Zetes, brother of Calais

ARGOS (or ARGOLIS) A district of the northern PELOPENNESUS, today known as the Argive Plain. For many centuries Argos dominated the Pelopennesus, rivaling ATHENS, SPARTA and CORINTH. It was known as HERA's city from the magnificent temple built in her honor. In mythology, Argos was known as the place where the 50 daughters of DANAUS killed their bridegrooms, except for one, who became the ancestor of PERSEUS. Another descendant of the Danaids was the hero HERACLES. AGAMEMNON was the famous king of Argos and MYCENAE who fought in the TROJAN WAR.

ARGUS (or ARGOS) (1) In Greek mythology, a giant with a hundred eyes. He was set by the goddess HERA to watch over the maiden IO, who had been transformed into a beautiful white heifer by the god ZEUS. Zeus sent HERMES to rescue Io. Hermes played upon his lute and sang songs until all of the hundred eyes of Argus closed in sleep. Then Hermes slew Argus and set Io free. (See *Io, the White Heifer*, under IO.) Hera placed the eyes of Argus on the tail of the peacock, where they remain to this day. The peacock is sacred to Hera.

ARGUS (or ARGOS) (2) In Greek mythology, the builder of the ship ARGO, of the ARGONAUTS.

ARGUS (or ARGOS) (3) In Greek mythology, the faithful old dog of ODYSSEUS, who alone recognized his master after 20 years of absence (see *Odysseus Returns to Ithaca*, under ODYSSEY.)

ARIADNE In Greek mythology, daughter of MINOS and PASIPHAË of CRETE; sister of ANDROGEUS, PHAEDRA and others.

Ariadne fell in love with the hero THESEUS when he came to Crete to kill the MINOTAUR, a monstrous creature, half-human, half-bull, that lived in the tortuous maze of the LABYRINTH. The Labyrinth had been invented and built by DAEDALUS so that no one, once inside, could find the way out. Ariadne gave Theseus a ball of string to trail behind him so that he could follow it and escape. After Theseus had done battle and slain the dreaded beast (see *Theseus, Ariadne and the Minotaur*, under THESEUS), he emerged triumphantly from the Labyrinth and carried Ariadne off. Some stories say that Theseus deserted Ariadne on the island of NAXOS. Other stories say that it was the god DIONYSUS who commanded Theseus to leave because he wanted the beautiful Ariadne for himself. Scholars think that the second version

of the tale is an attempt to make the great hero Theseus less of a scoundrel for deserting Ariadne. Still other versions of the story say that Ariadne was slain by the goddess ARTEMIS; or that she was pregnant and died in childbirth. All the different stories seem to indicate that part of the original story of Ariadne was lost. She was probably a prehistoric goddess of whom little was known.

In any case, it is said that the god ZEUS gave her a crown and set her among the stars. She was accorded godlike honors: in Greece at Naxos, and in Italy, where, as a bride of Dionysus, she was identified with the wine-goddess Liberia.

Ariadne was the subject of numerous works of literature (for example, a novel by Mary Renault [1905–1983], *The King Must Die*), music (*Ariadne auf Naxos* by Richard Strauss [1864–1949]), and art.

ARION In Greek mythology, the swiftest of all horses; possibly winged. He was born from the union between DEMETER (who had changed herself into a mare) and the sea-god POSEIDON, who changed himself into a stallion. Arion belonged first to the hero HERACLES, and then to ADRASTUS, king of Argos. In the war called the SEVEN AGAINST THEBES, Adrastus was the only one to survive, thanks to his wonderful steed.

ARISTAEUS An ancient rural Greek deity, native to THESSALY. Son of APOLLO and the NYMPH Cyrene. Aristaeus was brought up by the Nymphs of the god HERMES (half-brother of Apollo), who taught him the arts of beekeeping, cheese-making and the cultivation of olives. Later the MUSES taught him healing, hunting and the care of herds and flocks.

Aristaeus tried to force his attentions on the dryad (tree nymph) EURYDICE. He was punished by the gods (or the nymphs), who destroyed his bees. Aristaeus sought the advice of PROTEUS, who advised him to sacrifice cattle to the gods. Aristaeus followed the counsel of Proteus and was rewarded when swarms of bees emerged from the rotting corpses of the slain cattle.

Aristaeus was honored as a god in ancient Greece because of the great knowledge of his crafts that he passed on to man.

ARTEMIS Greek goddess of the hunt and of childbirth and chastity; also associated with the moon; daughter of ZEUS and LETO; sister of APOLLO. One of the OLYMPIAN GODS. Her origins are very old, probably derived from the Great-Mother mythologies. She is identified with DIANA in Roman mythology.

Artemis was armed with a bow and a quiver of arrows made by the smith-god, HEPHAESTUS. Like Apollo, she had many sides to her nature—she could be wild and destructive with her arrows; she could cause deadly disease in animals. She was a deity of sudden death. (See *Artemis, the Vengeful One,* below.) On the other hand, Artemis could be benevolent: with Ilithya, she was helpful to women in childbirth. Like Apollo, Artemis loved music, song and dancing.

Artemis was worshiped throughout Greece, especially in ARCADIA, and also in CRETE, ASIA MINOR and MAGNA GRAECIA.

The Birth of Artemis

See *The Birth of Apollo,* under APOLLO.

Artemis, the Vengeful One

Artemis, Greek goddess of the hunt, was not only pure and virginal herself; she punished any of her attendant nymphs who fell in love and she punished any men who approached her or her nymphs with amorous intent.

In the legend of CALLISTO, a handmaiden of Artemis, the god ZEUS falls in love with Callisto, who bears him a child, ARCAS. Angry at her departure from chastity, Artemis changes Callisto into a she-bear.

ACTEON, a hunter who saw Artemis bathing, gazed at her with admiration. Outraged, Artemis changed Acteon into a stag, then set his own pack of hounds upon him; they tore him to pieces.

The ALOEIDS, two giants who were determined to overthrow the OLYMPIAN GODS, swore to capture both HERA and Artemis; in one legend, Artemis turned herself into a white doe and pranced between the brothers. The Aloeids aimed their darts at the doe and inadvertently killed each other, and thus were punished for lusting after the goddesses.

NIOBE, the mother of 12 children, was foolish enough to boast that she was superior to LETO, the mother of Apollo and Artemis, who had borne only two children. Enraged, Apollo and Artemis killed all Niobe's children.

When Artemis at last fell in love, it was with ORION, another great hunter. One day Orion went swimming and swam so far from shore that his head looked like a rock in the sea. Jealous of his sister's love for Orion, or perhaps wanting to preserve his sister's chastity, Apollo challenged Artemis to hit the rock with her arrow. The arrow of Artemis pierced Orion's head, killing him. Another legend says that Artemis sent a scorpion to sting Orion, as a punishment for having gazed upon her amorously.

Artemis and the Amazons

The AMAZONS were a mythical race of female warriors who had a leader named Artemis and who worshiped at EPHESUS, in Ionia, ASIA MINOR (today's western Turkey). The temple built to Artemis (c. 550 B.C.) was considered one of the Seven Wonders of the ancient world. It was said that the Amazons removed their right breast in order to draw the bow more easily. Although the Amazons were warlike, fierce and seemed to have a horror of men, and therefore had a resemblance to Artemis, it is unlikely that they had anything to do with the Greek goddess; her name was merely conferred upon their leader.

ASCANIUS In Roman mythology, the son of AENEAS and his wife, Creusa. When Troy fell (see TROJAN WAR), Ascanius fled with his parents and his grandfather, ANCHISES. He is said to have founded ALBA LONGA, a city of ancient LATIUM near Lake Albano, southeast of Rome. Since he is also called Iulus or Julus, the family of Julius Caesar, mighty Roman emperor, claimed descent from him. The story of Ascanius is told by the Latin poet VIRGIL in the AENEID.

ASCLEPIUS Greek god of medicine and healing; son of APOLLO and CORONIS; father of Hygeia and others. The Roman spelling of his name is Aesculapius. The center of his cult was EPIDAURUS (northeast PELOPONNESUS), but there were many others, including Cos and Pergamum, where treatments were given to the sick.

Snakes (symbols of renewal because of the frequent shedding of their skin, to reveal glossy new skin underneath) were his emblem, usually depicted as twined about a wand called a CADUCEUS.

According to legend, Asclepius learned the art of healing from CHIRON, the wise and gentle CENTAUR. He mastered his craft so well that eventually, it was said, Asclepius could raise the dead. The god ZEUS, afraid that mere men might become immortal, struck Asclepius with a thunderbolt, but then made him a minor god in charge of medicine and healing.

ASIA MINOR The peninsula at the extreme tip of western Asia, usually synonymous with Asian Turkey or Anatolia. It is washed by the Black Sea in the north, by the Mediterranean in the south and by the Aegean Sea in the west. It was the intersecting point between East and West in ancient times: to the east lay Mesopotamia and China, to the west, Europe, especially nearby Greece. It was the site of the ancient kingdoms of LYDIA and PHRYGIA. At the entrance to the DARDANELLES, the sea passage that led from the Mediterranean to the Black Sea, was the city of TROY.

ASTERION (or ASTERIUS) (Starry) In Greek mythology, king of CRETE who married EUROPA and adopted her three sons: MINOS, RHADAMANTHUS and SARPEDON. (See *Europa and the Bull*, under EUROPA.)

ATALANTA In Greek mythology, a renowned huntress, daughter of Iasus, king of ARCADIA, and Clymene. Disappointed at the birth of a daughter, Iasus put the infant on Mount Parthenon and left her to die. (This was a common fate for girl babies in ancient Greece). ARTEMIS, goddess of the hunt, sent a she-bear to suckle the baby. The child was then reared by a band of hunters who found her on the mountainside.

Her hunting skills were so great that Atalanta dared to join the all-male group of hunters who were going after the Calydonian Boar at the request of MELEAGER, prince of Calydon. Atalanta scored the first thrust at the ferocious boar. Meleager killed the boar and presented its coveted hide and tusks to Atalanta, thus causing anger and strife among the men. (See CALYDONIAN BOAR HUNT.)

Now that she was famous, King Iasus recognized Atalanta as his daughter. He insisted that she must marry. Atalanta, having been warned by an ORACLE that she would find no happiness in marriage, set a condition on her marriage: Her suitor must be able to beat her in a footrace, or else die. Many tried to win her but failed and died. Finally MELANION, a prince from Arcadia, sought the help of APHRODITE, goddess of love. She gave him three golden apples that he dropped, one at a time, throughout the race. Atalanta couldn't resist picking them up and lost the race. Atalanta bore Melanion a son, Parthenonpaeus.

In some versions of this legend it is said that Atalanta and Melanion were turned into lions by Aphrodite and forced to pull the chariot of CYBELE, a goddess of earth and nature.

It is said that Atalanta was one of the ARGONAUTS, a fabled crew of sailors who sought the GOLDEN FLEECE. (See *Jason and the Argonauts*, under JASON.)

ATHAMAS In Greek mythology, one of the sons of AEOLUS; brother of SISYPHUS and Salmoneus; king of Orchomenus in BOEOTIA. With NEPHELE he had two sons, PHRIXUS and Leucon, and a daughter, HELLE.

Athamas tired of the phantomlike Nephele and took INO, daughter of CADMUS, to be his second wife. It was this marriage and the subsequent flight of Phrixus and Helle that brought about (a generation later) Jason's quest for the GOLDEN FLEECE (see *Jason and the Argonauts*, under JASON), for the two youngsters had fled from Boeotia on the back of a winged ram that bore a golden fleece on its back.

Athamas and Ino looked after the infant DIONYSUS, son of ZEUS and SEMELE. For this they earned the gratitude of Zeus but also the wrath of his wife, HERA, who visited madness upon Athamas and Ino.

Athamas and Ino had had two sons, Learchus and Melicertes. In a fit of madness, Athamas killed Learchus and ate his still-warm flesh. Stricken with grief, Athamas left his kingdom and wandered from country to country. After many years he founded a city called Alos, in

EPIRUS, an ancient country of Greece, on the Ionian Sea.

The conflict between the two wives of Athamas, Nephele (made by Zeus in the likeness of Hera) and Ino, may represent the conflict between early Ionian farmers (who worshiped the corn-goddess) and later Aeolian invaders, who reared sheep and worshiped the thunder-god Aeolus (represented by the cloudlike Nephele).

ATHENE (OR ATHENA) In Greek mythology, daughter of ZEUS and METIS. One of the most important OLYMPIAN GODS. Identified as MINERVA by the Romans.

Athene was a deity of many different functions and attributes. On the one hand, she was a goddess of war, the female counterpart of ARES. However, she was also associated with peace and compassion; she was a patroness of the arts and crafts, especially spinning and weaving (see ARACHNE); a patron of cities, notably ATHENS, which was named after her; and a goddess of wisdom.

The cult of Athene went back to the Cretan civilization, which predated that of classical Greece by about 1500 years. In CRETE and MYCENAE she was an earth-goddess. However, the Athenians firmly claimed her as their own, and dedicated the Parthenon, the temple on the Acropolis in Athens, to her. (See *Athene and Poseidon*, below.) Athens acknowledged Athene as the ancestor of their first king, ERICHTHONIUS (1).

Athene appears in innumerable myths, but none better displays her unique intellectual qualities than her role in the ODYSSEY as the constant friend and adviser of the clever and imaginative ODYSSEUS. She also offered help to other heroes, such as JASON and DIOMEDES (1). Other myths associated with Athene include those of BELLEROPHON; Perseus and the Medusa, (see *Perseus and the Medusa*, under PERSEUS); ARGUS and the ship ARGO; CADMUS and the dragon's teeth (see *Cadmus and the Dragon*, under CADMUS); and heroes HERACLES, Diomedes and Tydeus.

Athene appears in HOMER, VIRGIL, the Homeric Hymns, Pausanius, OVID, AESCHYLUS, SOPHOCLES and in English literature, usually under her Roman name, Minerva.

(See *The Birth of Athene*, and *Athene and Poseidon*, below).

The Birth of Athene There are many different stories about the birth and parentage of Athene. In the most familiar story, she sprang fully armed from the head of ZEUS when HEPHAESTUS split it open with an ax. Zeus had previously swallowed his consort, METIS, on learning that she would soon bear a child who would rule the gods. Metis was renowned for her wisdom. The myth may be a way of saying that when Zeus came to power he absorbed wisdom (Metis), and from this wisdom came the knowledge from which the arts (Athene) developed. This myth in some tellings develops the story of Zeus having violent headaches that made him howl with pain and rage. HERMES found him on the banks of the Triton river and summoned Hephaestus to help relieve his pain.

In CRETE they said that the goddess Athene had been hidden in a cloud and that by striking the cloud with his head, Zeus had caused Athene to emerge. This event was supposed to have happened beside a stream called the Triton.

According to the Pelasgians (prehistoric peoples inhabiting Mediterranean lands), Athene was born beside the lake or river Triton, and nurtured by three NYMPHS. As a girl, Athene accidentally killed her playmate, Pallas. In token of her grief, Athene set the nymph's name before her own, and is often known as Pallas Athene. This legend probably belongs to pre-Hellenic times.

Athene and Poseidon In this myth (see *Poseidon and Athene*, under POSEIDON), Athene challenges the sea-god Poseidon, as to who should rule over Athens. Zeus judged Athene the winner because she bestowed upon Athens the olive tree, while Poseidon produced only a salty stream. The rivalry for the possession of Athens may have been a folk memory of the collision between new people (migrants) with their new gods, and the ancient people (symbolized by Athene, earth-goddess of the Cretans and Mycenaeans). The triumph of the ancient mother-earth figure over the male god, Poseidon, shows that the myth goes back to archaic times, long before the Hellenes (Greeks) and other migrants arrived on the peninsula (the

Peloponnesus), bringing with them belief in dominant male gods.

ATHENS Capital of modern Greece; situated in ATTICA. It was named after the goddess ATHENE. Athens was inhabited even before the Bronze Age (2000–1000 B.C.). It is the site of many architectural and archaeological wonders, such as the Acropolis, an ancient fortress, and the Parthenon, one of many temples surviving from antiquity. Athens was (and is) the cultural center of the Greek world.

ATLAS In Greek mythology, a TITAN, the son of Iapetus and Clymene. He was the leader of the Titans in their battle against the gods. (See *The War with the Titans*, under ZEUS.) The Titans were defeated and all but Atlas were confined to TARTARUS, a section of the UNDERWORLD. Atlas' punishment was to carry the sky upon his shoulders throughout eternity. In the myth of the great hero HERACLES, Heracles took the burden from the shoulders of Atlas so that the Titan could fetch for him the golden apples of the HESPERIDES. When he returned, Heracles tricked him into taking back the weight of the heavens. (See *The Twelve Labors of Heracles*, under HERACLES.) In another myth, the hero PERSEUS turned the Titan into stone by showing him the head of MEDUSA. Because of his gigantic size, the petrified Atlas became a mountain range.

A book of maps is called an atlas because a picture of Atlas supporting the world upon his shoulders appeared on the title page of the book of Flemish mapmaker and geographer, Mercator (1512–1594).

ATREIDS The stories concerning the house of PELOPS. (See ATREUS AND THYESTES.)

ATREUS AND THYESTES In Greek mythology, the sons of PELOPS and HIPPODAMEIA; the Pelops family, of which they were a part, was doomed to tragedy and bloodshed through the generations until the fall of MYCENAE and the death of their descendants, AGAMEMNON and MENELAUS. The stories concerning the tragedies of the house of Pelops are sometimes called the ATREIDS, after Atreus. One of the stories tells how Atreus became king of Mycenae. (See *The Golden Fleece*, below.)

ATLAS, THE TITAN, WAS DOOMED TO CARRY THE SKY UPON HIS SHOULDERS FOR ALL ETERNITY. (NEW YORK PUBLIC LIBRARY PICTURE COLLECTION)

The Golden Fleece The people of Mycenae had been advised by an ORACLE to choose a ruler from the house of PELOPS. They considered Atreus and Thyestes, the sons of Pelops and Hippodameia. The brothers had been rivals since childhood.

Atreus laid claim to the throne, being the older brother, and also the owner of the lamb with the golden fleece that had been given to the brothers by the god HERMES. Atreus sacrificed the lamb to the gods but kept the valuable fleece for himself.

Thyestes then persuaded Aerope, the wife of Atreus, to steal the golden fleece for him. Because of the valuable fleece, the elders of Mycenae chose Thyestes as their ruler; but the great god ZEUS revealed to them that Thyestes had obtained the fleece by treachery. Thyestes fled in terror of punishment, leaving his home and children behind, and the throne of Mycenae was awarded to Atreus.

Not content with his victory, Atreus plotted revenge on his brother's treachery. He invited his brother back from exile, pretending forgiveness, and served him a banquet that consisted of Thyestes' own children. When he found out what he had eaten, Thyestes went mad with grief. He threw a curse upon the house of Atreus, thus compounding the one already laid upon it by the charioteer, MYRTILUS, who had been tricked by Pelops, the father of Atreus and Thyestes. The children of Atreus, AGAMEMNON and MENELAUS, would suffer from these curses.

Thyestes then consulted an ORACLE and was advised to beget a child upon his own daughter, Pelopia (the only one not cooked in the stew served up by Atreus). Thyestes, in disguise, seduced his own daughter, who managed to wrest his sword from him. Years later, when Thyestes was a captive of his brother Atreus, a boy of seven appeared before him bearing a sword. Thyestes recognized the sword as his own, and the boy, AEGISTHUS, as his son with Pelopia. Aegisthus, upon learning the truth of his ancestry, was persuaded to acknowledge Thyestes as his true father and to turn the sword upon Atreus.

Thyestes then reigned as king of Mycenae, with Aegisthus as his heir. But this being the accursed house of Pelops, Agamemnon (the eldest son of Atreus) drove Thyestes out of Mycenae and deposed Aegisthus; it was only at the death of Aegisthus and CLYTEMNESTRA (see under AGAMEMNON) that the FURIES and FATES were satisfied and put an end to the atrocities of murder and incest that had plagued the house of Pelops and of Atreus.

ATTICA Triangular area at the eastern end of central Greece. Its capital is ATHENS.

ATTIS A Phrygian vegetation god, the beloved of the great earth-mother CYBELE. His cult was more important in Roman than in Greek mythology. Attis was born of a virgin mother, Nana, by springing from a ripe almond or pomegranate that she had placed on her bosom. As a young man he was beloved by Cybele, but Attis reneged on his vows to the goddess and espoused the daughter of a river-god. In some accounts, Cybele struck Attis in jealous anger, and in the ensuing frenzy Attis wounded himself and bled to death, whereupon Cybele (or ZEUS) turned him into a pine tree. Around the tree grew masses of violets, nourished by his blood. According to another tradition, Zeus set a wild boar upon Attis, and Attis was gored to death.

In any case, Attis went to the UNDERWORLD. All through the dark months of winter, Attis was mourned. Then, in the spring he returned to the earth and was worshiped, only to be sacrificed again at the end of the season.

In ancient times the birth, death and resurrection of Attis were celebrated with wild music and bloody rituals in the shrines sacred to Cybele. The worship of Attis was rare in Greece, but the cult flourished in Rome, where Attis was regarded as a supreme deity.

The myth of Attis, like that of ADONIS, is plainly the development of an ancient fertility festival that celebrated the corn-god, born anew each year, then killed and planted underground, only to reappear the following spring.

AURORA (Dawn) The Roman goddess of dawn, known by the Greeks as the "rosy-fingered" EOS.

The aurora borealis (known as the northern lights), the bands of light seen at high latitudes, is caused by electrically charged solar particles. A similar phenomenon in the Southern Hemisphere is called the aurora australis (known as the southern lights).

AUTOLYCUS In Greek mythology, the son of HERMES and CHIONE. Autolycus, like his father, was a notorious thief. Some said that he could change his shape at will. From his father, Autolycus received the gift of making things invisible. In this way he was able to commit numerous thefts. He stole the cattle of EURYTUS and sold them to the hero HERACLES; and he stole the cattle of SISYPHUS, who took revenge upon ANTICLEA, the daughter of Autolycus.

Anticlea was the mother of ODYSSEUS, which made Autolycus the grandfather of Odysseus. In HOMER'S ODYSSEY, Autolycus helps to nurse his grandson when he is wounded by a wild boar. Autolycus also makes an appearance as a villain in a play of William Shakespeare (1564–1616), *The Winter's Tale*.

B

BACCHANALIA In Roman mythology, the Latin name for the orgiastic rites of BACCHUS (see DIONYSUS). The excesses with which they were accompanied led to a senatorial decree banning them in Italy in 186 B.C. In spite of severe penalties, the rites continued to be celebrated for a long time. Numerous paintings depict the bacchanalia; among the most famous are those by Flemish painter Peter Paul Rubens (1577–1640) and French painter Nicolas Poussin (1594–1665).

BACCHANTS (or BACCHANTES) In Roman mythology, the women (also called MAENADS) who followed the god BACCHUS (DIONYSUS). In their ritual orgies the Bacchants were said to sacrifice wild animals and humans, tearing them apart and eating their flesh. Their cult was banned by the Roman Senate in 186 B.C. The *Bacchae*, a tragedy by EURIPIDES, deals with the cult of the Bacchae.

BACCHE In Greek mythology, one of the five NYMPHS who looked after the infant DIONYSUS on Mount Nysa. The other nymphs were Macris, Nysa, Erato and Bromie. Collectively they were called the BACCHANTS; later their name was used to describe followers of Dionysus.

In gratitude for the nymphs' service in rearing Dionysus, the god ZEUS placed their images among the stars, naming them the Hyades, a constellation in Taurus.

BACCHUS The Roman name for DIONYSUS. He was also known as Liber. The cult of the Dionysian religion spread all over Italy in the 2nd century B.C., causing alarm to the Romans. The rites were suppressed in 186 B.C., but the cult of Bacchus continued for many years.

Bacchus was portrayed by many artists, including the Italian painter Caravaggio (1573–1610), who portrayed him, in *The Young Bacchus,* as a sensual youth, the god of wine and revelry.

BACCHANTS WERE THE FOLLOWERS OF BACCHUS. THIS IS A DETAIL FROM A GREEK VASE PAINTING, C. 420 B.C. (NEW YORK PUBLIC LIBRARY PICTURE COLLECTION)

Roman bacchanalia were festivals in honor of Bacchus, characterized by wild and drunken revelry.

BELLEROPHON In Greek mythology, son of the Corinthian king GLAUCUS (2); grandson of SISYPHUS. In one story, Bellerophon, a very handsome young man loved by many women, is sent on a seemingly impossible mission to

23

kill the CHIMERA, a fire-breathing monster with the head of a lion, the body of a goat and a serpent's tail. The seer Polyeidus advises the young hero to capture the winged horse, PEGASUS. This Bellerophon does, with the help of the goddess ATHENE, who gives him a golden bridle. Pegasus and Bellerophon kill the monster.

Bellerophon and his fabulous horse have many adventures. But the young man makes a mistake when he decides to ride Pegasus up to OLYMPUS, the home of the gods. Stung by a gadfly sent by ZEUS, Pegasus throws his rider and Bellerophon falls to earth. He spends the rest of his life as a cripple and an outcast.

BOEOTIA   An ancient region of central Greece, north of ATTICA and west of Megaris and the Gulf of CORINTH. The early inhabitants were from THESSALY. The city of THEBES dominated the region. DELPHI, the most celebrated ORACLE of antiquity, had her abode in Boeotia, on Mount PARNASSUS. Mount HELICON, sacred to the god APOLLO, was the abode of the nine MUSES. It was from Boeotia that the children of King ATHAMAS fled, leading (a generation later) to the quest for the GOLDEN FLEECE (see *Jason and the Argonauts*, under JASON).

BOREAS   In Greek mythology, the North Wind, offspring of the dawn-goddess, EOS, and the TITAN Astreus. He was the father of the fleet-footed Calais and Zetes, who sailed with JASON and the ARGONAUTS.

BRISEIS (also called HIPPODAEMIA)   The daughter of a Trojan priest, Briseus. A captive and lover of the Greek hero ACHILLES, she was stolen from him by AGAMEMNON, the leader of the Greek army, by an act of trickery. Furious, Achilles withdrew his troops from the battle (see TROJAN WAR), causing the Greeks to lose ground to the Trojans. These acts marked the beginning of HOMER'S ILIAD, his great epic about the Trojan War.

BRITOMARTIS (Sweet Virgin)   A very ancient Cretan deity, later said to be a daughter of the god ZEUS. A huntress, she pursued wild beasts in the forests of CRETE. King MINOS of Crete fell in love with her and pursued her for nine months. Finally Britomartis flung herself off a cliff into the sea, but was caught in a net and rescued by fishermen. She escaped to the island of Aegina, where she was given the name DICTYNNA (Lady of the Nets). The goddess ARTEMIS (also a virgin huntress) rewarded her chastity by making her immortal. It is said that Britomartis appears at night to navigators to guide them. In Greek mythology Dictynna-Britomartis is called the Cretan Artemis.

C

CADMUS (From the East) In Greek mythology, the founder of the city of THEBES, in BOEOTIA. He was the son of King AGENOR and Telephassa; brother of EUROPA, CILIX and PHOENIX; married HARMONIA; father of INO, Agave, Antonoë and SEMELE (daughters), and Polydorus (a son). When Europa was carried off by the god ZEUS (disguised as a bull [see *Europa and the Bull,* under EUROPA]), Agenor sent his three sons to search for her, warning them not to return home without their sister. Not being able to find her, each of the brothers settled down elsewhere. Cadmus, on the advice of the Delphic oracle (see below), eventually founded the city of Thebes and married Harmonia.

Cadmus and the Delphic Oracle When Cadmus was sent to find his sister after she had been stolen away by a white bull (see *EUROPA AND THE BULL, UNDER EUROPA*), he and a few companions crossed the sea and went to DELPHI to consult the ORACLE who resided there. The pythoness-oracle told Cadmus that he would found a city, and that he should give up the search for his sister and follow the tracks of a cow that would show him where to build the city. After a battle with a dragon (see *Cadmus and the Dragon,* below) and years of slavery under the war-god ARES, Cadmus founded the city of THEBES (see *Cadmus Builds the Citadel,* below).

Cadmus and the Dragon Cadmus, son of King AGENOR, was searching for his sister EUROPA; she had been carried off by a white bull. (See *Europa and the Bull,* under EUROPA.) The Delphic oracle (see above) advised Cadmus to give up the search for his sister and instead to follow the tracks of a cow who would show him where to found a new city.

Cadmus, with a few companions, followed a cow that had moon-shaped markings on its head. The cow went deep into BOEOTIA before she rested. Cadmus knew that her resting place was to be the site of the citadel, or fortress, of the city that the oracle had told him he would found. He decided to sacrifice the cow to ATHENE, goddess of wisdom. He sent his companions to get some purifying water from a nearby spring. The men were attacked by a dragon, the guardian of the spring, who killed them all before Cadmus could reach them. Cadmus then crushed the dragon's head with a rock. He sacrificed the cow and was rewarded by a visit from Athene. She told him to pull out the dragon's teeth and plant them in the ground. Cadmus did this, and in a very short time a host of fully armed men sprang up eager to fight, for the dragon is sacred to the war-god, ARES, the god who loved to fight. The men were called the Spartoi (Sown Men).

Cadmus threw a stone into the midst of the Spartoi and at once the men started to attack each other, bellowing, until all but five were dead.

Ares was angry with Cadmus for killing his serpent-dragon and a divine court sentenced Cadmus to become the slave of Ares for "a Great Year," which may mean as much as eight years.

Cadmus Builds the Citadel Cadmus served many years of slavery under the war-god, ARES, who was angry because Cadmus had killed one of his dragons. When the term of bondage was over, Cadmus and the Spartoi (the warriors born from the dragon's teeth [see *Cadmus and the Dragon,* above]) built the great citadel, or acropolis, called Cadmea in honor of Cadmus. Around the fortress rose the city of THEBES. The Spartoi were to be the ancestors of the Theban nobility.

Cadmus Marries Harmonia After Cadmus founded the city of THEBES, he married HARMONIA, the daughter of ARES and APHRODITE. This was the first wedding of mortal beings ever attended by all 12 of the OLYMPIAN GODS. Cadmus had 12 golden thrones set up for them in his house. All the gods brought gifts: Aphrodite gave Harmonia a golden necklace (made by HEPHAESTUS) that would make her irresistibly beautiful; Athene gave her a golden robe that would make her wise; HERMES gave her a lyre; and all the gods blessed Harmonia.

Cadmus and Harmonia had four daughters; INO, Agave, Antonoë and SEMELE, and a son, Polydorus.

In their old age the royal house of Thebes was destroyed and Cadmus and Harmonia made their way to Illyria, an ancient region of the Balkan Peninsula, generally taken to mean the Adriatic Coast north of Albania and west of the Dinaric Alps. There they eventually turned into serpents. In mythology, serpents are considered to be of the earth, so the transformation of Cadmus and Harmonia into serpents may simply be another way of saying that they died and were buried in the earth.

Cadmus and the Alphabet Cadmus, founder of Thebes, is said to have introduced the alphabet, and therefore writing, into Greece from his native Phoenicia. It is known that early Greek alphabets were derived from the Phoenician alphabet.

CADUCEUS In Greek mythology, the wing-topped staff with two snakes winding around it, carried by HERMES (and in Roman mythology, MERCURY). Two snakes intertwined is a very ancient symbol, associated since Babylonian times (3rd millennium B.C.) with fertility, wisdom and healing. The staff was carried by Greek heralds and ambassadors as a symbol of peace and neutrality. In later times, the staff became the emblem of ASCLEPIUS, god of healing. Today the caduceus is the insignia of the medical profession in many countries, including the United States and Britain.

CALCHAS In Greek mythology, the sinister seer who keeps prophesying doom throughout HOMER'S ILIAD. He is a priest of APOLLO and is called the son of Thestor. He accompanies the Achaeans (Greeks) on their expedition to Troy during the TROJAN WAR. It is Calchas that advises AGAMEMNON to sacrifice his daughter IPHIGINIA to gain fair winds for the expedition

to Troy; and it is Calchas who asserts that there will be no victory for the Greeks without the help of ACHILLES.

CALLIOPE (Beautiful Voice) One of the Greek MUSES, generally considered as the first and most important, Calliope was the patroness of epic (heroic) stories and poems. She was the daughter of MNEMOSYNE and ZEUS and, some say, the mother of ORPHEUS. She is portrayed in art with a tablet and stylus and sometimes with a trumpet. The name calliope is given to a kind of whistling steam-organ once played at circuses.

CALLIRHOË In Greek mythology, daughter of OENEUS (Oeneous), king of CALYDON. Callirhoë married ALCMAEON, not knowing that he was already married to Arsinoë, a princess of ARCADIA, a mountainous, isolated region in the PELOPONNESUS. However, Callirhoë did learn about the fabulous treasure of HARMONIA, a necklace and a robe, that Alcmaeon had inherited from his greedy mother, ERIPHYLE. As Alcmaeon's wife, Callirhoë asked that the treasure be given to her (see under ALCMAEON).

CALLISTO The handmaiden of the Greek goddess ARTEMIS and the lover of the god ZEUS, with whom she bore a child, ARCAS, the ancestor of the Arcadians. Artemis, angry at Callisto's loss of virginity, changed her into a she-bear. One day as the grown-up Arcas was hunting in the woods he saw the she-bear and was about to kill her. Zeus, to prevent the young man from killing his own mother, changed them both into stars: Callisto became Ursa Major, the Great Bear; Arcas became ARCTURUS, Guardian of the Bear.

CALYDON A town of AETOLIA, in western Greece. In Greek myth, it was founded by AETOLUS and was the site of the CALYDONIAN BOAR HUNT.

CALYDONIAN BOAR HUNT, THE In Greek mythology, the boar was a ferocious creature sent by the goddess ARTEMIS to ravage CALYDON, an ancient city in Aetolia, western Greece. OENEUS, the king of Calydon, had offended the goddess by failing to offer her proper sacrifices; the boar was sent as punishment. MELEAGER, the son of Oeneus, was ordered to kill the boar. He sent messengers far and wide asking princes and sportsmen to come to his aid. Among those that came were the hero of Athens, THESEUS; his friend Peirithous; JASON; and ATALANTA. Atalanta, the only woman in the hunt, was the first to wound the boar, which was finally killed by Meleager. He presented the boar's hide to Atalanta, thus causing anger and quarrels among the men.

The Calydonian Boar Hunt is a heroic saga, probably based upon a real boar hunt that degenerated into bitter feuds between rival clans from different parts of ancient Greece.

CALYPSO In HOMER'S ODYSSEY, the nymph-queen of the island of Ogygia in the Ionian Sea. She detained the shipwrecked ODYSSEUS for seven years but finally, at the command of the god ZEUS, she helped him on his way back to ITHACA, his home.

CAMILLA In Roman mythology, a virgin queen of the Volscians. She was the daughter of Metabus and Casmilla. Her father, Metabus, dedicated his infant daughter to the goddess DIANA. It is said in VIRGIL'S AENEID that she ran so swiftly over a field of corn that not a single blade of grass was bent and that she ran over the sea without even wetting her feet. Camilla joined TURNUS in the struggle against the Trojan hero AENEAS and was killed by a spear.

CAPRICORN (The Goat) A constellation between Sagittarius and Aquarius; the 10th sign of the zodiac. Capricorn is named after the goat-nymph AMALTHEA who, in Greek mythology, tended the god ZEUS when he was an infant. In gratitude, Zeus set Amalthea among the stars. (See *The Childhood of Zeus*, under ZEUS.)

CARTHAGE An ancient city on the north shore of Africa, near modern Tunis. In mythology, as told in VIRGIL'S AENEID, Carthage was founded by DIDO, who became its queen.

CASSANDRA In Greek mythology, daughter of King PRIAM of TROY and of Queen HECUBA; sister of Hellenus. The god APOLLO gave Cassandra the gift of prophecy, but when she rejected his advances he ordained that no one would ever believe her prophecies (which were always accurate). Before the fall of Troy, Cassandra warned the Trojans that the gift-horse of the Greeks was a trick, but no one believed her, and the Trojans were defeated (see TROJAN WAR). At the fall of Troy, Cassandra was given as booty to the victorious AGAMEMNON, king of ARGOS and MYCENAE. Cassandra warned the king that he would be killed by his wife, CLYTEMNESTRA, but Agamemnon would not believe her. He brought Cassandra back to Mycenae. Both Agamemnon and Cassandra were murdered by Clytemnestra.

Cassandra appears in many works of literature, including HOMER'S ILIAD and ODYSSEY, VIRGIL'S AENEID, OVID'S *Metamorphoses* and many others.

The word *cassandra* has come to mean someone who is a prophet of doom.

CASSIOPEIA In Greek mythology, wife of King CEPHEUS of ETHIOPIA; mother of ANDROMEDA and of Atymnius, by ZEUS. Cassiopeia boasted that she and her daughter were more beautiful than the sea NYMPHS, or nerieds, daughters of the god POSEIDON. This aroused the wrath of Poseidon, who sent a monster to punish Ethiopia. An ORACLE declared that only the sacrifice of Cassiopeia's daughter, Andromeda, would appease the monster and save the country. (See *Perseus and Andromeda*, under PERSEUS). Cassiopeia, along with Cepheus and Andromeda, was set among the stars as a constellation visible in the Northern Hemisphere.

CASTOR AND POLLUX Twin gods known to the Greeks as the DIOSCURI (sons of ZEUS and brothers of HELEN). They were adopted by the Romans as the "Heavenly Twins" when they were said to have fought on the side of the Romans against warring Latin tribes, bringing victory to Rome at Lake Regillus (496 B.C.). Castor and Pollux became popular Roman gods, associated with commerce and, eventually, symbols of life and death. Many legends grew up around them and magnificent temples were erected in their honor.

CELEUS In Greek mythology, legendary king of ELEUSIS; father of DEMOPHON and TRIPTOLEMUS; husband of Metaneira. He and his wife were hosts to the goddess DEMETER when she wandered the earth in search of her daughter PERSEPHONE. Demeter became the nurse of Demophon and subsequently bestowed great gifts upon Triptolemus. Celeus is described as the first priest and his daughters as the first priestesses of Demeter at Eleusis.

CENTAURS In Greek mythology, these were creatures half-man and half-horse, sons of CENTAURUS. Their origin is said to be as follows: IXION, a LAPITH of THESSALY was in love with the goddess HERA, wife of ZEUS. Zeus was angry. He fashioned a likeness of Hera out of a cloud and called her NEPHELE. Ixion, convinced that the beautiful cloud-woman was Hera, mated with her. Nephele produced a son, Centaurus. This son mated with the mares of Thessaly, producing creatures that were half-man and half-horse—the centaurs.

The myth of the centaurs probably stems from the time of the migrations and the coming of the horse to Greece—the horse was unknown in Greece until about 2000 B.C. The horse was enormously important to migratory people and was a cult animal in many parts of the world. In remote regions where the wild horses lived, there must have been primitive peoples who were so skilled at catching, taming and riding the horses that the sight of them awed all who saw them. Many may have believed that they were looking at a single, magical creature, with the head and trunk of a man and the hind quarters of a horse, particularly since a skilled rider and a horse can give the impression of being as one.

Usually depicted as unruly, the centaurs are notorious in legend for their disorderly behavior among the Lapiths, the mythical people of Thessaly. The result was a battle. The centaurs were expelled from their native Thessaly and took refuge on Mount Pindus, on the frontiers of EPIRUS. Centaurs are often associated with the SATYRS and SILENI, followers of the wine-god, DIONYSUS. However, CHIRON, the most famous of the centaurs, was wise and gentle. Because of their human-animal form, centaurs were often thought of as depictions of humankind's dual nature.

CENTAURUS In Greek mythology, son of IXION and NEPHELE; father of the CENTAURS, created after Centaurus mated with the mares of THESSALY.

CEPHALUS In Greek mythology, son of HERMES; husband of Procris; loved by the dawn-goddess EOS. Eos tricked Cephalus into leaving his beloved wife. The unhappy Procris sought the protection of ARTEMIS, goddess of the hunt. By the devious methods of Artemis, Cephalus was presented with two magnificent gifts: a spear that never missed its mark and a hound (named LAELAPS) that never lost the scent of its quarry. Cephalus inadvertently cast the spear at Procris and killed her. He then killed himself by leaping from a cliff into the sea.

CEPHEUS In Greek mythology, king of ETHIOPIA; husband of CASSIOPEIA; father of ANDROMEDA, who was to marry the hero PERSEUS. (See *Perseus and Andromeda,* under PERSEUS.) After their deaths, Cepheus, Cassiopeia and Andromeda were all set among the stars as constellations.

CERBERUS In Greek mythology, the hound of HADES, guardian of the UNDERWORLD. Cerberus was the offspring of TYPHON and ECHIDNA. In some accounts Cerberus had three heads; in others, as many as 50. He was a fearsome creature, but it is said he could be calmed by music or offerings of food.

For HERACLES, bringing Cerberus from Hades to the upper world was his 12th and most difficult labor (see *The Twelve Labors of Heracles,* under HERACLES). It is said that when he was captured, the monstrous dog dripped venom from his fangs and thus infected certain herbs, including the aconite, called wolfsbane. Evil magicians then used these herbs to prepare poisonous brews.

The idea of a fearsome guardian-dog probably had its origin in the custom of the Egyptians, who guarded the graves of the dead with large, dangerous dogs. Cerberus is associated with the

HERACLES CAPTURES THE THREE-HEADED DOG, CER-BERUS. (NEW YORK PUBLIC LIBRARY PICTURE COLLECTION)

dog-headed Egyptian god Anubis, and also with Hecate, an ancient goddess of death.

CERCOPES In Greek mythology, twins, sons of OCEANUS and Theia. They were mischievous, clever thieves, sometimes depicted as monkeys. They teased the great hero HERACLES. Heracles took them captive, tying them onto a pole that he carried across his shoulders. Heracles was so disarmed by the jokes and good humor of the twins that he set them free.

CERES Roman corn-goddess, "Mother Earth," protector of agriculture and all fruits of the earth. She was identified with the Greek goddess DEMETER, who was one of the OLYMPIAN GODS. Ceres had a daughter, PROSERPINA, the Roman equivalent of PERSEPHONE.

From Ceres we get the word *cereal*, which denotes the grasses—such as wheat, oats and barley—that are cultivated for their edible grains.

CHAOS In Greek mythology, the empty, unfathomable space at the beginning of time. GAIA, the original Earth Mother, sprang from Chaos, as did Nox (Night) and EREBUS (Darkness). Eventually the word chaos came to mean great confusion of matter out of which a supreme being created all life. In modern parlance, chaos has come to mean a confusing mess of any kind.

CHARON In Greek mythology, the ferryman of the UNDERWORLD. Son of EREBUS (darkness personified) and NOX (Night), the hideous old man ferried the shades, or spirits, of the dead across the rivers ACHERON and STYX. If not presented with an *obolus* (a small coin), that is, a bribe, the old man would drive away the hapless intruder, who was then condemned to wander the bleak shores of Acheron and Styx. Hence comes the custom of the Greeks (and others) placing a coin on the mouth or eyelids of the dead.

CHIMERA (She-Goat) In Greek mythology, a fire-breathing monster with a lion's head, a goat's body and a serpent's tail; the offspring of the monsters ECHIDNA and TYPHON. It is said that BELLEROPHON destroyed the Chimera by mounting on his winged horse, PEGASUS, and shooting the monster with arrows or lumps of lead.

The word *chimera* is used in English for an illusory fantasy or a wild, incongruous scheme.

The origin of this creature may be a volcano in LYCIA, ASIA MINOR, whose eruptions created as much havoc as did the mischief of Chimera until she was slain by the Lycian, BELLEROPHON.

CHIONE Daughter of Daedalion, mother of AUTOLYCUS by HERMES and of Phillamon by APOLLO.

CHIRON In Greek mythology, a CENTAUR of great wisdom and kindness, friend of both men and gods. Possibly the son of CRONUS and Phylira, Chiron lived on Mount PELION in THESSALY. He received his education from the divine twins, APOLLO and ARTEMIS. In turn, he was entrusted with the education of ASCLEPIUS, god of healing, and the heroes JASON and ACHILLES.

Chiron was inadvertently wounded by HERACLES during a brawl with the centaurs, who were mostly wild and unruly. Heracles rushed to the side of Chiron but there was nothing either he or Chiron could do, for the arrow of Heracles had been dipped in the poisoned blood of HYDRA, the many-headed water-serpent. Since Chiron was immortal he was doomed to suffer eternal pain. The dilemma was solved by the

CERES WAS THE ROMAN CORN-GODDESS, IDENTIFIED WITH THE GREEK GODDESS DEMETER. (NEW YORK PUBLIC LIBRARY PICTURE COLLECTION)

god ZEUS. He allowed Chiron to confer his immortality on PROMETHEUS in return for the peace of dying. Zeus then placed Chiron in the heavens as part of the SAGITTARIUS constellation.

Chiron, half-man and half-horse, represented ancient wisdom: He was the symbol of the wild horse, full of strength, tamed to be of enormous help to man.

CHRYSEIS In Greek mythology, the daughter of Chryses, a priest of APOLLO. She was taken prisoner by Greek war hero ACHILLES. Considered as war booty, Chryseis was then seized by AGAMEMNON, leader of the Greeks. Her father, Chryses, came to the Greek camp to rescue his daughter, but was repulsed by Agamemnon. Thereupon Apollo sent a plague among the Greeks. Many died and Agamemnon at last released Chryseis to her father to appease the anger of the god Apollo.

CILIX In Greek mythology, son of AGENOR and Telephassa, brother of CADMUS, EUROPA and PHOENIX. When Europa was stolen away by ZEUS, King Agenor sent his three sons to search for her. The brothers could not find her, and not daring to return to their father, settled down elsewhere. Cilix is said to have founded the nation of the Cilicians, an ancient region of southeast ASIA MINOR. Modern Cilicia is an area of southern Turkey lying between the Mediterranean Sea and the Taurus range of mountains.

CIRCE In Greek mythology, daughter of the sun-god HELIOS, sister of PHAETON and AETES. The witch-goddess of HOMER'S ODYSSEY, she cast powerful spells. Circe turned all Odysseus's men into swine. Odysseus escaped the curse with the help of a herb called *moly* and spent a year with the enchantress. Eventually he persuaded Circe to restore his men to their former shapes and they all escaped from the witch. Circe also appears in the story of JASON (see *Jason and the Argonauts* under JASON).

In post-Homeric stories Circe bore Odysseus a son, TELEGONUS.

CLYTEMNESTRA In Greek mythology, daughter of Tyndareus, king of SPARTA, and of LEDA. Leda had been loved by the god ZEUS, who had come to her in the form of a swan. Leda bore HELEN as well as Clytemnestra and others, so Clytemnestra and Helen were half-sisters. Clytemnestra was the mother of Chrysothemis, IPHIGENIA, ELECTRA and ORESTES.

Clytemnestra married AGAMEMNON, king of ARGOS and MYCENAE, of the accursed house of PELOPS. When Agamemnon went to the TROJAN WAR as commander of the Greek forces, Clytemnestra became the lover of AEGISTHUS, another descendant of Pelops. Clytemnestra hated Agamemnon, for he had sacrificed their daughter Iphigenia to ARTEMIS, and to the wind-god, AEOLUS, in order to get fair winds for the Greek fleet to sail to Troy and many years of war.

CHARON WAS THE BOATMAN WHO FERRIED THE SOULS OF THE DEAD OVER THE RIVER STYX TO THE UNDERWORLD. (NEW YORK PUBLIC LIBRARY PICTURE COLLECTION)

When the victorious Agamemnon returned from Troy, he brought with him Princess CASSANDRA as one of the spoils of war. He and Cassandra were murdered by Clytemnestra and Aegisthus, who were themselves murdered by Electra and Orestes, the children of Clytemnestra and Agamemnon.

Although Clytemnestra has little mythology of her own, she is a major tragic figure in the plays of AESCHYLUS, SOPHOCLES and EURIPIDES.

CONSUS Ancient Roman god of fertility. He was also worshiped in connection with horses. On the day of his feast, horses and asses were garlanded with flowers and allowed to rest. Eventually his cult was forgotten and he became regarded as a god of good counsel (Latin *consilium*).

CORINTH A city in the northeast PELOPONnesus, strategically situated on the isthmus connecting Peloponnesus with central Greece. Corinth was one of the largest and most powerful cities of ancient Greece, a rival of ATHENS and traditionally allied with SPARTA. Corinth traded with both east (across the Aegean Sea) and west (across the Ionian Sea) and founded numerous colonies. Corinth is mentioned many times in Greek mythology. For example, the hero JASON and his sorceress wife, MEDEA, fled to Corinth when they were forced to leave Iolcus. In Corinth Jason fell in love with GLAUCA, daughter of King Creon of Corinth.

CORNUCOPIA (Horn of Plenty) In Greek mythology, the horn of the goat-nymph, AMALTHEA, who had tended the infant ZEUS (see *The*

Childhood of Zeus under ZEUS). The horn was as large and full as that of a cow's, and would remain forever filled with food and drink for its owners. Zeus gave the horn to the ash-nymphs, Adrastia and IDA (1), who, along with Amalthea, had tended him when he was an infant. The cornucopia remains a symbol of plenty, generosity, hospitality and general well-being.

CORONIS In Greek mythology, daughter of Phlegyas, king of the LAPITHS of THESSALY; mother of ASCLEPIUS, with the god APOLLO.

Apollo fell in love with Coronis when he saw her bathing in a lake. Coronis seemed to accept the love of Apollo. He left a white bird, a crow, to watch over her. But Coronis then fell in love with Ischus. The crow sped off to tell the news to Apollo, who struck the crow in his anger and turned its white feathers to black. ARTEMIS, the sister of Apollo, shot her arrows at the faithless Coronis and killed her. But Apollo managed to snatch the infant Asclepius from the funeral pyre. The child was brought up by the god HERMES, or, some say, by CHIRON, the gentle CENTAUR, to become a god of healing and medicine.

CORYBANTES In Greek mythology, the worshipers of CYBELE who celebrated their goddess with wild dances and loud music. They were identified with the GALLI and later with the Cretan CURETES.

CRETE An island southeast of Greece in the eastern Mediterranean. Crete had one of the world's earliest civilizations, and one of the most brilliant: the Minoan civilization, named after the legendary King MINOS. It is believed to be the birthplace of classical Greek language and literature. In mythology, Minos was the son of the god ZEUS and EUROPA. He married PASIPHAE, who fell in love with a bull. Pasiphaë gave birth to the MINOTAUR, half-man and half-bull. In order to hide the Minotaur, Minos had DAEDALUS build the famous LABYRINTH. Young men and maidens were said to be sacrificed to the bull. In the great palace of Knossos, beautiful murals depict these young people vaulting over the back of the Minotaur. Minoan culture was at its prime between 2200 and 1450 B.C.

CRONUS In Greek mythology, TITAN, the son of URANUS (Heaven) and GAIA (Earth). With his sister-wife, RHEA, Cronus fathered three daughters: DEMETER, HESTIA and HERA; and three sons: HADES, POSEIDON and ZEUS, who became OLYMPIAN GODS. The Roman SATURN is identified with him. Cronus dethroned his father, Uranus (see *Cronus Overthrows Uranus*, below), and was in turn dethroned by his son, ZEUS (see *The War with the Titans*, under ZEUS).

Cronus was probably a corn-god in very ancient times and is often depicted holding a sickle or scythe—the same weapon that he used to render Uranus impotent.

Cronus is sometimes spelled Kronos.

Cronus Overthrows Uranus URANUS and GAIA had many children, including the TITANS, the CYCLOPES and the HECATONCHEIRES (Hundred-Handed Ones). But Uranus grew jealous of his children and had them confined under the earth. Their mother Gaia was very unhappy about losing all her children. Finally she gave a sickle to her bravest son, Cronus, and encouraged him to use it on his father. This Cronus did, mutilating his father horribly so that Uranus became impotent. From his blood were born the FURIES and the GIANTS; from parts of his flesh, which Cronus had cut off and thrown into the sea, arose the goddess APHRODITE. The defeated Uranus left his realm to Cronus, but warned him that one of his sons would in turn overthrow him (see *The War with the Titans*, under ZEUS).

The Children of Cronus Cronus, the TITAN, married his sister, RHEA, with whom he fathered daughters DEMETER, HESTIA and HERA and sons HADES, POSEIDON and ZEUS. Remembering the prophecy of his defeated father, URANUS, Cronus swallowed his children as soon as they were born so that none could overthrow him. In despair Rhea sought the advice of her mother, GAIA, who advised her to give Cronus a stone to swallow the next time a child was born to her. When Zeus was born, Rhea hid him away (see *The Childhood of Zeus*, under

ZEUS) and presented Cronus with a large stone wrapped in baby clothes. Cronus promptly swallowed the stone, thinking it was his child.

When Zeus grew to be a young man he tricked Cronus into coughing up all the siblings—and the stone—that he had swallowed (see *Zeus Rescues His Siblings*, under ZEUS). Then the siblings gathered together with Zeus, the CYCLOPES and the HECATONCHEIRES, (Hundred-Handed Ones) to fight a long war with Cronus and finally defeat him. (See *The War with the Titans*, under ZEUS.) The era of the Titans was over and Zeus and his brothers and sisters founded the Olympian dynasty (see OLYMPIAN GODS).

There are various versions of the story of Cronus. The oldest and most often cited is found in the writings of HESIOD.

CUPID (Desire) Roman god of love, son of VENUS and possibly of VULCAN, the fire-god. Cupid is usually represented as a winged boy or fat baby, often blindfolded to denote his irresponsible nature, and carrying a bow and arrows, used to shoot his victims. Cupid is a Roman adaptation of the Greek god EROS. He was of no great importance except to writers such as VIRGIL (in the AENEID) and to many artists. (See *Eros and Psyche*, under EROS.)

CURETES (Young Men) In Greek mythology, the young Cretan warriors, possibly sons of RHEA, who guarded the infant ZEUS when he was hidden on Mount IDA in central CRETE (see *The Childhood of Zeus*, under ZEUS). The young men danced wildly and clashed their weapons together to drown out the sound of the infant's crying. It is thought that there may have been a cult in Crete devoted to the god Zeus as a youth *(kouros)* and that its devotees were the Curetes. There is further mention of the Curetes in several Greek myths, including that of ZAGREUS.

The Curetes were sometimes identified with the CORYBANTES who performed with dancing, shouting and clashing of armor at the rites of the goddess CYBELE, as did the Curetes at the rites of Rhea and of the young Zeus. (See also GALLI.)

CYBELE A Phrygian (Asiatic) goddess of fertility who found favor in Greece (in the 4th or 5th century B.C.) and Rome (in the 3rd century B.C.). She was sometimes associated with RHEA, the ancient TITAN, as she, too, personified the earth in its primitive state. Cybele was sometimes known as AGDISTIS, who had some of the attributes of both a male and a female. Her attendant god was ATTIS; her priests were the GALLI. The cult of Cybele had a strong appeal for women. With GORDIUS, king of PHRYGIA (ASIA MINOR), Cybele bore a son, MIDAS. (See *Cybele and Attis* and *Cybele and Midas*, below).

Cybele and Attis ATTIS was a lesser god with whom the great goddess Cybele fell in love. He is represented as a young, handsome shepherd. Cybele chose Attis as her priest and imposed upon him a vow of chastity. But Attis broke his vow and in a fit of rage Cybele changed him into a pine tree, or an almond tree. (Stories differ.) The death of Attis and his rebirth as a tree were celebrated every year in ancient Greece, and later, in Rome. This myth of Attis obviously has its origins in ancient fertility rites, based on the belief that Cybele or AGDISTIS,

CYBELE WAS AN ANCIENT EARTH-GODDESS. HER ATTENDANT WAS THE HANDSOME YOUTH ATTIS. (NEW YORK PUBLIC LIBRARY PICTURE COLLECTION)

personification of the Earth, kills and then resurrects vegetation.

Cybele and Midas The goddess Cybele mated with GORDIUS, king of PHRYGIA, with whom she bore a son, MIDAS. Midas inherited his father's throne. By the god DIONYSUS, Midas was granted the wish that everything he touched should be turned to gold. (See *Midas and the Golden Touch*, under MIDAS.)

CYCLOPES (Round-Eyed) In Greek mythology, three giant sons of URANUS (Heaven) and GAIA (Earth). According to HESIOD, their names were Arges (Bright), Brontes (Thunderer) and Steropes (Lightner). They had one round eye each, set in the middle of the forehead. The Cyclopes were master craftsmen. They made thunderbolts for the god ZEUS to help him defeat CRONUS and the TITANS (see *The War with the Titans*, under ZEUS). They also forged a helmet of invisibility for HADES and a trident for POSEIDON.

In later mythology the Cyclopes were said to have been the builders of gigantic walls ("Cyclopean walls") that are found in the ruins of ancient cities of Greece. (The word *cyclopean* has come to mean gigantic.) Some said that their ghosts inhabited the caverns of the volcano Mount Etna, in Sicily, and that the fire and smoke that came from the crater were evidence that their forges were still at work. In HOMER'S ODYSSEY a one-eyed giant named POLYPHEMUS, from the island of Cyclops (thought to be Sicily), entraps the hero Odysseus and his companions. (see *Odysseus and the Cyclops*, under ODYSSEY, THE.)

CYCLOPS In Greek mythology, the dangerous one-eyed giant POLYPHEMUS, who, in HOMER'S ODYSSEY, ensnares the hero ODYSSEUS and his companions. Odysseus manages to blind Polyphemus and thus escape from the mythical island of Cyclops, which is thought to be Sicily. (See CYCLOPES and *Odysseus and the Cyclops*, under ODYSSEY, THE.)

CYNCUS In Greek mythology, son of ARES by Pelopia or by Pyrene. Cyncus was cruel and aggressive like his father, the god of war. Cyncus attacked and killed travelers in the region of TEMPE, in THESSALY. He used their bones to build a temple for his father. One day he challenged HERACLES. In the fearsome battle that followed, Heracles killed Cyncus and severely wounded Ares, who had tried to help his son.

CYRENE In Greek mythology, Thessalian NYMPH, carried off by the god APOLLO to the country that came to be called Cyrenaica. Here she bore Apollo a son, ARISTAEUS.

D

DAEDALUS (Cunningly Wrought) In Greek mythology, a legendary Athenian, descendant of the god HEPHAESTUS (who was known as "the divine artificer"). Daedalus was a great craftsman, architect, sculptor and inventor. His nephew, TALUS, was also a gifted craftsman and became the apprentice of Daedalus. When the boy invented the saw, Daedalus became jealous, murdered his nephew and fled from ATHENS to the island of CRETE.

Daedalus entered the service of King MINOS of Crete, for whom he constructed the amazing LABYRINTH (or maze) that was to hide from the world the existence of the MINOTAUR, a monster, half-man, half-bull, the offspring of Minos's wife PASIPHAË and a bull. (See *Minos and the Minotaur*, under MINOS.)

Once the Labyrinth was completed Minos kept Daedalus prisoner so that he couldn't reveal the secret of the maze to anyone. Daedalus made wings from the feathers of birds and wax and escaped from Crete with his son, ICARUS. Icarus ignored his father's advice and flew too near the sun, which melted the wax and rendered the wings useless. Icarus fell into the sea and was drowned.

Daedalus landed in Sicily and entered the court of King Cocalus, where he constructed beautiful and imaginative toys for the king's daughters.

Minos went in search of Daedalus. He carried with him a triton shell and a piece of linen thread, saying that he would reward the person who could thread the linen through the shell. Minos knew full well that only the talented Daedalus could find a way to do this impossible task. Sure enough, when he reached Sicily, King Cocalus boasted of the wonderful inventor at his court and asked Daedalus to perform the task. This Daedalus did by boring a minute hole in the triton shell, smearing it with honey and sending an ant, harnessed to the thread, through the hole and all the way through the shell's spirals to its opening.

Minos demanded the surrender of Daedalus, but with the help of Cocalus's daughters, Daedalus contrived a horrid death in a hot bathtub for Minos.

The story of Daedalus ends there. Scholars don't know whether there was a real Daedalus, so skillful that legends grew around his memory, or whether he was a purely fictitious invention.

The word *daedalian*, meaning tortuous, inventive, cunning, perpetuates the name of Daedalus.

DAFFODIL (in botany, *Narcissus pseudo-narcissus*) The flower of the UNDERWORLD. Legend has it that the Greek maiden PERSEPHONE (her Roman counterpart was PROSERPINA) wreathed her head with these lilylike flowers. She was captured by the god of the Underworld and carried off in his chariot. The white flowers fell from her head and turned golden yellow. The flowers were called asphodels by the Greeks, and later, affodils, then daffodils, by the English.

DANAE (or DANAË) In Greek mythology, daughter of Acrisius, king of ARGOS; mother of PERSEUS, who would one day kill his grandfather in fulfillment of a prophecy made by an ORACLE. (See *Perseus and Acrisius*, under PERSEUS.) The oracle had told Acrisius that he would be killed by a son of Danae. Acrisius imprisoned Danae in a tower or chamber of bronze, safe from the advances of men. But the great god ZEUS was undeterred in his amorous pursuit of Danae. He appeared to her in her prison as a shower of gold, which impregnated her. She bore a son, Perseus.

Scholars think that the story of Zeus and Danae is a pastoral allegory, in which water is the "gold" of the Greek shepherd or farmer. Hence Zeus was thought to send thunder and showers onto the earth (Danae) to make her fertile.

Daedalus, a great craftsman, invented wings so that he and his son, Icarus, could flee from Crete. (Alinari-scala/art resource)

DANAUS In Greek mythology, a king of Egypt who had 50 daughters demanded by their cousins in marriage. Danaus fled with his brood to ARGOS, where he became king. The cousins came in pursuit. Danaus gave a dagger to each of his daughters so that they could murder their bridegrooms. Only one of the youths (Lynceus) survived. He became the king of Argos after he had killed Danaus, and became the ancestor of PERSEUS. As for the daughters, according to legend, they were punished in HADES by being compelled to try and fill a sieve with water for all eternity. The daughters are sometimes known as the Danaids.

DAPHNE (Laurel) In Greek mythology, a NYMPH, daughter of the river-god Ladon, or of Peneus, and GAIA (Mother Earth). Pursued by the god APOLLO, Daphne begged her mother for help. Gaia opened up the earth and Daphne disappeared. In her place a laurel tree sprang up. Apollo embraced the tree and adopted it as his sacred tree and emblem. This story is told by the poet OVID.

In some legends, Daphne was also loved by Leucippus, a mortal man who had disguised himself as a girl to pursue the nymph, but was discovered to be a man when he went bathing with the maidens. Leucippus was torn to pieces by the angry nymphs.

DAPHNIS In Greek mythology, the son of HERMES and a Sicilian NYMPH; inventor of bucolic (that is, simple, countrylike) poetry. Daphnis was a shepherd loved by the nymph Nomia. In one account Daphnis was untrue to his love and she blinded him in revenge. After that Daphnis sang the sad but beautiful songs that are associated with pastoral music. His father, Hermes, at last took pity on his son and led him up to OLYMPUS. Another account has it that Daphnis was incapable of love, a fact that made APHRODITE, goddess of love, so angry that she afflicted him with everlasting sadness and longing.

Some say that PAN taught Daphnis to play the pipes, and that Daphnis was beloved by APOLLO, and hunted with ARTEMIS, though other accounts have it that it was Daphnis's father, Hermes, who enjoyed these privileges.

DARDANELLES (construed as plural) The strait between Europe and Asian Turkey, connecting the Aegean Sea with the Sea of Marmara. It is 40 miles long and one to five miles wide. In ancient times it was called the HELLESPONT, which means "bridge to the Hellenes," or Greece.

DARDANUS The founder of the city of TROY, according to HOMER. He was the son of ZEUS. His son was ERICHTHONIUS (2), the richest king on earth, who owned thousands of horses. The son of Erichthonius was Tros, who had three sons: Ilus, GANYMEDE and Assaracus. King PRIAM of Troy was a descendant of Ilus.

DEIANIRA In Greek mythology, daughter of OENEUS, king of CALYDON; sister of MELEAGER. She became the second wife of the hero HERACLES and unwittingly caused his death. (See *Heracles, Deianira and the Centaur*, under HERACLES.) Deianira killed herself in despair at what she had done to Heracles.

DEIPHOBUS In Greek mythology, son of PRIAM and HECUBA. He married HELEN (or took her by force) after the death of PARIS, his brother. He was slain by MENELAUS at the fall of Troy (see TROJAN WAR); or, some say, he was killed by Helen.

DELOS The smallest of the Greek islands known as the Cyclades, in the Aegean Sea. One legend says that Delos was a drifting island until the god ZEUS anchored it so that LETO could comfortably give birth to their children, ARTEMIS and APOLLO.

DELPHI The most venerated shrine in ancient Greece and probably the oldest. It lies on the remote slopes of Mount PARNASSUS, high above the Gulf of Corinth, which separates mainland Greece from the Peloponnesus. The oldest objects found at Delphi date back to 1600 B.C., but it is thought that this cleft in the hills was sacred long before that time. (See *The Origins of Delphi*, below.) The ruins of the temple of APOLLO, the presiding god, may still be seen. Nearby is the stadium where the PYTHIAN GAMES were held in honor of the ancient PYTHON vanquished by Apollo (see *Apollo and Python*, under APOLLO).

The Origins of Delphi

According to one myth, two eagles sent by the god ZEUS from opposite ends of the earth established Delphi as the center of the world. A stone marked like a navel (OMPHALOS in Greek) was recognized as the place from which the ORACLE (a wise being, capable of speaking words of the gods and foretelling the future) would speak.

Long before that, the site of the shrine was sacred to GAIA (Mother-Earth). At that time Delphi was called Pytho. It was guarded by a female serpent-dragon, PYTHON. The young god Apollo slew Python and commanded her spirit to be his oracle at Delphi (see *Apollo and Python*, under APOLLO).

Delphi was in fact Apollo's chosen land. Having killed the serpent Python, he built an altar in the sacred grove. According to one legend, Apollo was looking for priests to minister to his shrine when he saw a ship manned by Cretans (a very ancient race, [see under CRETE]). Apollo turned himself into a dolphin and sped after the ship. He captured the ship and persuaded the sailors to guard his temple, which was then called Delphi in honor of the dolphin (Greek *delphin*).

The decline of Delphi and its oracle is paralleled by the decline of Greece and of the justice and moral excellence represented by Apollo. Some efforts were made to restore Delphi's influence but finally, in A.D. 385, the Emperor Theodosius silenced the voice of Apollo forever, in the name of Christianity.

DEMETER In Greek mythology, daughter of CRONUS and RHEA, one of the 12 great deities of OLYMPUS. With her brother ZEUS she became the mother of PERSEPHONE. Goddess of earth, agriculture and crops, especially corn, who in ancient rites presided over the harvest. Her Roman name is CERES.

Demeter and Persephone

Demeter is most famous for her suffering over the loss of her daughter PERSEPHONE, or Kore. Persephone was the daughter of Demeter by ZEUS. Unbeknownst to Demeter, Zeus had promised Persephone to HADES, god of the UNDERWORLD. One day when the maiden was gathering flowers in the fields of Nysa, the earth opened and Persephone was seized by Hades and dragged underground.

Demeter was demented with grief at the loss of her daughter. She wandered the earth, searching for her child, until at last HELIOS (the Sun, who sees everything) told her what had happened. In anger and grief at the treachery of Zeus, Demeter left OLYMPUS and went to live among mortals, disguised as an old woman. Demeter's sojourn at ELEUSIS (see *Demeter and the Eleusinian Mysteries*, below) was the chief episode in the course of her wanderings on Earth.

Meanwhile the earth was suffering from her grief, and bore no fruit. Finally Zeus sent HERMES into the kingdom of Hades to bring Persephone back to her mother. Before leaving the underworld Persephone had been persuaded to eat four seeds of the pomegranate fruit. In ancient mythology, to eat the fruit of one's captor meant that one would have to return to that captor or country. So Persephone was doomed to return to the underworld for four months (a third) of the year. But she was allowed to spend the remaining two-thirds of the year with her Earth Mother, Demeter.

There was great rejoicing on earth at Persephone's return, for now Demeter allowed the earth to bear crops once again.

The meaning of this myth is obvious: It has its basis in the four seasons of the Northern Hemisphere. The time when Persephone goes underground is winter; the time when she returns is spring, which leads to the fruit of summer and the seeds of autumn, which in turn lead inevitably to the new growth of the next spring.

Demeter and the Eleusinian Mysteries

The mysteries were secret rites practiced by initiates in honor of certain gods. By far the most important of these were the ones held in honor of Demeter. Her daughter, PERSEPHONE, or Kore, had been stolen away by HADES and taken to the UNDERWORLD. According to legend, Persephone was the embodiment of the corn-seed that hides underground until its rebirth in the spring, when it returns to Demeter, Mother-Earth.

The disappearance and the return of Persephone were the occasions of great festivals in ancient Greece, among them the Eleusinian rites, whose secrets were so closely guarded that little is known about them. It is thought that the rites or mysteries fostered the idea of a more perfect life after death, and thus helped to lay the groundwork for the advent of Christianity, which upholds the idea of everlasting life.

Demeter's Suitors Demeter, the corn-goddess, was loved by ZEUS and bore him a daughter, PERSEPHONE (see above). She was also loved by the sea-god, POSEIDON, who pursued her even after she had turned herself into a mare and hidden in a flock owned by King Oncus of ARCADIA. Demeter bore Poseidon a daughter, Despoena.

Demeter, in turn, loved Iason, and bore him a son, PLUTUS. Zeus was jealous of Iason and struck him with a thunderbolt; but some say that Iason lived for a long time with Demeter and introduced her cult into Sicily.

Demeter at Eleusis Demeter, the sorrowing mother of PERSEPHONE, wandered the earth in search of her daughter, not knowing that Persephone had been carried off into the UNDERWORLD by HADES. One day Demeter arrived in ELEUSIS, at the palace of King CELEUS. Demeter disguised herself as an old woman, wearing a hood. The king's wife, Metaneira, welcomed Demeter and asked her to look after her newborn son, DEMOPHON.

Demeter nourished the infant on ambrosia (food of the gods), and each night placed him in the fire in order to destroy all that was mortal in him, so that he would grow up like a god. One night Metaneira spied upon her nurse and saw her place the child in the fire. Metaneira screamed with terror. Demeter was angry at the intrusion. (In some accounts Metaneira's screams broke the magic spells and the child was destroyed in the flames.) Demeter threw back her hood and revealed herself as the goddess. She demanded that a temple be built for her in Eleusis. (See *Demeter and the Eleusinian Mysteries*, above.)

Before she left the palace of Eleusis, Demeter showed her gratitude to Celeus and Metaneira by giving TRIPTOLEMUS, Celeus's elder son, the first grain of corn. She taught him how to sow it and harvest it. (In some accounts Triptolemus is identified with Demophon.)

Demeter's stay at Eleusis was the chief episode in the course of her wanderings on earth.

DEMOPHON In Greek mythology, the son of METANEIRA and King CELEUS of ELEUSIS. DEMETER, the sorrowing mother of PERSEPHONE, was given refuge by the king and his wife, who asked her to look after their infant son, Demophon. This Demeter did, performing some goddesslike magic along the way. (See *Demeter at Eleusis*, under DEMETER.)

DEUCALION In Greek mythology, a son of PROMETHEUS, the TITAN champion of mankind. Prometheus warned Deucalion that ZEUS was so angry with the evils of men that he was plotting the annihilation of mankind. Deucalion, the Greek equivalent of the Old Testament's Noah, built an ark. After nine days of rain, the ark landed safely on Mount PARNASSUS. Deucalion and his wife PYRRHA, gave sacrifice to Zeus. They were instructed by the spirit of the TITAN THEMIS to re-people the earth. This they did by casting stones (the bones of Mother-Earth) behind them. Those cast by Pyrrha became women; those cast by Deucalion became men. The eldest son was Hellen, the ancestor of the race of Hellenes, later called the Greeks.

Scholars say that the Deluge of this myth is undoubtedly the same one as the Flood quoted in the Old Testament and the Gilgamesh epic of Babylon, and reflects a dim memory common to all peoples of the Mediterranean.

DIANA Roman goddess of hunting and the woodlands, identified with the Greek goddess ARTEMIS and possibly SELENE. She was worshiped especially in groves and woodlands by women, and was regarded as a protector during childbirth.

DICTYNNA (Lady of the Nets) In Greek mythology, a very ancient Cretan goddess, perhaps the goddess of Mount Dicte, which was later said to be the birthplace of the Greek god ZEUS. She was the mother-goddess of CRETE, later associated with BRITOMARTIS, the huntress and patron of navigators.

DICTYS In Greek mythology, the fisherman, some say the brother of POLYDECTES, who rescued the hero PERSEUS and his mother, DANAE, from the sea. Dictys took the mother and child to the court of King Polydectes of the island of SERIPHOS, in the Aegean Sea. Later he would rescue Danae once again, this time from the unwelcome attentions of Polydectes. Perseus turned Polydectes into stone with the head of MEDUSA as his weapon, and Dictys became the new king of Seriphos.

DIDO (also known as ELISSA) In Greek mythology, the founder and queen of CARTHAGE. She was the daughter of the Tyrian king Belus, and sister of PYGMALION. Dido was married to her wealthy uncle Acerbas. Acerbas was murdered by Pygmalion. Dido fled to Carthage. Here she was allowed to purchase as much land as could be enclosed with the hide of a bull. Dido cleverly had the hide cut up into narrow strips so that the area they enclosed was great. Her citadel was called Byrsa, and around it the city of Carthage arose.

The best-known story about Dido is that of her love for the hero AENEAS, told by VIRGIL in his AENEID. In it, she hears tales of the adventures of the hero and falls in love with him. Aeneas deserts her to pursue his destiny and Dido kills herself. The story of Dido is much older than *The Aeneid*, dating back at least to the 2nd century B.C.

DIOMEDES (1) In Greek mythology, son of Tydeus and successor of ADRASTUS as king of ARGOS. Diomedes sailed against Troy in the TROJAN WAR, and was, next to ACHILLES, the bravest of the Greeks. The war-goddess ATHENE favored him.

DIOMEDES (2) In Greek mythology, a son of ARES; king of the Bistones in Thrace. He raised man-eating mares who were carried off and tamed by HERACLES (see *The Twelve Labors of Heracles*, The Horses of Diomedes, under HERACLES), after Heracles had killed Diomedes and fed him to the mares.

DIONE An obscure, ancient divinity of prehistoric Greece, said to be a daughter of OCEANUS and TETHYS, closely associated with the cult of the god ZEUS. Scholars point out that her name is a feminine form of the name Zeus. HOMER said that she was the mother, with Zeus, of the goddess APHRODITE, though most sources say that Aphrodite, goddess of love and fertility, was born from URANUS and GAIA. Dione was venerated at DODONA as the consort of Zeus.

DIONYSUS (BACCHUS in Roman mythology) A Greek fertility god, god of vegetation, especially the vine, god of wine and later of the pleasures of civilization. Son of ZEUS; his mother is variously thought to be SEMELE, DEMETER, PERSEPHONE, or IO, DIONE or LETHE. The most common myth identifies his mother as Semele (see *The Birth of Dionysus*, below).

In early times Dionysus was associated with orgiastic rites and generally wild behavior. As the cultivation of the vine spread throughout Greece, so did the worship of Dionysus and the ensuing orgies, called Dionysian or Bacchic festivals. Later, however, Dionysus was also celebrated as a cultivator of the soil, a lawgiver, a peacemaker and a patron of tragic art.

Among his followers were the CENTAURS, MAENADS, SATYRS and SILENI, all of whom were depicted in ancient art as enthusiastically, sometimes frighteningly demented, carrying staffs and wearing animal skins and crowns of ivy and grape leaves.

Dionysus is usually depicted as a semi-nude, youthful god with a softly rounded body, his head crowned with vine leaves and grapes, and carrying a goblet of wine in one hand and a thyrsus staff headed with a pine cone in the other. In earlier art he was shown as a mature, bearded man crowned with ivy.

The young Dionysus was not honored as a god and he was forced to flee from Greece. He traveled through Europe, ASIA MINOR and North Africa. Many adventures marked his passage

DIONYSUS, THE GREEK GOD OF WINE (ROMAN: BACCHUS), WAS OFTEN ASSOCIATED WITH WILD REVELRY AND FEASTING. (NEW YORK PUBLIC LIBRARY PICTURE COLLECTION)

through the countries he visited as he spread his knowledge of the cultivation of the vine and the making of wine. Dionysus learned to use the divine power he had inherited from his father, ZEUS. He inspired devotion, especially among women, and finally returned to Greece in triumph as a true god. APOLLO, beautiful god of the arts, admitted Dionysus to his shrine at DELPHI. Thus Dionysus joined the OLYMPIAN GODS.

The acceptance of Dionysus into Greece after many struggles probably refers to the conflict between old and new religions in the ancient world. Dionysus represents the very ancient cult of the spirit of nature and fertility. It found expression in human sacrifice, nature worship and orgiastic rites, as did the cult of Dionysus. Apollo represents the Dorians and other mi-

grants who invaded peninsular Greece. These newcomers brought with them their own gods and cults but learned to accept the ancient deities and rites.

The Birth of Dionysus Though the name of Dionysus's mother is in doubt, the most common myth identifies her as SEMELE. The great god ZEUS had come down to earth disguised as a mortal. He wooed and won Semele. HERA, the wife of Zeus, was jealous. When Semele was six months pregnant, Hera, disguised as an old nurse, persuaded Semele to ask Zeus to reveal himself in his true form. This she did. At first Zeus refused Semele's request but finally presented himself in all his glory as a mighty god, flashing lightning and hurling thunderbolts. No mortal could withstand such power, and Semele perished in flames. Zeus snatched the unborn child from the fire and sewed it into his thigh so that it could mature for another three months. In due course Zeus gave birth to a boy, Dionysus, who is sometimes called DITHYRAMBUS (child of the Double Door), referring to his two births, once from his mother's body and again from his father's.

Some scholars believe that this myth represents Zeus asserting his power over mortals by killing Semele and taking her child under his protection.

The Childhood of Dionysus ZEUS entrusted the care of his newborn child to SEMELE's sister, INO and her husband ATHAMAS. Although her rival, Semele, was dead (see *The Birth of Dionysus*, above), HERA, wife of Zeus, was still jealous; she transferred her hatred to Dionysus. She caused the child's foster parents to become insane. But Dionysus survived their madness, and Zeus gave him to HERMES to take to the nymphs of Nysa. It is not known whether Nysa was a mountain near HELICON, the highest point in BOEOTIA, or a purely imaginary spot. The nymphs were BACCHANTS. They took good care of the child and Dionysus grew to manhood in Nysa.

Hera's hatred of Dionysus and his wife may reflect conservative opposition to the ritual use of wine and the extravagant orgies of the Bacchants and MAENADS. Although Dionysus was eventually admitted to OLYMPUS (see above), he never ceased to be anything but a demigod.

DIOSCURI (Lads of Zeus) Joint name, in Greek mythology, for Castor and Pollux (whose Greek name is Polydeuces), the twin sons of LEDA and ZEUS; brothers of HELEN and CLYTEMNESTRA. (See CASTOR AND POLLUX.) Some say that they were the sons of Leda and Tyndareus, her husband. The best known legend of their origin is that Leda mated with a giant swan who was the god Zeus in one of his many disguises.

One myth (recounted by PINDAR) says that Castor was mortally wounded in battle and that his twin brother, Polydeuces, begged Zeus to allow him to share his brother's suffering. Zeus granted them a single life, to be shared and lived on alternate days. The god also created the constellation Gemini in their honor.

In other myths the twins rescue their sister Helen from the hero THESEUS; take part in the expedition of the ARGONAUTS; and are given special powers by the sea-god, POSEIDON, and so were venerated by mariners, to whom they appeared as what is now known as Saint Elmo's fire, an atmospheric phenomenon regarded by seamen as a portent of good weather.

Twins are featured in mythologies around the world. The origin of the Dioscuri may lie in stories of real men who were regarded as heroes and eventually honored as gods themselves. One of the superstitions connected with twins was that one was fathered by a man, the other by a god; this belief explained the semidivine attributes they were thought to possess.

DIS (or DIS PATER) A Roman god of the UNDERWORLD, related to the Roman god PLUTO and the Greek god HADES.

DITHYRAMBUS (Child of the Double Door) In Greek mythology, a name for the god DIONYSUS, referring to the legend that he was born twice (see *The Birth of Dionysus*, under DIONYSUS).

In literature a dithyramb is a Greek song or chant of wild character and irregular form, originally sung in honor of Dionysus, god of wine. Verse described as dithyrambic is most irregular in form.

DODONA The oldest and most famous sanctuary of the god ZEUS, situated in EPIRUS, in northwestern Greece. Since the times of the Pelasgians (the most ancient peoples of the land that is now called Greece), people had come here to consult the ORACLE who was said to live in a sacred oak tree (some said it was a beech tree) and to represent Zeus. The ancient goddess DIONE was also worshiped at Dodona along with Zeus. Her presence at Dodona suggests that the oracle of Dodona was of greater antiquity than Zeus; her oracle was taken over by a male god in the course of the Indo-European migrations.

The Dodona oracle is referred to several times in HOMER's ILIAD. A beam from the sacred tree formed part of the ARGO, the ship crewed by JASON and the ARGONAUTS.

E

ECHIDNA In Greek mythology, a monster-child of GAIA and TARTARUS (or, in some tellings, of Ceto and Phorcys). Echidna was half-woman and half-serpent. She once lived in a cave where she ate the flesh of men. With TYPHON, another monster, she had a brood of frightful children. In one story, she was slain by the hundred-eyed ARGUS, who killed her while she slept.

Among the offspring of Echidna and Typhon were CERBERUS (the Hound of Hell); HYDRA (the many-headed serpent of Lerna); and the CHIMERA (a fire-breathing goat with a lion's head and a serpent's body). By Orthos, a two-headed hound, Echidna begot the SPHINX and the Nemean Lion (see *The Twelve Labors of Heracles*, 1. The Nemean Lion, under HERACLES).

In zoology an echidna is a porcupine anteater, found in Australia, Tasmania and New Guinea, and is related to the platypus. Among marine animals the spiny sea urchin belongs to the phylum of Echinoderms.

ECHO In Greek mythology, an oread or mountain-NYMPH, daughter of GAIA. The goddess HERA, in a fit of jealousy, deprived her of speech, except for the ability to repeat the last words spoken by somebody else. Echo fell in love with NARCISSUS. But Narcissus loved only his own reflection; Echo faded away until there was nothing left of her except her voice, which may still be heard in the mountains and caves of the world.

The story of Echo and Narcissus is told in OVID's *Metamorphoses*. It belongs to later Greek mythology.

EILEITHYA (or ILITHYA) Greek goddess of childbirth. Daughter of HERA and ZEUS. Eileithya is met in accounts of the births of Heracles and of LETO's delivery of her divine twins, APOLLO and ARTEMIS. Eileithya is probably a pre-Olympian goddess whose function was to take care of women in childbirth. She was sometimes identified with Hera, sometimes with Artemis.

ELECTRA (1) In Greek mythology, daughter of AGAMEMNON and CLYTEMNESTRA; sister of IPHIGENIA and ORESTES. Agamemnon was the leader of the Achaean (Greek) forces in the TROJAN WAR. Clytemnestra took a lover, AEGISTHUS. When Agamemnon finally returned from the war he brought with him the lovely CASSANDRA. Abetted by Aegisthus, Clytemnestra murdered both Agamemnon and Cassandra. To avenge their father's death, Electra and Orestes murdered Clytemnestra and Aegisthus. Electra eventually married Pylades.

The story of this tragic mythical family is told by many great playwrights, including AESCHYLUS, SOPHOCLES and EURIPIDES, and in modern times in *Mourning Becomes Electra*, by Eugene O'Neill (1883–1953).

ELECTRA (2) One of the PLEIADES; daughter of ATLAS and Pleione; mother, by ZEUS, of DARDANUS, the founder of TROY. Some say that Electra was the lost Pleiad, who faded away with grief after the TROJAN WAR and the destruction of Troy.

ELECTRA (3) A sea-NYMPH, daughter of OCEANUS and TETHYS. Mother of IRIS (Rainbow) and the HARPIES.

ELEUSIS Ancient city in ATTICA, in ancient Greece, famous for being the site of the Eleusian Mysteries (see *Demeter and the Eleusinian Mysteries*, under DEMETER).

ELIS An area of the PELOPONNESUS whose chief city was Elis. Nearby Olympia was the scene of the OLYMPIC GAMES.

ELYSIUM A conception of after-life, the pre-Hellenic paradise that the Greeks identified with their mythical Isles (or Islands) of the Blessed. It was believed to be at the ends of the earth—"the far west"; people (or their shades) transported there led a blessedly happy life rather than remaining in the oblivion of the truly dead of the UNDERWORLD. RHADAMANTHUS and CRONUS were joint rulers of this paradise. In HOMER, Elysium was a place for elite heroes; in HESIOD, it was a place for the blessed dead; and from the time of PINDAR, it was believed that admission to Elysium was the reward of a good life.

ENDYMION   In Greek mythology, according to various sources, the son of ZEUS and Calyce or the shepherd son of Aethlius; prince or king of ELIS, a region of the PELOPONNESUS; he was a beautiful young man, loved by SELENE (the Moon). In one myth, Endymion begged Zeus to give him immortality so that he could be with Selene forever. Zeus granted his request with the condition that he remain eternally asleep. Another myth has it that Selene herself imposed eternal sleep on Endymion so that she might enjoy his beauty forever. In another story it is said that Selene had 50 daughters by Endymion. Selene visited Endymion on many nights of the month, personifying the gentle radiance of the moon that caresses the sleep of mortals.

English poets Michael Drayton (1563–1631), John Keats (1795–1821), John Lyly (? 1554–1606) and many others wrote poems based upon the legend of Endymion and Selene.

EOS (Dawn)   The Greek goddess of dawn. She was the daughter of HELIOS (Sun), or, some accounts say, the sister of Helios and SELENE (Moon), begotten by TITANS, HYPERION and Thea. She was known as AURORA by the Romans. Eos was married to TITHONUS, but she had many other lovers. Eos is depicted as a beautiful young woman, sometimes riding the dawn skies on the winged horse, PEGASUS, sometimes in a chariot drawn by two horses.

With the Titan Astraeus, Eos bore the winds Zephyrus and BOREAS and various astral bodies.

Memnon was one of her sons with Tithonus; and CEPHALUS, one of her partners in a tragic love affair.

EPAPHUS   The son of the Greek god ZEUS and IO. Epaphus was born in Egypt. HERA, wife of Zeus, was jealous of Io and had tormented her endlessly until Io, in the shape of a white heifer, eventually escaped to Egypt, where Zeus restored her to her human shape. There, Io bore her son. (See *Io, the White Heifer*, under IO.) Hera, still jealous, ordered the CURETES to abduct Epaphus. This they did, but Zeus destroyed the Curetes and rescued the child. Epaphus later became king of Egypt, where he built the great city of Memphis, capital of the Old Kingdom of ancient Egypt.

EPHESUS   An ancient Greek city of ASIA MINOR (today, Turkey, south of Izmir). Once a wealthy seaport, it was the site of a temple to the goddess ARTEMIS (Roman DIANA); the temple was considered one of the Seven Wonders of the World.

EPIDAURUS   A city in southern Greece (northeastern PELOPONNESUS) celebrated in ancient times as the sanctuary of ASCLEPIUS, god of medicine and healing. Epidaurus was (and is) also famous for its magnificent theater, dating from the 4th century B.C.

EPIGONI (Descendants, that is, the younger generation)
In Greek mythology, the sons of the SEVEN AGAINST THEBES, an expedition launched by ADRASTUS and Polynices to capture the throne of THEBES. The effort failed and Adrastus was the only survivor. When the sons of the Seven (the Epigoni) were old enough to bear arms, Adrastus rallied them to make a second attack. This one succeeded. Thebes was destroyed. It was a bitter victory for Adrastus, for his son Aegialeus was killed.

EPIMETHEUS (Afterthought)   In Greek mythology, brother of PROMETHEUS, a TITAN. Epimetheus accepted PANDORA as his wife, in spite of the warnings of his wiser brother. Pandora had been created by the gods to punish mankind for accepting the forbidden gift of fire from Prometheus.

EPIRUS An ancient country of Greece, on the Ionian Sea, west of Macedonia and THESSALY. It was the home of the ORACLE at DODONA and refuge of the CENTAURS when they were expelled from their native Thessaly.

EREBUS (Darkness) In Greek mythology, the personification of darkness. Erebus sprang from CHAOS at the beginning of time. He was the father of CHARON, NEMESIS and others. His name was given to the gloomy underground cavern through which the dead had to walk on their way to the UNDERWORLD.

ERICHTHONIUS (1) In Greek mythology, legendary king of ATHENS. According to HOMER, Erichthonius was the son of the lame god, HEPHAESTUS, and GAIA (Earth). He grew out of seed spilled by Hephaestus when he tried to force his attentions on the goddess ATHENE. Earth nourished the seed and the child, Erichthonius, was born. In a later story, Athene placed the child in a basket and gave it to the daughters of Cecrops to look after. She forbade them to open the basket but the women could not resist. When they saw what was inside they ran off screaming, for the child was half-serpent. It is common in Greek mythology for men born of the soil to be represented as half-serpent, for serpents were regarded as the essential earth creatures in ancient times.

When Erichthonius became king he established the worship of Athene in Athens.

ERICHTHONIUS (2) The son of DARDANUS, the founder of TROY. Erichthonius was said to be the richest king on earth. He owned thousands of magnificent horses that had been sired by the North Wind. He was the father of Tros and the grandfather of Ilus, GANYMEDE and Assacarus. King PRIAM of Troy was a descendant of Ilus.

ERIGONE In Greek mythology, daughter of King Icarius of ATTICA (in ancient Greece, the area of the southeastern mainland where modern ATHENS now stands). Her father was slain and buried by shepherds drunk with the wine of DIONYSUS. Erigone and her faithful dog, Maera, set out in search for the vanished king. When Erigone discovered the tomb of Icarius she was grief-stricken and hanged herself from a nearby tree. She was transformed into the constellation Virgo, and Maera became Procyon, the brightest star in Canis Minor.

ERINYES (Furies) In Greek mythology, the three avengers of wrong, generally known by their Roman name, the FURIES. They were also called EUMENIDES (Good-Tempered Ones) by the wise and tactful Greeks, who feared their wrath.

ERIPHYLE In Greek mythology, wife of AMphiaraus, mother of ALCMEON, sister of ADRASTUS. Eriphyle was given the magic necklace of HARMONIA, a guarantee of unfading beauty, for persuading her husband, Amphiaraus, and her brother, Adrastus, to join in the disastrous rebellion known as the SEVEN AGAINST THEBES. Eriphyle was killed by her son, Alcmeon. Her dying curse was that no land would ever shelter him.

ERIS (Discord) In Greek mythology, the spirit or goddess of strife; the sister of ARES, accompanying him into battle and helping to cause quarrels and lawlessness. In HESIOD she is the daughter of Nox (Night). Later legends say that she helped to cause the TROJAN WAR by flinging her "apple of discord" among the guests at the wedding of PELEUS and THETIS. Three jealous goddesses competed for the golden apple. PARIS awarded the prize to APHRODITE, goddess of love and beauty. (See *The Judgment of Paris*, under PARIS.)

EROS (Erotic Love) Greek god of love and fertility, called CUPID by the Romans. In ancient times Eros was a force to be feared: He represented the havoc and misery that could be brought about by love and desire. In later times Eros was depicted as an overweight baby, winged, and carrying a bow and a quiver of arrows, which he would shoot off randomly. The parentage of Eros is confused and obscure. He is often thought of as the son of the goddess of love, APHRODITE. His father may have been the great god ZEUS, the god of war, ARES, or the god of fertility, HERMES; older traditions say that he is the son of GAIA (Mother-Earth), and therefore

EROS, GREEK GOD OF LOVE (KNOWN AS CUPID TO THE ROMANS), LOVED PSYCHE, A BEAUTIFUL PRINCESS. (BILDARCHIV FOTO MARBURG/ART RESOURCE)

almost as old as Earth herself. Though he appeared in many legends, Eros was never considered important enough to be set among the 12 great OLYMPIAN GODS. Nevertheless he is depicted as the constant companion of the goddess Aphrodite. The most famous tale about Eros is *Eros* (or Cupid) *and Psyche* (see below).

Eros and Psyche Eros was a Greek god of love, perhaps the son of APHRODITE, goddess of love. PSYCHE was a mortal princess. She was so beautiful that Aphrodite, in a jealous rage, ordered Eros to punish the maiden. Eros fell in love with Psyche and carried her off to a magnificent palace. He didn't reveal his identity to her and commanded her never to try and see his face. But Psyche couldn't resist and uncovered his face as he slept. Eros and all the beautiful surroundings immediately disappeared. From then on Psyche was pursued by an angry Aphrodite. She came through terrible ordeals, helped by some mysterious force. Finally Eros pleaded with ZEUS to put an end to her suffering. Zeus consented and conferred immortality on Psyche. The wedding of Psyche and Eros was celebrated on OLYMPUS, and Aphrodite, it is said, joined in the festivities.

ETHER In Greek mythology, the daughter of Nox (Night) and EREBUS (Darkness); sister of Hemera (Day). Ether was supposed by the ancients to occupy the upper regions of space. Intangible and heavenly ("ethereal"), Ether was the essential being of the universe.

ETHIOPIA A country in northeast Africa. In Greek mythology, ANDROMEDA was the daughter of CEPHEUS and CASSIOPEIA of Ethiopia. Chained to a rock in the sea, Andromeda was rescued by the hero PERSEUS. Memnon, a hero of the TROJAN WAR, was a king of Ethiopia.

EUMENIDES (Good-Tempered Ones) The ironic appellation given by the Greeks to the ERINYES, fearsome creatures whose name means FURIES, the term by which they are generally known in literature.

EURIPIDES One of the great Greek tragedians, ranked with AESCHYLUS and SOPHOCLES, though his attitudes were very different from theirs. His was a questioning, probing nature. He found it hard to believe that the gods and goddesses, with their capricious, all-too-human ways, were the creators of the universe. To him, mortal men and women were more interesting and noble, and their triumphs and tragedies more worthy of notice and of compassion. Among his surviving plays are *Andromache, The Bacchae, Electra, Hecuba, Heracles, Medea* and *The Trojan Women.* Euripides lived from 480 to 406 B.C.

EUROPA In Greek mythology, daughter of AGENOR, king of Tyre (a seaport in PHOENICIA) and Telephassa, and the sister of CADMUS, PHOENIX and CILIX. Mother of MINOS, RHADAMANTHUS and SARPEDON with ZEUS; and of Euphemus with POSEIDON; wife of ASTERION, king of CRETE. (See *Europa and the Bull,* below.)

Europa and the Bull Europa was the daughter of King AGENOR of PHOENICIA (an ancient kingdom at the eastern end of the Mediterranean) and of Telephassa. She had three brothers: CADMUS, PHOENIX and CILIX. Europa was famed for her beauty. The god ZEUS fell in love with her and, knowing that the maiden liked to wander on the shore, devised a plan. He turned himself into a snow-white bull and grazed peacefully on the grass near the shore. Europa was enchanted by the beautiful animal. She caressed him and twined garlands of flowers upon his horns. When the bull gracefully knelt

THE GOD ZEUS TURNED HIMSELF INTO A BULL IN ORDER TO CARRY OFF THE BEAUTIFUL MAIDEN EUROPA. (NEW YORK PUBLIC LIBRARY PICTURE COLLECTION)

before her, she climbed upon its back, whereupon the bull dashed into the sea (the Mediterranean) and swam with Europa to the island of CRETE, which lies south of Greece. There he turned himself into an eagle and mated with Europa. She bore him three sons: MINOS, RHADAMANTHUS and SARPEDON. Then she married ASTERION, the king of Crete, who adopted her sons. She was worshiped as a goddess after her death.

The story of Europa and the Bull is very old. It probably harks back to a time when the bull, a symbol of strength and fertility, was the principal cult animal of the eastern Mediterranean. It seems possible that the figure of Zeus was grafted onto an ancient Cretan story, as often happened when old myths were embroidered upon by later storytellers.

Zeus's capture of Europa may refer to an early Hellenic raid on Phoenicia by Hellenes from CRETE, when Taurus (Bull), king of Crete, assaulted Tyre (seaport in Phoenicia) during the absence of Agenor and his sons. The Hellenes took the city and carried off many captives, including the king's daughter. The story also represents the contribution of Phoenician civilization to that of Crete, which is symbolized by the bull-god.

EURYDICE In Greek mythology, a beautiful dryad (tree-NYMPH) who became the wife of ORPHEUS. While being pursued by ARISTAEUS she was bitten by a serpent and died. Stricken with grief, Orpheus charmed his way into the UNDERWORLD and persuaded HADES to release his wife. Seduced by the beautiful music of Orpheus, Hades let Eurydice go, on the condition that Orpheus would not look back to see if she was following. The pair had almost reached the entrance to the world when Orpheus looked back. Eurydice disappeared instantly and was never seen again. The tragic story of Orpheus and Eurydice is the subject of many plays and operas (see under ORPHEUS).

EURYLOCHUS In Greek mythology, one of the crewmen of ODYSSEUS and, apart from Odysseus himself, the only one to escape the spell of CIRCE, the witch who turned men into swine. (See *Odysseus and Circe,* under ODYSSEY, THE.) Eurylochus, who had been the head of the party exploring Circe's island, hid, saw what happened to his shipmates and fled to warn Odysseus. Later, when Odysseus and his crew had escaped both Circe and the UNDERWORLD (see *Odysseus in the Underworld,* under ODYSSEY, THE), it was Eurylochus who led the crew to feast on the sacred cattle of HYPERION, god of the Sun, thus bringing about the destruction of the entire crew, except for Odysseus.

EURYSTHEUS In Greek mythology, the king of ARGOS and MYCENAE who imposed the Twelve Labors upon his cousin, HERACLES (see *The Twelve Labors of Heracles,* under HERACLES). Eurystheus was the son of Sthenelus, a descendant of the hero PERSEUS, and Nicippe. Not much is known about Eurystheus, except that he became king because of the wiles of HERA, the angry and jealous wife of the god ZEUS: On the day that Heracles was to be born, Zeus proclaimed before the OLYMPIAN GODS that the descendant of Perseus born on that day would become ruler of Greece. Zeus fully expected that his son with ALCMENE, to be named Heracles, would qualify for the role of ruler. But Hera, knowing that Nicippe was about to give birth, caused her child, Eurystheus, to be born ahead of Heracles. Thus it was Eurystheus, not Heracles, who became ruler of Greece.

The chagrined Zeus decreed that if Heracles could perform the Twelve Labors imposed by Eurystheus he would become a god.

EURYTUS In Greek mythology, king of Oechalia, father of IOLE. Eurytus was a renowned archer. He promised his daughter to anyone who could shoot better than he. The great hero HERACLES won the contest; but Eurytus accused Heracles of using poisoned arrows and furthermore of being a slave of EURYSTHEUS and therefore unworthy of a king's daughter. Eurytus refused to honor Heracles's right to the hand of Iole. For this he died at the hand of Heracles. But Heracles was also to die because of Iole. (See *Heracles, Deianira and the Centaur,* under HERACLES.)

F

FATES, THE In Greek mythology, the three goddesses who controlled the destiny of men and women. Also called Moirae and Moirai, they were the daughters of ZEUS and Themis. Clotho spun the web of life; Lachesis measured its length; Atropos cut the web at the end of life. Some say that the power of the Fates was even greater than that of Zeus.

The Roman Fates were the Parcae. Their names were Nona, Decuma and Morta.

FAUNUS One of the oldest Roman gods; god of nature and fertility, protector of farmers and shepherds. He also had the gift of prophecy. Faunus was identified with the Greek god PAN. He probably evolved into a single deity from the original idea of the *fauni*, spirits of the countryside. He was usually depicted as a young man with the horns and legs of a goat, similar to the SATYR of Greek myth. His female counterpart was FLORA.

In natural history, the word *fauna* is used to denote the animals of a region or specific area, as the word *flora* denotes vegetation.

FERONIA Ancient Roman deity, thought to be a goddess of fertility and childbirth. Although little is known about her, inscriptions show that Feronia was popular in central Italy. Her most famous shrine, near Terracina, was used for the ceremony of bestowing freedom on slaves. (Terracina is an ancient town on the Tyrrhenian Sea, midway between modern Rome and Naples.)

FLAMEN In ancient Rome, a special priest ordained to offer daily tributes to particular gods in the Roman pantheon, the most important of which were JUPITER, MARS and QUIRINUS. The flamens were responsible for organizing daily sacrifices to the gods, and were exempt from taxation and military duty. It was a peculiarity of Roman dictators and emperors that they accepted deification during their lifetimes, and so were allowed to have their own flamens who would honor them. Thus Mark Antony was a flamen of Julius Caesar.

The flamens are historical, rather than mythological people, but they carried on some of the traditions of ancient peoples, such as the ritual sacrifices to particular gods.

FLORA Roman goddess of flowers and plants. Her male counterpart was FAUNUS, god of nature and fertility. Springtime feasts held in honor of Flora were said to be very lively.

The word *flora* denotes the vegetation native to a region or specific area.

FORTUNA (Fate; also called FORS FORTUNA) Roman goddess of destiny and chance, of great antiquity. She was identified with the Greek Tyche. Fortuna was represented with a horn of plenty (a horn or basket filled with fruit and flowers, a symbol of fruitfulness), and a rudder, because it is Fortune that "steers" men's lives as a rudder steers a boat. Fortuna's most important temple was at Praeneste Palestrina, where she was called Primigenia (First Born, possibly of the god JUPITER, though there is some confusion about this). The Praeneste Palestrina in Latium, founded about 800 B.C., was one of the largest sanctuaries in Italy. Crowned with the round temple of Fortuna, it was visible for miles around.

FURIES, THE The Roman appellation for the Greek name ERINYES (Furies). They were said by HESIOD to be the daughters of Earth Mother GAIA; they sprang from the blood of URANUS. In other accounts they were the daughters of Night or of Darkness. Their numbers varied but there were generally thought to be three Furies: Alecto (She Who Rests Not), Megaera (Jealous One) and Tisiphone (Avenger of Blood). The Furies were merciless avengers of any crimes committed, especially those that involved bloodshed in a family or among kin. It is said that their punishment continued even after death and descent into the UNDERWORLD. The Furies were called by the name EUMENIDES (Good-Tempered Ones) by the Greeks, who feared punishment if they called them by their rightful name, Erinyes, literally, Furies.

G

GAIA (also GAEA or GE) (Earth) The personification of Mother Earth in Greek mythology, known to the Romans as Terra. She was born out of CHAOS at the beginning of time, and in turn bore URANUS, the starlit sky. Gaia was the mother of the seas, the mountains and valleys and all the other natural features of the earth. Once the earth was formed, Gaia mated with her son Uranus and produced the TITANS, the first race on earth. Then came the CYCLOPES and the HECATONCHEIRES (Hundred-Handed Ones). Uranus was horrified by his monstrous offspring and banished them all to the UNDERWORLD. At first Gaia mourned for her children but then she became angry with Uranus. She fashioned a sharp sickle and gave it to CRONUS, her youngest and bravest Titan son, bidding him to attack Uranus. Cronus did mutilate his father's body and cast its parts into the ocean. From the blood that dropped upon the earth sprang the FURIES, the GIANTS (Gigantes) and the ash-NYMPHS (the Meliae).

According to HESIOD and others the primitive Greeks worshiped the Earth, which they pictured as a bountiful Mother. She was the supreme deity not only of men but of gods. Later, when the OLYMPIAN GODS were established, Gaia was still held in reverence. She presided over marriages and was honored as a prophetess. She was offered gifts of fruits and grains at her many shrines. Gaia was represented as a gigantic, full-breasted woman.

GALLI In Greek mythology, priests of the deity CYBELE. They celebrated her with wild dances, loud music and noise created by the clashing of shields and swords. They were akin to the CORYBANTES and were later identified with the CURETES of CRETE.

GANYMEDE In Greek mythology, Trojan prince, great-grandson of DARDANUS, the founder of TROY. The god ZEUS, enraptured by the beauty

GANYMEDE WAS A BEAUTIFUL YOUTH CARRIED OFF BY ZEUS (IN THE FORM OF A HUGE EAGLE) TO BECOME A CUPBEARER TO THE GODS. (NEW YORK PUBLIC LIBRARY PICTURE COLLECTION)

of young Ganymede, carried him off to OLYMPUS to be a cupbearer to the gods. Some say that Zeus took the form of an eagle for this exploit; others that the god came as a storm wind. There are many famed depictions of this picturesque event.

GENIUS (plural, GENII) (Creative Force, Guardian Spirit) In Roman mythology, the spirit

50

that attended a man from birth until death. (A JUNO spirit accompanied a woman.) The genius determined the person's character, his happiness and his fortune. The word *genial* (good-natured) comes from the genius who presided over pleasures. The genius was the source of creativity; hence the word *genius* is used to describe an exceptionally talented person. In some accounts each person was thought to have both a good and a bad genius. Bad luck was the work of the evil genius.

(The genie of Eastern mythology were jinns [fallen angels] and had nothing to do with the genii of Roman mythology.)

GERYON   In Greek mythology, a monster with three heads, three bodies and six hands; Geryon owned red cattle, which were guarded by the two-headed dog, Orthrus, and the herdsman, Eurytion. In his Tenth Labor, the hero HERACLES slew the dog and the herdsman. Only after a fearsome battle did Heracles defeat Geryon. (See *The Twelve Labors of Heracles*, under Heracles.)

From Geryon's blood sprang a tree that produced a stoneless, cherrylike fruit that yielded a blood-red dye.

GIANTS (GIGANTES)   In Greek mythology, the offspring of GAIA and the blood of the wounded URANUS. Gaia prompted the giants to attack the gods, and the War of the Giants ensued. It was finally won by the gods, with the help of the hero HERACLES, who used his bow to good effect. ZEUS killed Porphyrion with a thunderbolt, ATHENE killed Enceladus and HEPHAESTUS hurled red-hot iron. DIONYSUS tripped up the giants with his vines; APOLLO, HERMES and POSEIDON joined in and the giants were completely defeated. Scholars say that the battle represented the conflict either between barbarism and order, or between man and the forces of nature.

GLAUCA (also called CREUSA)   In Greek mythology, daughter of King Creon of CORINTH. She married the hero JASON. In revenge, MEDEA, Jason's former wife, used her magic powers to kill Glauca. Medea sent her a wedding dress soaked with poison. When Glauca put it on it burned into her flesh and killed her. Creon, Glauca's father, also perished from the poison.

GLAUCUS   (1) In Greek mythology, the most famous Glaucus was the grandson of BELLEROPHON, a hero in the ILIAD. Glaucus fought on the Trojan side during the TROJAN WAR. But he and the Greek hero DIOMEDES (1) discovered that their grandparents had been friends; and so the two exchanged armor and vows of friendship with each other. Another of Glaucus's friends was SARPEDON. When Sarpedon was killed, Glaucus appealed to the god APOLLO to help him retrieve the body. This he did, with the help of the hero HECTOR. Glaucus was eventually killed in battle by AJAX.

GLAUCUS   (2) In Greek mythology, the son of SISYPHUS (and father of BELLEROPHON) and owner of a famous herd of mares. However, he refused to let them breed, thus incurring the anger of APHRODITE, goddess of love. Aphrodite drove the mares mad and they tore Glaucus to pieces in their frenzy.

GLAUCUS   (3) In Roman mythology, a sea-god, father of the Sibyl of Cumae. He designed the ship ARGO and went to war with the ARGONAUTS.

GOLDEN BOUGH   In Roman mythology the hero AENEAS was sent by the Sybil of Cumae to obtain the Golden Bough, which would give him safe passage to the UNDERWORLD. The Golden Bough is thought to be the MISTLETOE, a plant that appears in many mythologies.

GOLDEN BOUGH, THE   A monumental study of mythology by Sir James G. Frazer (1854–1941). It was published in 12 volumes between 1890 and 1915. (It is now available in one abridged volume.) *The Golden Bough* is a vast study of the beliefs of mankind, suggesting that the thinking person progresses from the magical and superstitious to scientific thought and analysis. Frazer's works had an influence on many literary figures. He was one of the founders of modern anthropology.

GOLDEN FLEECE, THE In Greek mythology, this fabled fleece was worn on the back of an extraordinary ram. The ram could talk and think; it could move through the air as easily as on land; and it had a fleece of gold. The ram was sent by the god HERMES to rescue PHRIXUS and HELLE, children of ATHAMAS, king of BOEOTIA. The hero JASON and his companions, the ARGONAUTS, overcame enormous obstacles to capture the precious fleece and bring it back to King PELIAS of IOLCUS, in Boeotia. (See *Jason and the Argonauts*, under JASON.)

Many scholars think that the "golden fleece" represented either gold amber or perhaps the alluvial gold found in riverbeds near the Black Sea and collected by the natives in fleeces laid on the river beds.

GORDIAN KNOT, THE In Greek mythology, a puzzling and intricate knot tied by GORDIUS (king of PHRYGIA, in ASIA MINOR) in a rope linking the yoke and the pole of the ox-cart that had borne him to the temple of ZEUS. Zeus, obeying the words of an ORACLE, made the peasant Gordius the new king of Phrygia. It is said that the ox-cart remained at Gordium, the capital city of Phrygia founded by Gordius, for centuries. A superstition grew up around the knot: Whoever could untie the knot would become the ruler of Asia. The knot was never untied, but in legend, Alexander the Great slashed through the knot with his mighty sword and did indeed become the ruler of Asia. The legend of the Gordian Knot seems to demonstrate that, in some cases, the power of the sword is greater than that of superstition. "To cut the Gordian knot" has come to mean resolving a difficult problem with one decisive, forceful step.

Scholar Robert Graves (1895–1985) points out that the town of Gordium was the key to Asia (that is, in those days, Asia Minor) because its citadel commanded the trade route from TROY to Antioch. Whoever controlled this route would be in a position of great power.

GORDIUS In Greek mythology, a peasant who became king of PHRYGIA (in ASIA MINOR), married CYBELE and fathered MIDAS. He is most famous for the GORDIAN KNOT, an intricate and puzzling knot tied by Gordius in the ropes that bound the yoke and the pole of the ox-cart that had brought Gordius to the temple of ZEUS.

GORGONS (Grim Ones) In Greek mythology, three female monsters (the Euryae); daughters of Ceto and Phorcys; sisters of the GRAEA. Their names were Euryale, Stheno and MEDUSA. They had the bodies of women, brazen claws for hands and snakes for hair. Two were immortal, but Medusa was not. The hero PERSEUS killed her and cut off her head. (See *Perseus and Medusa*, under PERSEUS.)

GRACES, THE THREE Greek goddesses of beauty and charm, they were themselves embodiments of both. They are usually thought to be the daughters of the god ZEUS and Eurynome. The names given to them by the poet HESIOD were Thalia (Flowering), Euphrosyne (Joy) and Aglaia (Radiance). The Three Graces were the personification of joy and well-being. They were present at human and divine marriages, and constantly attendant upon the goddess of love, APHRODITE. They were also associated with the god APOLLO.

The Three Graces are often depicted as mingling with NYMPHS in joyous dances celebrating the bounties of nature.

GRAEA (Gray Women) In Greek mythology, daughters of Phorcys and Ceto; sisters of the GORGONS. Their names were Dino, Enys and Pemphredo. The personification of old age, they had only one eye and one tooth to share among themselves. The eye was stolen by the hero PERSEUS as they passed it from one to another. He gave it back to them after they had told him the whereabouts of their sister, MEDUSA, and where to find the helmet, winged sandals and magic wallet he needed to complete his quest (see *Perseus and Medusa*, under PERSEUS).

H

HADES Greek god of the UNDERWORLD, associated in Roman mythology with PLUTO, ORCUS and DIS. Hades was the son of CRONUS and RHEA, and like his sisters DEMETER, HERA and HESTIA, and his brother POSEIDON, was swallowed by Cronus. His brother ZEUS escaped and eventually rescued his brothers and sisters from Cronus. (See *Zeus Rescues His Siblings*, under ZEUS.)

After the defeat of Cronus, Zeus, Poseidon and Hades drew lots to see who should rule the various parts of the universe. To Hades fell the Underworld.

Hades seldom left his underground realm (or if he did, no one knew about it, for he had a helmet that made him invisible). But when he fell in love with PERSEPHONE, he came above ground to pursue her as she gathered flowers in a field. He carried her off into the dark earth, and there she was forced to remain for four months of the year. (See *Demeter and Persephone*, under DEMETER.)

On another occasion Hades came above ground to woo the NYMPH, MINTHE. In a fit of anger, Persephone, or perhaps Demeter, trod the maiden underfoot. A sorrowful Hades transformed her into the fragrant mint plant.

Essentially a god of terror, of inexorable death, there were few temples built to Hades and he had few worshipers.

The cypress and the narcissus were sacred to Hades.

The word *Hades* is often used as a euphemism for Hell.

HARMONIA In Greek mythology, daughter of APHRODITE and ARES; wife of CADMUS, king of THEBES. All the OLYMPIAN GODS attended the wedding of Harmonia and Cadmus. Harmonia was blessed with many gifts from the gods, including a golden necklace from Aphrodite, made by the smith-god, HEPHAESTUS. The necklace had the power of giving unfading beauty to its wearer, but would also bring misfortune in the later history of Thebes (see SEVEN AGAINST THEBES, THE, and ERIPHYLE).

Some scholars, such as Robert Graves (1895–1985), say that while Harmonia (which means peace) may seem a strange name for a daughter born of Aphrodite, the goddess of love, and Ares, god of war, then, as now, more than usual affection and therefore harmony are generated among people in times of stress such as war.

The children of Cadmus and Harmonia were INO, Agave and SEMELE, daughters, and Polydorus, a son.

HARPIES (Snatchers) In Greek mythology, supernatural winged beings, probably originally winds and spirits that carried people off. In later stories they were depicted as large birds with the faces and breasts of women, who were said to snatch food from tables and spread stench and filth. The word *harpy* has come to mean a scolding, nagging woman. A harpy is also a large, powerful eagle of tropical America.

Harpies attack Aeneas and his Trojan crew in VIRGIL'S AENEID, they plague JASON and the ARGONAUTS, and are mentioned in the ODYSSEY of HOMER.

HEBE Daughter of the Greek gods ZEUS and HERA and cupbearer to the gods. She became the wife of the hero HERACLES after he was deified and transported to Olympia. Later she was represented as the goddess of youth, with the power to rejuvenate, that is, bring back youth. In Roman mythology she is called Juventas (Youth).

HECATONCHEIRES (or HECATONCHIRES) In Greek mythology, the hundred-handed giants, offspring of GAIA and URANUS. Their names were Briareus, Cottus and Gyges. They helped ZEUS in the war against the TITANS. The Hundred-

Handed Ones are thought by some to represent early bands of warriors, who were organized in groups of one hundred men. In Latin their name is Centimanes.

HECTOR In Greek mythology, great hero of the Trojans (see TROJAN WAR); eldest son of PRIAM, king of TROY, and of HECUBA; husband of ANDROMACHE; father of Astyanax. Hector has very little mythology except in HOMER'S ILIAD, yet he comes across as a likable and warm-hearted man. Numerous passages in literature, for example, his combat with AJAX and his farewell to his wife and infant son, show him as a sympathetic character. His death, the violation of his body by ACHILLES and his magnificent funeral bring the epic of *The Iliad* to an end. There are references to Hector in VIRGIL'S AENEID, OVID'S *Metamorphoses* and Shakespeare's *Troilus and Cressida*.

HECUBA In Greek mythology, wife of King PRIAM of TROY; daughter of the king of PHRYGIA; mother of many, among them HECTOR, leader of the Trojans in the TROJAN WAR, and PARIS, whose abduction of HELEN was a leading cause of the war. Hecuba was written about in HOMER'S ILIAD and by the tragedian EURIPIDES in *Hecuba* and *The Trojan Women*.

HELEN In Greek mythology, daughter of ZEUS and LEDA, said to have been born from an egg, since Zeus came to Leda and mated with her disguised as a swan. Often called Helen of TROY, Helen was in fact from SPARTA. She was the sister of the DIOSCURI (Castor and Polydeuces) and of CLYTEMNESTRA. She became the wife of MENELAUS, king of Troy. Helen was said to be the most beautiful woman in the world, a symbol of womanly beauty. Her abduction by the Trojan prince PARIS was a leading cause of the TROJAN WAR. (See also *The Judgment of Paris*, under PARIS.) In Marlowe's *Faustus*, (c. A.D. 1592), Helen's face is called "the face that launched a thousand ships," that is, the ships of the Greek expedition that went to fight in the Trojan War.

There are varying accounts of the end of Helen. Some say that after the fall of Troy she was reconciled with her husband, Menelaus.

Others say that she married DEIPHOBUS; or that she was hanged by a vengeful queen; or that she hanged herself from a tree. She was venerated as a goddess of beauty on the island of Rhodes (in the eastern Mediterranean) under the name Dendritis (Tree).

It seems likely that Helen was an ancient goddess of fertility in LACONIA, which may account for the half-human, half-divine stories that were told about her.

HELENUS In Greek mythology, son of PRIAM and HECUBA. The brother of CASSANDRA, he shared with her the gift of prophecy. In HOMER'S ILIAD he gives good advice to HECTOR, leader of the Trojans in the TROJAN WAR. In the play *Andromache*, by EURIPIDES, Helenus weds his fellow captive ANDROMACHE after the fall of TROY. In some accounts Helenus becomes king of EPIRUS. In VIRGIL'S AENEID he warns the Trojan hero of SCYLLA AND CHARYBDES and urges him to consult with the SIBYL of Cumae.

HELICON The highest mountain in BOEOTIA, in the southern part of the Greek mainland. It was celebrated in Greek mythology as the haunt of the nine MUSES. The poet HESIOD lived on the slopes of Mount Helicon. In later mythology, the spring of Hippocrene, created when the winged horse PEGASUS stamped his hoof, was just below the summit.

HELIOS The sun-god of the Greeks. He was husband to Rhodos, the NYMPH of the island of RHODES, which he chose as his favored abode. Their children—CIRCE, Acetes and Phaeton—were the first inhabitants of Rhodes. Helios is usually depicted as a charioteer who drove the sun across the earth from east to west each day. Helios was all-seeing and often called upon as a witness (see *Demeter and Persephone*, under DEMETER). Helios (called Hyperion by HOMER) appears in both the ILIAD and the ODYSSEY; in the latter, the cattle of Helios (Hyperion) are victims of ODYSSEUS and his crew of hungry mariners.

In later times Helios was identified with APOLLO, and, in the late Roman empire, with Sol, one of the principal gods of the Romans.

HELLE In Greek mythology, daughter of ATHAMAS and NEPHELE; sister of PHRIXUS. Helle and her brother fled from INO, their stepmother, on the back of the winged ram sent to them by HERMES. (See the GOLDEN FLEECE.) One story has it that Helle fell from the air and was drowned at a place that came to be called the HELLESPONT in her honor.

HELLEN In Greek mythology, the son of DEUcalion and PYRRHA, survivors of the Flood. He was the father of AEOLUS, Dorus and Xuthus, and through them the ancestor of all the HELLENES (Greeks).

HELLENES The name given to the people now called Greeks. It was derived from HELLEN, the son of DEUCALION, who became, after the Flood, the ancestor of all the Greeks. There is no good explanation of why the people of ancient Greece should be called Hellenes, rather than Achaeans, Argives or Danaans. As modern British scholar Michael Stapleton points out (in *The Illustrated Dictionary of Greek and Roman Mythology*), the word *Greek* is not Greek at all: It comes from the Latin *Graecia*, the country from which many "Greek" settlers came to live in Italy.

HELLESPONT (now known as the DARDANELLES) The long narrow channel or strait leading from the Aegean Sea into the Sea of Marmara and the Black Sea. It was an important trade route for ships traveling between Asia and Europe. There were many battles and wars for control of this channel; the most famous such war of ancient times was the TROJAN WAR.

The Hellespont got its name because HELLE, the sister of PHRIXUS, was said to have drowned there when she and her brother were fleeing from their stepmother, INO. (See GOLDEN FLEECE, THE.)

HEPHAESTUS (Roman VULCAN) The Greek god of craftsmen, especially smiths, and of fire; called "the divine artificer." In some accounts he was the son of ZEUS and HERA, in some of Hera alone. Hephaestus was lame from birth and not as handsome as the other gods in OLYM-

PUS. It is said that Zeus or Hera flung him from Mount Olympus in anger. He landed on the island of Lemnos, where the sea-goddesses THETIS and Eurynome rescued him and looked after him until he was grown.

Although lame, Hephaestus had strong shoulders and was an excellent craftsman, the patron of all smiths, and perhaps something of a magician. Some scholars say that in fact every Bronze-Age (c. 3000 B.C.) tool, weapon or utensil was believed to have magical properties and that the smith who made them was thought to be a sorcerer. In many mythologies, from West Africa to Scandinavia, the smith-god is depicted as lame; in primitive cultures the craftsmen may have been purposely crippled in order to keep them from running off and joining rival tribes. Another theory has it that the limping gait of the smith personifies the zigzag path of lightning, an aspect of fire.

In HOMER'S ODYSSEY, Hephaestus was married to the beautiful goddess of love, APHRODITE. But she was unfaithful to him, and had many lovers, including ARES, the god of war. Hephaestus used his craftsmanship to get the better of Ares. (See *Ares and Aphrodite*, under ARES.)

Another story has it that Hephaestus cracked open the head of Zeus in order to release the goddess ATHENE. (See *Birth of Athene*, under ATHENE.)

In other accounts (including Homer's ILIAD) the wife of Hephaestus is Aglaia, one of the three GRACES.

Hephaestus is an ancient god—whose origins are probably in ASIA MINOR—thought to be kindly and peace-loving. His smoky, flaming workshop was supposed to be located beneath Mount Etna, the volcano in Sicily, an idea that the Romans adapted for their similar god, VULCAN. With Athene, the cult of Hephaestus was important in the life of the city of ATHENS.

HERA (Lady) In Greek mythology, queen of OLYMPUS, sister and wife of ZEUS, daughter of CRONUS and RHEA. Known as JUNO by the Romans. Mother of ARES, HEBE, HEPHAESTUS and EILEITHYA. The patroness of marriage, Hera was the goddess most concerned with the welfare of women and children.

Hera was an ancient goddess, existing long before the time of the migrations and their new gods, including Zeus. Her original name is unknown: Hera is a title, meaning "Lady." Her original cult was so strong that the newcomers from the north had to acknowledge it and absorb it into their own religion by making Hera the consort of Zeus, the king of the OLYMPIAN GODS.

Hera was depicted as a young woman, fully clad and of regal beauty, sometimes wearing a high, cylindrical crown. Her emblems include a scepter surmounted by a cuckoo (see *Hera and the Cuckoo*, below), and a pomegranate, symbol of married love and fruitfulness. The bird sacred to Hera is the peacock, testifying to the services of the hundred-eyed ARGUS (see *Hera and Io*, below).

The marriage of Hera and Zeus was not a happy one, for Zeus was unfaithful to his wife and Hera was angry and jealous. She sought to avenge herself on Zeus and his loves in various ways (see *Hera and Her Rages*, below). The many quarrels between Hera and Zeus may reflect the conflicts between the old gods, where woman was the Great Mother and Queen, and the new (Zeus and the Olympians), where men became dominant.

Hera and the Cuckoo

There are several legends about how the marriage of ZEUS, chief god of the Olympians, and Hera, queen of OLYMPUS, came about. The most famous is told by the writer Pausanius: Zeus appears before Hera in the shape of a cuckoo—in this story, a small, shivering bird, drenched with rain. Tender-hearted Hera takes the poor creature to her bosom to warm it. Zeus at once resumes his normal form and Hera finally agrees to become his wife. The marriage is solemnly celebrated on Olympus, but it does not put an end to the amorous adventures of Zeus (see *The Loves of Zeus*, under ZEUS). With Zeus, Hera had two sons, ARES and HEPHAESTUS, and a daughter, HEBE. Some legends say that Hera conceived and gave birth to Hephaestus without any help from Zeus. Some say that she was also the mother of EILEITHYA, about whom little is known.

Hera and Ixion

Hera, wife of ZEUS, was ever faithful to her fickle husband. However, she was very beautiful and men found her desirable. Ephialtes, one of the ALOEIDS, was determined to capture Hera and make her his wife. Thus he and his brother precipitated a war with the Olympians. Another admirer was King IXION of Lapith. Invited to a banquet at Olympus, he fell in love with Hera. When Zeus found out about his advances, he was angry and jealous. Zeus used his magic to shape a cloud in the likeness of Hera. Ixion made love to the cloud, whose name was NEPHELE, and from this union was born CENTAURUS, father of the CENTAURS. Ixion was bound to a fiery wheel and doomed to whirl perpetually through the sky.

Hera and Io

One of the loves of ZEUS was the maiden IO. Zeus turned Io into a beautiful white heifer to protect her from Hera, but Hera was not deceived. She demanded to be given the heifer and Zeus could not refuse her. Hera then tied up the heifer and had her guarded by the hundred-eyed ARGUS (1). The god HERMES rescued Io by using songs and stories to close all the eyes of Argus in sleep, and then killing him. But Io remained a heifer, relentlessly pursued by a gadfly sent by Hera, until she reached Egypt. Hera transferred the eyes of Argus onto the magnificent tail of the peacock, where, legend has it, they remain to this day. The peacock is sacred to Hera. Some scholars believe that Io was a form of Hera as an ancient goddess dispossessed by the Olympians. In HOMER the goddess Hera is often described as "ox-eyed."

Hera and Her Rages

Hera, sister-wife of the OLYMPIAN GOD ZEUS, had to face the fact that her husband had a wandering eye (see *The Loves of Zeus*, under ZEUS, and *Hera and Io*, above). Hera fought back as best she could. (See LETO [the TITAN mother of APOLLO and ARTEMIS]; the story of SEMELE in *The Birth of Dionysus*, under DIONYSUS; and also the stories of ANTIGONE and PARIS, the Trojan, who preferred APHRODITE in the famous beauty contest on Mount IDA (see *The Judgment of Paris*, under PARIS].)

HERACLES (or HERAKLES) (Glory of Hera) The greatest hero of Greek mythology, he was called

HERCULES by the Romans. He was the son of the god ZEUS and of a mortal, ALCMENE, who was the wife of AMPHITRYON of THEBES; both parents were descendants of the hero PERSEUS. Heracles was the personification of physical strength and courage, a superman and demigod, a supreme athlete, but at the same time he had many human weaknesses. He performed seemingly impossible tasks (see *The Twelve Labors of Heracles*, below), fought in battle, loved many women including DEIANIRA (who would eventually cause his death) and was afflicted by murderous madness and sudden rages. Heracles was snatched from his funeral pyre by his father, Zeus, and taken to Olympia, where he was worshiped like a god, became immortal and married HEBE, about whom little is known.

Heracles' name (Glory of Hera) suggests an origin among ancient people who worshiped the goddess Hera, wife of Zeus. The myth of Heracles is based perhaps on a historical figure, perhaps a lord of TIRYNS (in ARGOS) whose military prowess led to the Homeric legend of his having met and conquered death. Later, invaders of the PELOPONNESUS (the southern peninsula of what is now called Greece) adapted the cycle of the Heracles-hero myths to fit their own ancestry.

Heracles' whole life—from the heroic deeds, the Twelve Labors and the crimes and atonements to the eventual elevation to OLYMPUS— seems to be a metaphor for victory over death, representing man's dream of achieving the immortality of the gods.

The Childhood of Heracles Heracles, the greatest hero of Greek mythology, was called HERCULES by the Romans. His father was the god ZEUS, his mother ALCMENE, a descendant of the hero PERSEUS.

ALCMENE was married to AMPHITRYON, also a descendant of Perseus. While Amphitryon was at war, Zeus visited Alcmene disguised as her husband. He wished to father a son that would be a champion of both men and gods. This son was Heracles. When Amphitryon came back the next evening, he, too, fathered a son with Alcmene. His name would be Iphicles.

HERA, the wife of Zeus, was, as usual, jealous and angry at the dallyings of her husband. Using her magic arts, she contrived the premature birth of EURYSTHEUS, another descendant of Perseus. Eurystheus was born a few minutes before Heracles and therefore became ruler of ARGOS. Heracles was obliged to serve him, and this he did most heroically (see *The Twelve Labors of Heracles*, below).

One legend has it that Hera sent two serpents to the cradle of the infant Heracles to kill him. But the baby managed to strangle both serpents with his supernormal strength. Another legend says that it was Amphitryon who sent the serpents, knowing that one of the twins belonged to Zeus. Thus, while his own son Iphicles cried pitifully, the son of the god was able to vanquish the serpents.

Amphitryon made sure that his godlike stepson was trained in all the arts of fighting, wrestling and boxing. Heracles became a supreme athlete.

Heracles, The Young Hero Heracles (Roman HERCULES) was the greatest of the Greek heroes. When Heracles was a boy, his stepfather

HERACLES SLEW THE MANY-HEADED HYDRA AS ONE OF HIS MIGHTY TWELVE LABORS. (NEW YORK PUBLIC LIBRARY PICTURE COLLECTION)

sent him to tend his cattle in the mountains and to develop athletic skills. A ferocious lion came from Mount Kithaeron to devour Amphitryon's cattle. Heracles killed the lion and ever after wore its pelt (though some say that the pelt worn by Heracles was that of the Nemean lion; see *The Twelve Labors of Heracles*, below).

Heracles then did battle with Erginus, king of Orchomenos, who attacked THEBES. Amphitryon was killed in this struggle. The victorious Heracles became the idol of Thebes. Creon, the new king of Thebes, gave his daughter MEGARA (2) to Heracles in marriage. The marriage was not a happy one, and in later years, in a fit of madness sent upon him by the goddess HERA, Heracles killed his children, and possibly his wife as well. He went to the ORACLE at DELPHI for advice. As atonement for the dreadful killings, the Oracle put Heracles into the servitude of his cousin, King EURYSTHEUS, who would impose upon the young hero the Twelve Labors (seemingly impossible tasks). (See *The Twelve Labors of Heracles*, below, and *The Childhood of Heracles*, above.)

The Twelve Labors of Heracles Like many a hero in mythologies from all over the world, Heracles, the greatest Greek hero, fought and won battles with extraordinary creatures that represented man's ancient strife with evil and the forces of darkness. Because of a fit of madness, in which he killed his children and possibly his wife, Heracles, son of the god ZEUS and the mortal ALCMENE, was put into the service of King EURYSTHEUS, a descendant of PERSEUS and ruler of ARGOS. To atone for his sins, Heracles had to perform 12 almost impossible tasks over the course of 12 years. In all of them he emerged as a victorious hero against unbelievable odds. The order of the Twelve Labors varies in some sources but are thought to begin with the killing of the ferocious Nemean lion and end with either the stealing of the apples of the Hesperides or the vanquishing of the dog CERBERUS.

1. *The Nemean Lion* The lion was gigantic, an offspring of SELENE. It lived in a cave with two entrances. After many futile battles Heracles sealed off one mouth of the cave and strangled the trapped lion with his bare hands. Ever afterward he wore the pelt and head of the lion. The two mouths of the lion's cave perhaps symbolize the entry of Heracles into the battles (the Twelve Labors) from which he would eventually escape, after death, into rebirth and immortality.

2. *The Hydra of Lernaea* The HYDRA was a many-headed monster who grew a new head each time Heracles lopped the previous one off. With the help of his companion IOLAUS, who burned the stumps of the heads and prevented them from growing again, Heracles vanquished the monster. He dipped his arrows in the blood of the Hydra, which contained a deadly poison. Heracles's destruction of the Hydra may represent the suppression of the ancient Lernaean fertility rites and the burning down of the forests where they were practiced. However, most mythographers are still puzzled as to the exact meaning of the Lernaean Hydra.

3. *The Wild Boar of Erymanthus* The boar was a huge beast that Heracles hunted through deep fields of snow. He vanquished the boar and brought it back to EURYSTHEUS. The king was so terrified at the sight of the beast that he hid himself in a bronze jar.

4. *The Hind of Ceryneia* This beautiful Arcadian deer had feet of bronze and antlers (surprising for a hind) that shone like gold, and ran so swiftly that it took Heracles a year to capture it. He brought it back unharmed to King EURYSTHEUS. The chase of the hind may represent man's pursuit of wisdom.

5. *The Stymphalian Birds* These monstrous birds had wings, beaks and claws of bronze. They fed on human flesh and were so numerous that when they took flight their hordes blotted out the sun. Heracles terrified them with the shattering noise from a bronze rattle that the goddess ATHENE helped him make. The birds flew away and were never seen again.

This legend may refer to Heracles's reputation as a healer, expert at getting rid of fever demons. In ancient times fevers were little understood and often proved fatal. Since they occurred frequently in marshy places they were identified with marsh birds such as cranes and ibises, large birds on which the Stymphalian birds may have been modeled.

6. The Augean Stables The Sixth Labor of Heracles was to clean, in one day, the pestilent, dung-filled stables of the cattle of King Elis of Augeus. Heracles did this by diverting the courses of two nearby rivers and sending their cleansing waters rushing through the stables. "Cleaning the Augean stables" has come to mean getting rid of superfluous, noxious rubbish in any area, whether physical, moral, religious or legal.

7. The Cretan Bull Heracles captured the bull that had been terrorizing the island of CRETE. He brought it back to king EURYSTHEUS. The bull was later killed by THESEUS. The combat of a man with a bull was one of the ritual tasks imposed on heroes (see the stories of THESEUS and also of JASON).

8. The Horses of Diomedes Heracles captured the horses (some say they were wild mares) of DIOMEDES (2) of Thrace. It was said that Diomedes fed the horses on human flesh. Heracles killed Diomedes and gave his flesh to the horses, after which, it is said, the beasts became quite tame. The taming of wild horses was an important rite in many ancient cultures.

9. The Girdle of the Amazon Heracles was asked to obtain the girdle of Queen HIPPOLYTA of the AMAZONS, for Admete, the daughter of King EURYSTHEUS. Some versions of the legend say that Hippolyta fell in love with Heracles and gave him her girdle. Other versions say that Hippolyta was later abducted by THESEUS. The conquest of the Amazons, a warlike tribe of women, may represent an early version of an attempt by men to achieve supremacy over rebellious women.

10. The Cattle of Geryon GERYON was a three-headed monster whose fine red cattle were the envy of everyone, including EURYSTHEUS, who ordered Heracles to capture them. Heracles did this, on the way erecting the Pillars of Hercules (now known as the Straits of Gibraltar), where Africa and Europe face each other at the western end of the Mediterranean Sea. Stealing another man's cattle was an ancient custom; a prospective husband bought his bride from the proceeds of a successful cattle raid.

11. The Stealing of Cerberus CERBERUS was the fearsome, three-headed dog that guarded the gates of the UNDERWORLD. EURYSTHEUS ordered Heracles to bring him the monster, never expecting the hero to return to the land of the living. However, with the help of the gods HERMES and ATHENE, Heracles overcame both HADES, god of the Underworld, and the monstrous dog. When Eurystheus saw the huge creature, he jumped into a bronze jar in terror.

The three heads of Cerberus may have represented the three seasons vanquished by the demigod who became immortal.

12. The Apples of the Hesperides Heracles's final task was to bring some of the golden apples of the HESPERIDES (daughters of ATLAS) to EURYSTHEUS. The apples belonged to HERA and were guarded by the dragon LADON. Only the TITAN Atlas, who carried the sky on his shoulders, knew where the apple orchard was. Heracles took the sky from Atlas and persuaded him to fetch some apples. He then tricked the Titan into taking back the weight of the sky upon his shoulders.

The explanation for this Labor may lie in the primitive ritual in which the candidate for a kingship or immortality (Heracles) had to overcome a monster (Ladon) and rob it of its treasure (the golden apples).

The Exploits of Heracles Heracles, the son of the god ZEUS and the mortal ALCMENE, was the greatest of Greek heroes. Even as an infant Heracles showed superhuman strength by killing two serpents (see *The Childhood of Heracles*, above). As a young man he performed miraculous services for EURYSTHEUS (see *The Twelve Labors of Heracles*, above).

There is no clear-cut chronology for the exploits of Heracles, but rather a patchwork of events, with some confusion about the order in which they took place. For example, it is not clear at what point the goddess HERA, wife of Zeus, angry at the dalliance of her husband with Alcmene, took revenge upon Heracles by sending him fits of murderous madness. Among his crimes were the killing of his own children and, some say, his wife MEGARA (2); and the killing of Iphitus, a guest in his house. Such deeds were unforgivable. Even the ORACLE at DELPHI refused to help Heracles after the killing of Iphitus. In another fit of madness, Heracles ravaged the oracle's shrine and attacked his half-brother, the god APOLLO. As a result of this outrage, Heracles became a slave to OMPHALE, queen of LYDIA.

Among his exploits for Omphale was the capture of the clever thieves called the CERCOPES; Heracles also killed Syleus, the king of Aulis, who had forced strangers to work in his vineyards and then, instead of paying them, cut their throats. Heracles rid the banks of the Sagaris from a gigantic serpent; and then killed Lityerses, another evil man who forced people to work for him and then killed them. Omphale so admired Heracles that she set him free.

After his servitude to Omphale, Heracles offered his services to LAOMEDON, king of TROY. Laomedon had incurred the wrath of the sea-god, POSEIDON, who sent a monster to ravage Troy. The oracle told Laomedon that only the sacrifice of his beautiful daughter, HESIONE, would appease the monster and save Troy. Laomedon chained the girl to a rock to await her fate. Heracles agreed to rescue the maiden in return for two magical horses that had been a gift from Zeus to Laomedon. But Laomedon, his daughter now safe, reneged on his agreement and Heracles killed him. Heracles then gave Hesione to his friend TELAMON in marriage. PRIAM, now king of Troy, demanded the return of his sister, Hesione. The Greeks refused to return her; the subsequent ill-feeling between the nations of Troy and Greece was one cause of the TROJAN WAR.

Heracles, Deianira and the Centaur

Heracles the mortal spent his life engaging in one heroic exploit after another (see *The Childhood of Heracles*, *The Exploits of Heracles*, *The Twelve Labors of Heracles*, and *Heracles, the Young Hero*, above). Sometimes Heracles sought adventure; sometimes he sought revenge for injustice; and sometimes he had to flee from the punishment due him for acts committed in madness.

After many bold deeds Heracles came to CALYDON, in Atolia, whose king, OENEUS, had a beautiful daughter, DEIANIRA. Deianira was constantly plagued by the attentions of ACHELOUS, who appeared to her in the form of a river, a dragon or a bull. After a furious contest Heracles vanquished Achelous and won the hand of the beautiful Deianira, with whom he bore a son, Hyllus.

Heracles, Deianira and Hyllus were forced to flee from Calydon when Heracles, again afflicted by rage, killed an innocent cupbearer, Eunomus.

When they came to the river Evenus a CENTAUR, NESSUS, offered to carry Deianira on his back, while Heracles swam across. When they reached the other side the centaur tried to carry Deianira off. Heracles shot him with his arrow. As he lay dying, Nessus told Deianira to collect some of his blood and use it as a love potion if she ever thought that her husband was straying. Deianira respected the wishes of the dying beast and took his blood in a vial that she carried. This so-called potion was to cause the death of Heracles (see *The Death of Heracles*, below).

The Death of Heracles

The last expedition of Heracles, the great Greek hero, was against his old enemy EURYTUS. Heracles slew Eurytus and carried off his daughter, IOLE, with whom he had been in love before he had met his present wife, Deianira. When Deianira heard about the beautiful maiden, she remembered the vial of blood that she had taken from a CENTAUR, NESSUS (see *Heracles, Deianira and the Centaur*, above). Innocently thinking that the potion would bring Heracles back to her, she soaked a shirt in a liquid made from the blood in the vial and sent it to her husband with his messenger, Lichas.

As soon as Heracles put on the fateful shirt he began to writhe with pain, for the potion was a deadly one, and proved fatal to Heracles. He commanded a funeral pyre to be built and laid himself upon it. His son, Hyllus, told him that Deianira had not intended his death and had killed herself in despair. Heracles, in his last throes of agony, gave Iole to his son in marriage. No one wanted to light the funeral pyre, but at last, PHILOCTETES (or his father,

Poeas) set the wood to light. Immediately a cloud descended from the sky, and in a display of thunder and lightning the god ZEUS snatched his son from death and bore him to OLYMPUS, where he would become immortal.

HERCULES Roman name for the Greek hero HERACLES. The cult of Heracles reached Rome at a very early period, having come from Latin towns with Greek commercial connections. ("So often religion goes hand in hand with trade," says 20th-century scholar Stewart Perowne in his *Roman Mythology*.) Heracles was as appealing in ancient times as modern "supermen" are today—somewhat godlike and yet human as well.

HERMAPHRODITUS In Greek mythology, the son of APHRODITE and HERMES. He was brought up by NYMPHS on Mount IDA, in CRETE. One of the nymphs, Salmacis, fell in love with him but Hermaphroditus scorned her. Salmacis prayed to be joined with him forever in one body. Her prayers were answered, for when she finally clasped him to her their two bodies became one.

The word *hermaphrodite* describes a person or other living form, such as a plant or insect, that has both male and female characteristics.

In terms of a mythological and religious concept, a young man with womanish breasts and long hair may represent the transition from matriarchy (the Earth Mother) to patriarchy (the rule of dominant males).

HERMES In Greek mythology, son of ZEUS and MAIA. The winged messenger of the gods, Hermes is also associated with fertility, and is god of flocks, roads, trading and thieves. In Roman mythology, he is known as MERCURY. Hermes was the inventor of the lyre and the guide of souls on the way to HADES. He was the father of many, including AUTOLYCUS, DAPHNIS and HERMAPHRODITUS.

In archaic art Hermes was depicted as a bearded man wearing a broad-brimmed hat and winged sandals, and carrying a herald's staff. From the 5th century B.C. on, he was depicted as a nude and beardless young man, typical of an accomplished athlete.

The earliest center of his cult was ARCADIA, where he was worshiped as a god of fertility with phallic images called *hermae*. These were heaps of stones set up the by the ancient Greeks to mark boundaries or distances along roads. With the development of artistic taste these crude piles became (in the 5th century B.C.) pillars crowned with the head of Hermes. In cities the hermae were erected at street corners and at the doors of houses.

The Childhood of Hermes Hermes, son of ZEUS and MAIA, was born in a cave in Mount Cyllene, in ARCADIA. He grew miraculously fast, and soon after his birth he was able to walk out of the cave, kill a tortoise and make the first lyre from its shell.

To complete the lyre Hermes needed strings. He stole a herd of cows belonging to APOLLO by making them walk backward so that their tracks would lead Apollo in the wrong direction. He killed the cows and made strings for the lyre from their guts.

When Apollo finally discovered the thief (now back in his baby-cradle), he brought Hermes before his father, Zeus. Zeus was more amused than angry at his infant son, and when Hermes produced the lyre and played it, even Apollo was charmed and offered the rest of his flock to Hermes in return for it.

Apollo also gave Hermes his CADUCEUS, a herald's staff of gold. HADES instructed Hermes to lay the golden staff on the eyes of the dying and lead them gently to the realm of the dead.

Some accounts say that Apollo taught Hermes how to prophesy, ARTEMIS taught him how to hunt and PAN taught him how to play the pipes. Hermes was undoubtedly a favorite with the gods.

The myth of Hermes's childhood may have an allegorical connection with a tradition of cattle raids made by crafty Messenians (personified by Hermes) on their neighbors (Apollo), and of a treaty by which the raids were discontinued.

HERO AND LEANDER In Greek mythology, the subjects of a tragic love story. Hero was a priestess of APHRODITE. Leander, a young man from Abydos, Mysia, in ASIA MINOR, was her lover. He swam across the HELLESPONT every night, guided by her light. One stormy night the light was blown out and Leander drowned. In her grief, Hero cast herself into the waves to be with him and perished. The story has been the subject of many literary works, including a long poem, *Hero and Leander*, by Christopher Marlowe (1564–1593).

HESIOD Greek poet, whose work is usually dated around 800 B.C., after HOMER. Hesiod was a poor farmer. His poem *Works and Days* gives us a vivid picture of everyday life in ancient Greece as it was lived by ordinary people, as opposed to the adventurers and courtiers of Homer's ILIAD and ODYSSEY. Hesiod's *Theogony* is concerned with mythology; it describes the Greeks' beliefs about creation, the universe, and the geneology of the gods and goddesses. Hesiod tells us also about sinister aspects of religion, such as witchcraft and human sacrifices. Both poems are invaluable sources for the study of Greek religion and mythology.

HESIONE In Greek mythology, daughter of LAomedon, king of TROY; sister of PRIAM. Laomedon offered his daughter as sacrifice to a seamonster to appease the gods POSEIDON and APOLLO. Hesione was rescued by the hero HERACLES, who slew the monster and gave Hesione in marriage to TELAMON, with whom she bore a son, TEUCER. Hesione's brother, Priam, now king of Troy, demanded her return. The refusal of the Greeks to return Hesione to her Trojan home was said to have caused some of the ill feeling that eventually led to the war between Greece and Troy (see the TROJAN WAR).

HESPERIDES In Greek mythology, the three sisters who guarded the golden apples that had been given to HERA as a wedding gift. They were the daughters of EREBUS (Darkness) and Nox (Night). The Hesperides lived to the far west of the river Oceanus, which was thought to be on the edge of the world and the entrance to HADES. The tree on which the apples grew was guarded by the dragon LADON.

In his Twelfth Labor, the hero HERACLES managed to steal the apples. (See *The Twelve Labors of Heracles*, 12. The Apples of the Hesperides, under HERACLES.)

Later mythologies say that the Hesperides were the daughters of the TITAN, ATLAS.

HESTIA (Hearth) In Greek mythology, daughter of CRONUS and RHEA; sister of ZEUS, POSEIDON, HADES, DEMETER and HERA; one of the 12 OLYMPIAN GODS; goddess of the hearth and fire, identified with VESTA in Roman mythology. Gentle, peace-loving and pure, Hestia kept away from all disputes. Hestia was the embodiment of a sacred principle—the household fire—and much honored as such, though there are few surviving stories about her. (See *Hestia and the Hearth*, and *Hestia and Priapus*, below.)

Hestia and the Hearth Hestia was the goddess of the hearth and the fire. It was a difficult task for primitive people to make and preserve fire; fire in the hearth was tended with care and worshiped. When a member of the family left home, he or she carried a glowing ember from the hearth, thus symbolizing the continuity of the family. When groups of people began to form villages and then towns, each community had a public hearth *(prytaneum)* where the fire was maintained. In later days the fire of the public hearth was used in religious sacrifices and took on a sacred character. Eventually the character of the *hestia* was personified as the deity HESTIA.

Hestia and Priapus Hestia was the goddess of the hearth. The hearth was the center of domestic life in early Greece. Hestia represented personal security and happiness and the sacred duty of hospitality. There are few surviving legends about Hestia, but one story emphasizes the importance of the hearth as a symbol of hospitality and protection.

One day, at a rustic feast, the drunken god PRIAPUS assaulted Hestia. The guests were extremely angry and drove Priapus away. This anecdote represents a warning against the illtreatment of guests, particularly women, who are under the protection of the domestic or public hearth.

HIPPODAEMIA In Greek mythology, the daughter of King OENOMAUS, who lost her in a chariot race to PELOPS (see *Pelops and the Charioteer*, under PELOPS). She and Pelops became the parents of Atreus and Thyestes (see under ATREUS AND THYESTES).

HIPPOLYTA   In Greek mythology, queen of the AMAZONS, wife of THESEUS, mother of HIPPOLYTUS. The hero HERACLES stole her girdle (see *The Twelve Labors of Heracles, 9. The Girdle of the Amazon*, under HERACLES). Heracles had been accompanied on this exploit by Theseus, king of ATHENS. Hippolyta and the Amazons waged war upon Athens and were vanquished by Theseus, who made Hippolyta his wife. She bore him a son, Hippolytus. Her other names were Antiope and Melanippe.

HIPPOLYTUS   In Greek mythology, son of THESEUS, the king of ATHENS, and of HIPPOLYTA, queen of the AMAZONS. In the tragedy *Hippolytus* by the Greek poet EURIPIDES (c. 429 B.C.), love-goddess APHRODITE desires Hippolytus, but he spurns her, worshiping only ARTEMIS, goddess of the hunt. In revenge, Aphrodite causes PHAEDRA, wife of Theseus, to fall in love with her stepson. Hippolytus is horrified at her advances and Phaedra hangs herself, leaving a letter for Theseus saying that his son tried to violate her. Furious, Theseus calls on the sea-god, POSEIDON, to punish his son. Poseidon causes a huge bull to rise up out of the sea. It ravages Hippolytus and his chariot. The dying prince is brought back to the palace, where Artemis has told the true story to the anguished king. Hippolytus forgives his father with his last words, ecstatic to be at last in the presence of his goddess.

This tragedy is one of many that shows the gods in a bad light—in this case it is Aphrodite who is shown to be mean and vengeful, causing pain, unhappiness and death among mortal men and women.

The tragedy by Euripides was the basis for many works, including a play in Latin by Seneca (c. 4 B.C.–A.D. 65) and the play *Phèdre* (Phaedra) by Jean Racine (1639–1699), considered a masterpiece of French classical drama.

HOMER   The great poet of ancient Greece to whom the epic poems the ILIAD and the ODYSSEY are usually attributed. Although he is Greece's most famous name, hardly anything is known about Homer. His birthdate is said to be some time between 1050 and 850 B.C. His birthplace is not known, though the island of Chios (off the coast of Ionia, in ASIA MINOR) has been deduced as likely from references in the poems. Some say that the work of Homer may have been a kind of anthology of ancient writings, gathered together with great genius by Homer, who is responsible for the poetical unity. Others (including recent studies by computers) say that *The Iliad* and *The Odyssey* were the work of a single poet, developed from older legendary material.

Whatever the origins of the poet, the poems had a tremendous influence on the Greeks, providing them with an elementary education in the mythology of their country. Homer's works have been of enormous value to historians, archaeologists and students of comparative religion. His stories preserve for us the social and religious customs of the late Bronze-Age Achaeans who invaded TROY (3000 B.C.). After the fall of the Achaeans there were three or four centuries of "darkness" until the great flowering of culture known to us as Classical Greece (5th century B.C.). Only Homer wrote about the period in between.

HORAE   In Greek mythology, daughters of ZEUS and THEMIS; goddesses of the seasons. According to HESIOD there were three Horae: Irene (peace), Dike (justice) and Eunomia (order). The names and numbers of the Horae differed from place to place in ancient Greece. The Horae controlled the four seasons, watched over agriculture, were goddesses of flowers and fruits and had many names, including Thallo (flowers) and Carpo (fruits). They were depicted as beautiful maidens, often in the company of the GRACES in the retinue of love goddess APHRODITE. They were especially tender toward children.

HYACINTHUS   A young man loved by the Greek god APOLLO; son of Amyclas, a Spartan king, and Diomede, or of Pierus and Clio, the MUSE. He was killed by a discus thrown by Zephyrus, the West Wind. Apollo created a fragrant flower, the hyacinth, in honor of his friend.

Hyacinthus was an ancient, pre-Hellenic fertility god, whose worship was absorbed by Apollo's cult in later years when the Hellenes were invaded by migratory tribes. A three-day festival, the Hyacinthia, was held at SPARTA in honor of the god, where boys and girls participated in games, competitions, sacrifices and various entertainments.

HYDRA (Water Creature) In Greek mythology, a many-headed serpent, the offspring of ECHIDNA and TYPHON. When one head was chopped off, another one grew in its place. The Second Labor of HERACLES was to kill the dreaded serpent. He did this by searing the creature's neck after he had cut off the head. Hydra's blood was venomous. Arrows or garments dipped in it killed CHIRON, the CENTAUR; NESSUS; PHILOCTETES; and, finally, HERACLES himself.

A hydra-headed situation is a difficulty that seems to get worse and worse.

In biology, hydras are small, freshwater coelenterate creatures, among the lowest of the many-celled animals. Most get their food by using venomous tentacles.

HYPERION (The One Above) In Greek mythology, one of the TITANS; son of URANUS and GAIA; father of HELIOS, SELENE and EOS (the Sun, the Moon and Dawn). Hyperion is sometimes used as the name for the sun itself. Earlier mythologies name Helios as the sun. In some accounts Hyperion, like Helios, is identified with APOLLO. (See also EURYLOCHUS and ODYSSEUS.)

I

ICARUS In Greek mythology, son of the great inventor DAEDALUS. When Daedalus wanted to escape from the island of CRETE, where he was being held prisoner by King MINOS, he invented and crafted wings from the feathers of birds, held together by wax. He and Icarus took flight. But Icarus ignored the warnings of his father and flew too near the sun. The heat of the sun melted the wax, and the wings of Icarus fell apart. Icarus plummeted into the sea and was drowned. The Icarian Sea, a part of the Aegean Sea between Turkey and the Greek islands of Patmos and Leros, is named after him. His name is sometimes used to describe a person who is rashly over-ambitious.

IDA (1) In Greek mythology, the NYMPH, who with her sister, ADRASTIA, and the goat-nymph, AMALTHEA, tended the infant god ZEUS on Mount IDA (2) in CRETE. (See *The Childhood of Zeus*, under ZEUS.)

IDA (2) Mountain in the center of CRETE, associated with the childhood of Zeus (see under ZEUS).

IDA (3) A mountain range in Mysia, northwest ASIA MINOR. It was from here that GANYMEDE was seized and taken to OLYMPUS to be a cupbearer to the gods; it was the scene of the *Judgment of Paris* (see under PARIS); and from here, the gods watched the battles of TROY during the TROJAN WAR.

ILIAD, THE The name of the epic poem by HOMER, who is thought to have lived during the 8th century B.C. The name derives from Ilion, one of the names for TROY, an ancient city on the northwestern tip of ASIA MINOR. *The Iliad* consists of 24 books. It tells of the last few days of the TROJAN WAR, focusing especially on the Greek hero ACHILLES, who withdrew from the conflict, causing severe setbacks

to the Greeks. However, he later rejoined the war, and slew HECTOR, the hero of the Trojans. *The Iliad* also tells of other leaders of the Greeks, such as ODYSSEUS, DIOMEDES, AJAX and MENELAUS, who was the leader of the Achaeans (Homer never called them Greeks). It does not tell of the beginning of the Trojan War, which was supposed to have been caused by the abduction of HELEN, a Spartan princess, by the Trojan PARIS.

The Iliad tells not only of the war, but of the peaceful lives of shepherds, fishermen and woodcutters of an era that is now supposed by historians and archaeologists to be between 1200 and 1300 B.C.

According to many scholars, *The Iliad* is one of the greatest works of literature, and certainly the earliest. Achilles is the first hero of Western literature and embodies (says modern critic Clifton Fadiman) man's prime idiocy: warfare. The poem tells of petty rages and jealousies, but also speaks of heroism and nobility in a memorable narrative.

ILIUM or ILIA Another name for TROY. In Greek legend, Ilus, son of Tros by CALLIRRHOË, was the founder of Ilium, which was also called Tros or Troy after his father. The ILIAD, by HOMER, means "about Troy."

INO In Greek mythology, daughter of CADMUS and HARMONIA; sister of Agave, Antonoë and SEMELE; wife of ATHAMAS. According to some scholars, including Robert Graves (1895–1985), Ino was Leucothea (White Goddess), a moon-goddess and a corn-goddess. She is important in the legend of Jason and the Argonauts (see under JASON) as the second wife of Athamas.

Ino hated her stepson PHRIXUS, the firstborn of Athamas and NEPHELE. Ino (as a corn-goddess) persuaded the women of BOEOTIA (the kingdom of Athamas) to roast the corn seeds secretly before they were sown, so that no new corn would grow from the dead seeds. She then bribed an ORACLE to tell Athamas that to make the barren fields fertile, his son Phrixus must be sacrificed to the corn-goddess. Terrified, Athamas agreed to the sacrifice. Phrixus was rescued by a winged ram that wore a GOLDEN FLEECE.

Ino and her husband Athamas took care of the infant DIONYSUS (son of Ino's sister SEMELE), which earned them the gratitude of ZEUS (father of Dionysus) but the wrath of HERA (wife of Zeus), who visited madness on both Ino and Athamas.

Io In Greek mythology, daughter of the river-god, Inachus; a priestess of HERA, and beloved by the husband of Hera, the great god ZEUS. Trying to protect Io from the wrath and jealousy of Hera, Zeus turned Io into a white heifer. Hera was not deceived and contrived to take the heifer from Zeus. Io was later rescued by HERMES and escaped to Egypt, where she gave birth to EPAPHUS, son of Zeus. (See *Io, the White Heifer*, below.)

Io, the White Heifer Io, the beautiful daughter of the river-god, Inachus, was a priestess of HERA. Hera's husband, the great god ZEUS, fell in love with Io. To protect Io from the wrath and jealousy of Hera, Zeus changed Io into a pretty white heifer (a young cow). Hera was not deceived. She asked Zeus for the heifer and Zeus was forced to hand her over. Hera put Io in charge of the hundred-eyed ARGUS (1), who kept watch on her night and day, for his eyes never closed.

Stricken with remorse, Zeus sent the god HERMES to rescue Io. This Hermes did by telling long stories and singing songs until all the eyes of Argus closed in sleep. Then Hermes cut off his head and released Io. Io fled, but Hera, still jealous, sent a gadfly to torment her. Io eventually reached Egypt, where at last she became a woman again and bore Zeus a son, EPAPHUS.

It is said that the Ionian Sea is named after Io, for she swam across it. The Bosporus, a narrow straight between the Black Sea and the sea of Marmara, is also named after her. (Bosporus means "cow-ford," that is, a crossing for cows.)

Some say that the strange story of Io had its origin in pre-Hellenic religion, when perhaps Io was a moon-goddess (it is said that moon-goddesses wore horns, as did Io as a heifer). The old Hellenic gods were deposed by the OLYMPIAN GODS. Some accounts say that Io was but one aspect of the goddess Hera, ancient Mother Earth, often described as "ox-eyed," deposed by the later gods.

IOLAUS In Greek mythology, the son of Iphicles (half-brother of HERACLES). Iolaus was the constant companion of Heracles and also his charioteer. Iolaus helped Heracles to slay the HYDRA (see *The Twelve Labors of Heracles*, 2. The Hydra of Lerna, under HERACLES).

IOLCUS A town in Magnesia, a region of THESSALY. In Greek mythology, it was the home of PELIAS and JASON, and the starting point for the expedition of the ARGONAUTS in search of the GOLDEN FLEECE.

IOLE In Greek mythology, daughter of EURYTUS, king of Oechalia. Iole was loved by the hero HERACLES. It was because of this love affair that DEIANIRA, the wife of Heracles, unwittingly caused the death of the hero by administering to him what she thought was a love-potion that would bring her husband back to her. (See *Heracles, Deianira and the Centaur*, under HERACLES.) After the death of Heracles, Iole married his son, Hyllus.

IPHIGENIA In Greek mythology, daughter of CLYTEMNESTRA and AGAMEMNON, king of MYCENAE and leader of the Greek forces in the TROJAN WAR; sister of ELECTRA and ORESTES. Agamemnon sacrificed Iphigenia to placate the goddess ARTEMIS, whom he had offended, and to ensure by this sacrifice fair winds on the voyage to TROY. Greek tragedians, notably SOPHOCLES and EURIPIDES, cited the death of Iphigenia as a motive for the murder of Agamemnon by Clytemnestra.

IRIS Greek deity personifying the rainbow; messenger of the gods, especially of ZEUS, and a devoted attendant of HERA. Daughter of the TITAN Thaumus; sister of the HARPIES.

ISLANDS OF THE BLESSED (or ISLES OF THE BLEST) In Greek mythology, a resting place of those favored by the gods. (See ELYSIUM.)

ITHACA A small island in the Ionian Sea off the coast of EPIRUS. It is thought by some to be the home of ODYSSEUS of Greek legend.

IXION In Greek mythology, king of the LAP-iths in THESSALY, the largest ancient region of north-central Greece. Ixion fell in love with HERA, wife of the god ZEUS. Angry at the advances of Ixion to his wife, Zeus tricked Ixion by creating a cloud, NEPHELE, in the likeness of Hera. Ixion made love to the cloud and from the union was born CENTAURUS, the ancestor of the CENTAURS. Zeus then hurled a thunderbolt at Ixion and had him tied to a fiery wheel, condemned to whirl forever through the heavens.

The poet OVID saw Ixion as symbolic of sensuality. Ixion appears in *The Divine Comedy* of Dante (1265–1321), *The Fairie Queen* by Edmund Spenser (c. 1552–1599), in *The Rape of the Lock* by Alexander Pope (1688–1744) and in *Ixion* by Robert Browning (1812–1889).

J

JANUS One of the principal Roman gods and one of the oldest. He was the guardian of gates and doors (and as such his name is used in the English word *janitor*, and in the name of the month of January, the gateway to the year). Janus is depicted as being two-faced or two-headed: One of his faces looks forward, into the future; the other looks backward, into the past. He was the opener and closer of all things. His name was mentioned in prayers even before that of JUPITER.

In the Forum in Rome there was a shrine dedicated to Janus in which the doors were opened only in time of war (to allow the warriors to march forward into battle).

The chief festival of Janus was on New Year's Day.

JASON The hero of one of the most famous Greek legends, often titled Jason and the Golden Fleece, or Jason and the Argonauts (see below). Jason was the son of AESON, king of IOLCOS (in THESSALY), and of Queen Alcimede. When PELIAS, the half-brother of Aeson, usurped the throne of Iolcus, threatening to kill any who disputed his claim, Jason was smuggled away from the kingdom and put into the care of CHIRON, the gentle CENTAUR.

After many years Jason made his way back to Iolcus to regain his kingdom. On his way he gave help to an old woman by carrying her across a river. He lost one of his sandals in the stream but earned the gratitude of the woman, who was the goddess HERA in disguise. Hera would always be an ally of Jason.

Pelias had been warned by an ORACLE to beware of a man wearing one sandal. When Jason appeared with one bare foot, Pelias sent him on an expedition to find the GOLDEN FLEECE, knowing it was unlikely that Jason would ever return. However, Jason came back triumphant (see *Jason and the Argonauts*, below). As well as the Fleece, Jason also brought with him the sorceress-queen MEDEA, who brought him disaster after he deserted her for GLAUCA. Jason lived a lonely and unhappy life, wandering about from place to place, until he finally died under the prow of his ship, the ARGO.

Jason and the Argonauts Jason was the hero of this, one of the most famous Greek myths. PELIAS, who had usurped the kingdom of IOLCUS, sent Jason to capture the GOLDEN FLEECE, a quest from which he thought Jason would never return.

But Jason had won the favor of the goddesses HERA and ATHENE. With their help Jason built the fabled ship ARGO, which had 50 oars; he recruited 50 remarkable people, called the ARGONAUTS. They included one woman, ATALANTA; HERACLES, the strongest man who ever lived; ORPHEUS, the poet from THRACE (northeastern Greece) who could sing more sweetly

TWO-HEADED JANUS, ONE OF THE OLDEST OF ROMAN GODS, LOOKED BOTH TO THE PAST AND TO THE FUTURE. (NEW YORK PUBLIC LIBRARY PICTURE COLLECTION)

JUNO WAS A GREAT GODDESS OF ANCIENT ROME AND THE WIFE OF JUPITER. (NEW YORK PUBLIC LIBRARY PICTURE COLLECTION)

than the SIRENS; and both the DIOSCURI, brothers of HELEN. They set sail for the Black Sea where the Golden Fleece was said to be.

After many adventures the Argonauts reached the kingdom of AETES. The king imposed seemingly impossible tasks upon Jason: One was to harness fire-breathing bulls with brazen feet and plow a field. Then he was to sow the plowed field with dragons' teeth, from which would spring fully armed warriors. Fortunately for Jason, MEDEA, daughter of Aetes, had fallen in love with him. She used her powers as a sorceress to help him. Jason was able to master the bulls; and when the armed men sprang from the dragons' seeds, Jason did what CADMUS had done before him (see *Cadmus and the Dragon*, under CADMUS). He threw a stone into the midst of the warriors, who accused each other of throwing the stone. They fought amongst themselves until all were dead.

Medea then led Jason to the place where the Golden Fleece hung, guarded by a terrible dragon. Using a magic potion, Medea put the dragon to sleep, allowing Jason to secure the precious trophy.

Jason and the Argonauts put to sea, accompanied by Medea, and pursued by King Aetes. Medea slew her brother, APSYRTUS, who had accompanied them. She cut his body into pieces and flung them into the sea and onto the surrounding land, knowing that Aetes would gather up the dismembered pieces of his son's body to give them a ceremonial burial. Thus the Argo-

JUPITER (OR JOVE), THE MIGHTIEST GOD OF ROMAN MYTHOLOGY, WAS ASSOCIATED WITH THE GREEK GOD ZEUS. (NEW YORK PUBLIC LIBRARY PICTURE COLLECTION)

nauts escaped with the Golden Fleece, and brought it back to Iolcus.

JOCASTA In Greek mythology, mother and wife of OEDIPUS. HOMER calls her Epicaste. (For her tragic story see under OEDIPUS.)

JOVE Another name for JUPITER, the chief god of Roman mythology. Jove gives his name to the word *jovial*, meaning of a hearty good humor. People born under the sign of the planet Jupiter are said to be good-natured.

JUNO One of the great goddesses of ancient Rome; moon-goddess, goddess of childbirth, and also a protector of the Roman state along with JUPITER and MINERVA. In later times Juno became identified with the Greek goddess HERA and so was regarded as the sister-wife of JUPITER (as Hera was the sister-wife of ZEUS).

Juno gave her name to the month of June, which was considered the most suitable time for marriage.

JUPITER (also called JOVE) The supreme god of Roman mythology. Son of SATURN (or CRONUS) and OPS (or RHEA). Jupiter was an ancient sky god of Italy, master of thunder, lightning, rain and light, and also the giver of victory and peace. However, like many of the Roman gods, he had little mythology of his own and became identified with the chief god of the Greeks, ZEUS.

Jupiter was the husband of JUNO; he was the special protector of Rome.

Jupiter is also the name of the largest planet in our solar system.

L

LABYRINTH The word *labyrinth* means any intricate building full of chambers and passages, or a maze of paths bordered by high hedges. In Greek mythology, the labyrinth designed by DAEDALUS for King MINOS to house the MINOTAUR may have been patterned on the design of the palace itself, which had a complex of rooms; in front of the palace was an open space that featured a dance floor with a maze pattern intended as a guide for performers in erotic spring dances. According to scholar Robert Graves (1895–1985), both the maze and the dances had their origin in the traditional brushwood maze built by hunters to decoy female partridges toward their mates, who were trapped in a central enclosure.

Labyrinthine has come to mean tortuous, elaborate, confusing, and may be used to describe, for instance, a literary style or an elaborate argument.

LACONIA A region in the southeast PELOPONNESUS whose capital was SPARTA. In Greek mythology, HELEN (wife of MENELAUS and legendary cause of the TROJAN WAR), was sometimes said to have been an ancient goddess of fertility in Laconia. She was worshiped there as a goddess of beauty.

LADON In Greek mythology, the dragon who guarded the garden where the apples of the HESPERIDES were kept. In this garden, on Mount Atlas, there was a tree that bore golden fruit. It was a present from Earth Mother GAIA to HERA on her marriage to ZEUS. No mortals knew the whereabouts of this sacred tree. It was the last task of the hero HERACLES to find and collect some of the apples (see *The Twelve Labors of Heracles*, 12. The Apples of the Hesperides, under HERACLES). This Heracles did with the help of ATLAS, the TITAN. Heracles then killed the dragon, incurring the wrath of Hera.

LAELAPS (also LELAPS or LALAPS) A marvelous hound in Greek mythology who could catch whatever he chased. The god ZEUS gave the dog to the NYMPH Procris, who then gave him to her husband, CEPHALUS, the hunter. Cephalus inadvertently killed Procris. A famous painting by Piero di Cosimo (1462–1521) shows Laelaps as a big red setter looking forlorn at the feet of the slain nymph. Laelaps was later sent out to hunt the Teumessian fox, which had been destined by the goddess HERA never to be caught. The seemingly impossible, unsolvable chase was resolved by Zeus, who turned both animals into stone.

LAERTES In Greek mythology, king of ITHaca, husband of ANTICLEA, father of the hero ODYSSEUS. Laertes was one of the ARGONAUTS, the gallant crew who helped JASON find the GOLDEN FLEECE. He was also present at the CALYDONIAN BOAR HUNT. Laertes was still alive when his son, Odysseus, returned from the TROJAN WAR.

LAESTRYGONIANS In Greek mythology, a race of giant cannibals who devoured many of the crewmen of the ships of ODYSSEUS when they anchored near their island. Only Odysseus's own ship escaped this terrible fate, since Odysseus had the foresight to anchor his vessel outside the harbor. In the ODYSSEY (Book X), HOMER describes how the giants threw rocks on the ships from the top of the cliffs and then harpooned the screaming men as if they were fish, and carried them off to be eaten.

LAOCOÖN In Greek and Roman mythology, a priest of APOLLO and POSEIDON; son of PRIAM, king of TROY, and of HECUBA. Laocoön made Apollo angry by marrying and begetting children, breaking his priestly vow of celibacy. Laocoön had been chosen by the Trojans to make

LAOCOÖN AND HIS TWO SONS WERE KILLED BY SEA SERPENTS WHILE OFFERING A SACRIFICE TO POSEIDON (NEPTUNE). (NEW YORK PUBLIC LIBRARY PICTURE COLLECTION)

sacrifices to Poseidon, whose priest they had murdered nine years before. Before he went to the altar with his two sons, Laocoön warned Priam to beware of the Trojan horse. (See *The Wooden Horse of Troy*, under TROJAN WAR.) Laocoön said that he feared the Greeks, especially when they brought gifts. From this, "a Greek gift" has come to mean a treacherous gift. As Laocoön and his twin sons, Antiphas and Thymbreus, stood at the altar of Poseidon, two gigantic serpents, sent by a vengeful Apollo, coiled about them and crushed them to death.

A famous statue of Laocoön and the serpents was discovered in Rome in 1506. It is believed to date from the 2nd century B.C., and it now stands in the Vatican Museum.

The story of Laocoön is told in VIRGIL'S AENEID.

LAOMEDON In Greek mythology, first king of TROY; father of PRIAM, HESIONE and others. He was slain by the hero HERACLES (see *The Exploits of Heracles*, under HERACLES). The gods APOLLO and POSEIDON had displeased ZEUS. As punishment they were sent to work for Laomedon for wages. Poseidon built the walls of Troy,

while Apollo tended the king's flocks on Mount IDA. (2) When the two gods had completed their tasks, Laomedon refused to pay them. In revenge the gods sent a sea-monster to ravage Troy. The monster could be appeased only by the sacrifice of a maiden. One of the maidens chosen was Hesione, the daughter of the king. She was rescued by Heracles; but again Laomedon refused to pay his debt to the hero, and was slain by him.

LAPITHS (plural, *Lapithae*) Mythical people of THESSALY, in north-central Greece. Their king, IXION, fathered with NEPHELE (a cloud that ZEUS had formed in the likeness of HERA) the half-human, half-horse creatures called CENTAURS. PIRITHOÜS, half-brother of the Centaurs, became the ruler of the Lapiths.

LATINUS In Roman mythology, the king of the Latini, ancient inhabitants of Latium. He was the father of LAVINIA, with his wife, Amata. He gave his daughter in marriage to the hero AENEAS, thus causing the jealousy of TURNUS, to whom she was already betrothed. The story is told in VIRGIL'S AENEID.

LATIUM A region of west-central Italy of which Rome is the capital. (See also ROMULUS AND REMUS, the legendary twins who in Roman mythology were the founders of Rome.)

LAVINIA In Roman mythology, the daughter of LATINUS and Amata. She had been betrothed to her relative TURNUS, but Latinus gave her instead to the hero AENEAS, who founded a city and named it Lavinium in her honor. Her story is told in VIRGIL'S AENEID.

LEDA In Greek mythology, the daughter of King Thestius of AETOLIA; wife of Tyndareus, king of SPARTA. She was the mother of the twin brothers, Castor and Polydeuces (POLLUX in Latin), known by the joint name of the DIOSCURI; and of HELEN and CLYTEMNESTRA. According to one myth Leda mated with the god ZEUS, who had disguised himself as a swan. Leda then laid an egg from which Helen and Polydeuces emerged. Castor and Clytemnestra arrived by normal delivery and were said to be the children of Tyndareus.

LEMURES Ghosts of the dead, malignant or mischievous spirits who returned to earth to terrify the living. They had their origin in the mythology of ROMULUS AND REMUS, the founders of Rome.

Romulus had murdered his twin brother Remus. He was tormented by the spirit of his sibling. He instituted the Lemuria, feasts of atonement. (It is thought that the feasts were originally called Remuria, after Remus; in time the first letter became corrupted into an L.) Families went through an extraordinary ritual at the Lemuria: Every father rose from his bed at midnight, snapped his fingers to scare away the spirits, then washed his hands three times. Next he filled his mouth with black beans, then tossed them behind him, chanting words of atonement. This performance he repeated nine times. Finally he washed his hands again, struck a gong and bade the evil spirits to depart. After that he could safely go back to bed.

(See also MANES.)

LETHE (Forgetfulness or Oblivion) In Greek mythology, one of the rivers of HADES. The souls of the dead were obliged to drink the waters of Lethe so that they could forget everything they had said or done when they were alive. Lethe is sometimes associated with DIONYSUS, god of the wine that encourages forgetfulness.

LETO In Greek mythology, a TITAN; daughter of Coeus and PHOEBE (in Roman mythology, Latona); mother, by ZEUS, of the twin deities, ARTEMIS and APOLLO. According to HESIOD, Leto was noted for her gentleness.

Leto was relentlessly pursued by HERA, the jealous wife of Zeus. She wandered from place to place, finally resting at DELOS, where she gave birth to the divine twins. It is said that Artemis was born first and immediately became mature enough to help her mother with the birth of Apollo. At one time Delos was a floating island in the Aegean Sea. In recognition of its being a haven for Leto and the children, Zeus made the island immovable and decreed that no one should be allowed to be born or to die there.

The harassment of Leto by Hera suggests the conflict between migrating tribes and the native tribes, who worshiped the Earth Mother (Hera).

LIBER (or LIBER PATER) In Roman mythology, an ancient god of fertility and the vine, sometimes identified with the Greek god DIONYSUS (Roman BACCHUS). His festival, the Liberalia, held on March 17, was associated with merrymaking and the day when adolescent boys entered their manhood.

LIBITINA Ancient roman goddess who presided over funerals. Her name is often synonymous with death. Originally she was perhaps an earth goddess or agricultural divity.

Undertakers in ancient Rome were called *libitinarii*. They had their places of work within Libitina's temple. Here deaths were registered and money paid by the bereaved to honor the goddess.

Libitina was sometimes identified with the Greek goddess PERSEPHONE.

LIBYA (1) In Greek mythology, mother, with sea-god POSEIDON, of AGENOR, king of Tyre. (See under EUROPA, who was the daughter of Agenor.)

LIBYA (2) The Greek name for North Africa, excluding Egypt and Ethiopia. In HOMER'S ODYSSEY, ODYSSEUS and his crew make landfall in Libya in the land of the LOTUS EATERS. In VIRGIL'S AENEID, AENEAS and his crew reach the coast of Libya, where Aeneas is visited by his mother, the goddess VENUS.

LITYERSES In Greek mythology, son of King MIDAS of PHRYGIA. Lityerses prided himself on his skill in the harvest. He challenged all to compete with him and was brutal to those that lost in the contest. In some legends the hero HERACLES defeated Lityerses, cut off his head with a sickle and threw his body into the Meander River.

LOTUS EATERS (Lotophagi) In HOMER'S ODYSSEY, people who lived on the fruit (or the roots) of the lotus plant. The food made them forget their past, their families and their future, so that they lived in a state of dreamy bliss. ODYSSEUS and his crew made landfall in the land of the Lotus Eaters on their way home to ITHACA. Several of the crew became addicted to the food of the lotus plant. They had to be dragged back to the ship by force.

"Lotus Land" was probably LIBYA (2), in North Africa. Lotus is a name given to many plants, especially water plants, such as water lilies. Some of them have edible roots.

LYDIA A wealthy kingdom of western ASIA minor (now northwestern Turkey). In Greek mythology, Lydia was the home of ARACHNE, the skillful weaver who rashly pitted her talents against those of the goddess ATHENE.

M

MAENADS WERE CRAZED WOMEN, FOLLOWERS OF DIONY-SUS. (NEW YORK PUBLIC LIBRARY PICTURE COLLECTION)

MAENADS In Greek mythology, the crazed women who followed the god DIONYSUS. (See under BACCHANTS, which was their Latin name.)

MAGNA GRAECIA (Great Greece) The collective name given to Greek city-states founded by settlers in southern Italy and the island of Sicily. The cult of the Greek hero HERACLES, and of other personages in Greek mythology, found their way into Roman mythology through the Greek colonists of Magna Graecia.

MAIA In Greek mythology, daughter of ATLAS and Pleione, the eldest and most beautiful of the PLEIADES (The Seven Sisters). Maia was the mother of HERMES (ZEUS was the father). She bore Hermes in a grotto on Mount Cyllene in ARCADIA. Maia's only appearance in Greek mythological writings is in HESIOD.

As a Roman goddess, Maia was identified with an ancient divinity of spring, also called

Maia, the cult-partner of Volcanus. The month of May, when most plants flower, undoubtedly gets its name from her.

MANES (Good Ones) In Roman mythology, the spirits of the dead. They were greatly feared and were called "Good Ones" to placate their anger. (Similarly, the greek FURIES were called the EUMENIDES, "good ones" or "good-tempered ones.")

Whenever a town was founded a pit was first dug within the site and then covered with a stone. The hole represented a gateway to the UNDERWORLD through which the Manes could pass when the stone was removed, three times a year.

MARS One of the most important Roman gods next to JUPITER. Mars was best known as the god of war (like his Greek counterpart, ARES), but he was originally a god of agriculture and fertility. The wolf, the woodpecker and the lance were his symbols. He was especially honored during the spring month of Mars (March in English).

The planet Mars was given his name because it has a reddish glow; the color red is identified with anger and war.

MEDEA In Greek mythology, a sorceress; daughter of King AETES of Colchis (ASIA MINOR); niece of CIRCE, the witch of the ODYSSEY. In his quest for the GOLDEN FLEECE, JASON fell in love with Medea, who helped him capture the precious fleece.

As Jason and Medea fled with the trophy they were pursued by Aetes, the father of Medea and her brother, APSYRTUS. Medea killed her brother and strewed pieces of him along the way, knowing that Aetes would stop to pick up his dismembered son. Thus she and Jason escaped from the angry king, Aetes.

Medea returned to Iolcus (Thessaly) with Jason. Her first deed was to destroy PELIAS, the

75

ROMAN MARS, LIKE HIS GREEK COUNTERPART ARES, WAS THE GOD OF WAR. (ARCHIVI ALINARI/ART RESOURCE)

king who had usurped the throne of Iolcus. She did this by suggesting to the daughters of Pelias that, if they killed him, cut him up into small pieces and cooked him in a stew, he would then be rejuvenated. She demonstrated her idea by cutting and cooking a ram and, by the use of magic, making a lamb spring forth from the pot. The daughters did as she suggested but of course Pelias did not survive. The people were so horrified at this deed that Jason and Medea had to flee the country.

Jason and Medea settled for a while in COR-INTH. Jason deserted Medea for GLAUCA, daughter of the Corinthian king Creon. Medea killed Glauca by sending her a wedding dress saturated with poison. Medea also killed the two sons she had borne with Jason, then fled to the court of King AEGEUS of ATHENS.

When the hero THESEUS arrived at his father's court Medea tried to murder him with a goblet of poisoned wine. Just in time, Aegeus recognized his son and dashed the cup from his hands. (See *Theseus and Medea*, under THE-SEUS.)

Medea fled from Athens and there is no record of where she went next. Some legends say that her son, Medus, was the ancestor of the Medes, an ancient people of Asia Minor.

MEDEA, THE BEAUTIFUL WITCH LOVED BY JASON. (NEW YORK PUBLIC LIBRARY PICTURE COLLECTION)

MINTHE In Greek mythology, a NYMPH of the Cocytus, a river that flowed to the UNDERWORLD. She was beloved by HADES (or PLUTO). In jealous rage the wife of Hades, PERSEPHONE (or perhaps her mother, DEMETER), stamped the nymph into the ground. Hades then transformed her into a fragrant herb, mint.

The legend of Minthe was probably the result of the use of herbs, especially mint, rosemary and myrtle, to sweeten the air during funeral rites in ancient times.

MISTLETOE A European plant *(Viscum album)* that grows as a parasite on trees, especially oak trees. For centuries it has been thought of as a mysterious and sacred plant, for it flourishes with bright green leaves atop bare-branched trees in the middle of winter. After it has been cut and kept for several weeks, its leaves and branches turn golden yellow, which may account for its name as the sacred GOLDEN BOUGH that gave the hero AENEAS safe passage to the UNDERWORLD.

MNEMOSYNE (Memory) In Greek mythology, a TITAN, daughter of GAIA and URANUS; with ZEUS, mother of the MUSES.

MUSES In Greek mythology, originally deities of springs, later designated as goddesses of various human inspirations. In later mythologies the Muses were the daughters of the god ZEUS and MNEMOSYNE (Memory).

The Muses sang and danced, led by the god APOLLO, at celebrations given by the gods and heroes. They were the personifications of the highest aspirations and intellectual minds and represented a remarkable and attractive conception in Greek mythology. Their separation into fields of inspiration was a Roman fancy of a later date. The word *museum* denotes a place of education and research, named after them.

The Muses and their various attributes are listed below.

Calliope: Muse of epic poetry. She carried a stylus and tablet and sometimes a trumpet.

Clio: Muse of history. She carried a trumpet and scrolls.

Erato: Muse of Lyric, or love-poetry, and hymns. She carried a lyre.

Euterpe: Muse of flute-playing.

Melpomene: Muse of tragedy. She carried the mask of tragedy.

Polyhymnia: Muse of mime. She had a pensive attitude.

Terpsichore: Muse of dance. She carried a lyre and plectrum.

Thalia: Muse of comedy. She carried the smiling mask and a shepherd's crook.

Urania: Muse of astronomy. She carried a globe and compass.

MYCENAE Ancient city of Greece situated in ARGOS, in the northern PELOPONNESUS. It was the center of the important Mycenaean civilization, which was roughly contemporary with that of the Minoan civilization of CRETE. In mythology, Mycenae was the royal city of AGAMEMNON.

MYRMIDONS Warlike people of ancient THESSALY (in the eastern part of the Greek mainland) who accompanied the hero ACHILLES into battle in the TROJAN WAR. According to some legends, the Myrmidons were ants who were turned into people by ZEUS to increase the population of Thessaly after a plague sent by his wife, HERA, had killed thousands. In modern English a myrmidon has come to mean a person who executes commands without scruple at a master's demand.

MYRTILUS In Greek mythology, son of the god HERMES and a mortal woman. He was the charioteer of King OENOMAUS of Pisa in ELIS (northeast PELOPONNESUS). He was in love with HIPPODAEMIA, the daughter of Oenomaus. When PELOPS came to compete in a chariot race with Oenomaus for the hand of the King's daughter, Pelops persuaded Myrtilus to fix Oenomaus's chariot so that it would overturn. Pelops promised the charioteer that, if he, Pelops, won the race, Myrtilus would be awarded an evening with the beautiful Hippodaemia. Myrtilus did as he was requested; Pelops won the race (and the hand of Hippodaemia); Oenomaus was killed when his chariot overturned. But Pelops had no intention of fulfilling his promise to the charioteer. He killed him. With his dying breath Myrtilus placed a curse upon Pelops and all his descendants. And the curse took hold, for Myrtilus was the son of the god Hermes; and the gods knew well how to make curses take hold. (See under PELOPS.)

One of the most famous and beautiful depictions of a charioteer is a life-size statue in bronze, dated around 470 B.C. (the Classical Period of Greek art) at DELPHI.

N

NARCISSUS In Greek mythology, the son of river-god Cephissus and Liriope. He was a beautiful man. When he rejected the love of ECHO, a NYMPH, he was condemned by NEMESIS to reject all love except that of his own image reflected in a pool. Narcissus pined away and was changed into a beautiful flower that bears his name. The story of Echo and Narcissus is told by OVID in *Metamorphoses*. It belongs to later Greek mythology.

NAUSICAA The daughter of ALCINOUS, king of the Phaecians. It was she who discovered ODYSSEUS when he was shipwrecked on the island of Scheria on his way back to ITHACA after the TROJAN WAR. She brought him as a guest to her father's court, a place of peace and luxury. The location of Scheria and the Phaecian kingdom is unknown.

NAXOS Island in the Aegean Sea southeast of Greece. It is famous in Greek mythology as the place where THESEUS abandoned ARIADNE, daughter of King MINOS, after she helped him find his way out of the LABYRINTH. (See *Theseus, Ariadne and the Minotaur*, under THESEUS.) Naxos was a center for the worship of DIONYSUS.

NEMESIS Greek goddess of vengeance; personification of the wrath of the gods toward those who had *hubris*, a Greek word meaning something like "over-self-confidence and pride in achievements and good fortune." Nemesis rewarded virtue and punished wickedness. One of those pursued by Nemesis was NARCISSUS. At first, Nemesis was an abstract concept. In later mythology she was personified as a daughter of Nox (Night) and EREBUS (Darkness), a powerful force.

In the English language word *nemesis* means an agent or an act of punishment that cannot be avoided or overcome.

NEOPTOLEMUS In Greek mythology, son of ACHILLES and Deidamia. Neoptolemus played no great part in HOMER's epics, except as one of the heroic Greek warriors who brought about the fall of TROY: He was hidden with the others inside the cunning wooden horse (see *The Wooden Horse of Troy*, under TROJAN WAR). However, as the son of the great hero Achilles Neoptolemus is mentioned in many myths: Some say that it was he who killed PRIAM, the vanquished king of Troy; others say that he won the Trojan princess, ANDROMACHE, as one of the prizes of victory. One tradition has it that he was killed at DELPHI by ORESTES. For many years there was a hero-cult dedicated to Neoptolemus at Delphi.

NEPHELE In Greek mythology, wife of ATHAMAS; mother of PHRIXUS, Leucon and HELLE. Nephele had started her life as a cloudlike form created by the god ZEUS to trick IXION, who was making advances to the god's wife, HERA. (See under IXION).

NEPTUNE Roman water-god; he became identified with the Greek sea-god, POSEIDON. He was represented as a bearded man, carrying a trident and often astride a dolphin or a horse.

NEREUS (Old Man of the Sea) A sea-god of Greek mythology, depicted as a very old man. His special dominion was the Aegean Sea. Nereus had 50 daughters, the nereids or sea-NYMPHS.

NESSUS In Greek mythology, the CENTAUR who caused the death of the hero HERACLES. Nessus carried DEIANIRA, the wife of Heracles, across the river Evenus when the couple were escaping from CALYDON (see *Heracles, Deianira and the Centaur*, under HERACLES). Nessus tried to force his attentions on Deianira, and Heracles shot him with an arrow. As he was dying, the Centaur told Deianira to take some his blood and use it as a love potion if Heracles ever seemed to be straying from her. Deianira used the potion when Heracles became interested in IOLE, not knowing that she would thereby cause his death.

NESTOR In Greek mythology, king of Pylos (on the west coast of Messenia, in the PELOPONNESUS) and, at 60 years old, the oldest and most experienced of the chieftains who fought in the TROJAN WAR. Nestor was greatly respected for his strength and wisdom; he was also famous for being garrulous, thus his name is sometimes applied as an epithet to an elderly, talkative man. He was one of the few heroes of TROY who returned safely to his kingdom in Greece. In HOMER'S ODYSSEY he tells TELEMACHUS, son of ODYSSEUS, of some of the adventures of the Greek leaders.

NIKE Greek winged goddess of victory, perhaps the daughter of the TITAN Pallas and STYX. Her Roman counterpart was VICTORIA. Nike's most famous temple was in ATHENS, Greece. Her most celebrated statue is Nike (or Victory) of Samothrace, in the Louvre, Paris.

NIOBE In Greek mythology, the daughter of TANTALUS; wife of AMPHION, king of THEBES. She was the mother of 12 children and the personification of maternal sorrow. She was unwise enough to boast about her numerous children in the hearing of LETO, who had only two children. But those children were the formidable twins APOLLO and ARTEMIS. They punished Niobe by slaying all her children. Niobe wept herself to death and was subsequently changed into a rock, from which water eternally flowed, symbolizing Niobe's tears. This story is told in HOMER'S ILIAD.

NYMPHS (Young Maidens) In Greek mythology, minor female spirits who were supposed to inhabit various places in the natural world. They were beautiful, and while not immortal they lived for a few thousand years and thus were supposed to have certain magical and oracular powers. Among them were:

Dryads and hamadryads (tree- and forest-nymphs);
Naiads (nymphs of freshwater fountains and rivers);
Naphaeae (nymphs of glens and valleys);
Nereids (sea-nymphs);
Oceanides (ocean-nymphs);
Oreads (nymphs of mountains and caves).

Among the best-known nymphs were AMPHITRITE, ARETHUSA, CALYPSO, ECHO, OENONE and THETIS.

The name nymphs was also given to the companions of certain goddesses such as ARTEMIS.

O

OCEANUS In Greek mythology, the TITAN son of GAIA and URANUS and the brother and husband of Titaness TETHYS; father of all the Oceanid NYMPHS and all the rivers and seas of the world. Like many ancient peoples, the Greeks believed that water encircled the world; they called this water Oceanus. Oceanus was represented sometimes as a serpent encircling the earth, its tail in its mouth, or as an old man with a long beard and with a bull's horns upon his head. With the ascendancy of the OLYMPIAN GODS, POSEIDON became the lord of the seas and rivers while Oceanus retired into oblivion, though his name was still used to denote the vast waters (that is, the Atlantic Ocean) that stretched beyond the known world of the ancients.

ODYSSEUS (called ULYSSES by the Romans) In Greek mythology, son of LAERTES, king of ITHACA, and ANTICLEA. Husband of PENELOPE; father of TELEMACHUS. Odysseus is one of the most famous characters in literature. His adventures on his homeward journey to Ithaca after the TROJAN WAR are recounted in HOMER'S ODYSSEY (see ODYSSEY, THE). Odysseus is depicted as a clever and resourceful hero, relying on his wits rather than on brute force to find his way out of predicaments, which are many. However, he could also be treacherous (for example, in his treatment of PALAMEDES). Thus Homer makes Odysseus a completely rounded, believable character, with faults as well as virtues.

ODYSSEY, THE The epic poem of HOMER that describes the adventures of ODYSSEUS (known as Ulysses to the Romans) on his homeward voyage to ITHACA after the TROJAN WAR. The action of *The Odyssey* occurs in no more than six weeks, but 20 years' adventures are related by means of flashback episodes told by Odysseus to the people he encounters.

The *Odyssey*, divided into 24 books, is considered to be a collection of folktales given

OCEANUS WAS THE TITAN FATHER OF ALL THE RIVERS AND SEAS OF THE WORLD. (NEW YORK PUBLIC LIBRARY PICTURE COLLECTION)

continuity and coherence by attributing the adventures to a single hero (Odysseus) and perhaps by reworking each incident so that it contributes to a consistent picture of the hero.

Some scholars say that *The Odyssey* is the first novel; that is, a fictional story with fictional characters, to be read and enjoyed. In this case, the novel had a sound base in history and mythology (see *The Trojan War: Fact or Fiction?*, under TROJAN WAR, THE). It was first written down by Homer in about the 8th century B.C. and thought to be a later work than the poet's ILIAD.

In *The Odyssey*, Homer supplies us not only with heroic adventures but with portraits of people who had superior wit and inventiveness,

85

usually substituting intelligence and ingenuity for brute force. (See below).

Odysseus and Circe

On their way back to ITHACA after the TROJAN WAR, ODYSSEUS and his crew made landfall on the island of Aeaea, on which dwelled the witch goddess CIRCE. Circe turned all the men into swine, except for Odysseus and EURYLOCHUS. Eventually Odysseus persuaded Circe to turn his men back into their human form. Under her spell, he dallied for a year on the island of the sorceress, who gave him warnings about the perils he would encounter on his way home. (See *Odysseus in the Underworld, Odysseus and the Sirens, Odysseus and Scylla and Charybdis,* and *Odysseus on the Island of the Sun,* below.)

Odysseus in the Underworld

On their way home from the TROJAN WAR, ODYSSEUS and his shipmates had been under the spell of the witch-goddess, CIRCE, for a year. (See *Odysseus and Circe,* above.) At last the crew grew restless and wanted to leave. On the advise of Circe, Odysseus and his crew visited the UNDERWORLD to consult the ghost of the blind seer, TIRESIUS. Tiresius had many warnings for Odysseus and his men, particularly about the danger of offending the gods on the island of Thrinacie, the Island of the Sun. (See *Odysseus on the Island of the Sun,* below.)

Terrified by the ghosts and the gloom of the Underworld, Odysseus and his crew fled.

Odysseus and the Sirens

ODYSSEUS, the hero, and the crews of his ships, had many adventures on their way home after the TROJAN WAR. The witch-goddess, CIRCE (see *Odysseus and Circe,* above), warned him about the SIRENS. These were beautiful NYMPHS who lured sailors to their destruction by singing so sweetly that the men would be driven mad and would be shipwrecked on the rocky coast where the Sirens lived. Always resourceful, Odysseus plugged the ears of his men with wax so that they wouldn't hear the singing. Then, because he himself wanted to hear the songs, Odysseus had himself tied to the mast of the ship while the men rowed on. They could hear neither the singing nor the pleas of their captain to be released so that he might go to the Sirens.

Odysseus and Scylla and Charybdis

One of the many dangers encountered by the hero ODYSSEUS on his way home after the TROJAN WAR was the narrow strait guarded by the monsters SCYLLA AND CHARYBDIS. The witch-goddess, CIRCE, had warned Odysseus and his crew about the danger. Odysseus steered his ship close to Scylla, to avoid being sucked into the boiling whirlpool of Charybdis. He lost six men to Scylla, the many-headed monster who lived high up on a cliff and sent down six long necks armed with ferocious teeth to devour any who came close.

Odysseus on the Island of the Sun

ODYSSEUS, the hero on his way home after the TROJAN WAR, had met with many dangerous adventures, and by his renowned cleverness had survived them. Both CIRCE, the witch-goddess, and TIRESIUS, the blind seer, had warned him about the Island of the Sun, which belonged to the sun-god, HYPERION. But in a state of despair and exhaustion Odysseus and his crew went there. While Odysseus rested, his crew disobeyed his orders and killed and ate the cattle of Hyperion. Odysseus was horrified when he awoke to the smell of roasting meat. But it was too late. Hyperion was furious and asked ZEUS to punish the men. This Zeus did, by causing the shipwreck of Odysseus's ship in a terrifying storm. Only Odysseus escaped alive. He was cast up on the island of CALYPSO, a NYMPH, where the hero stayed for seven years.

Odysseus and the Cyclops

On his way home from the TROJAN WAR, the hero ODYSSEUS and his crew landed on an island that had rich pastures and great flocks of sheep. The shepherd turned out to be one of the CYCLOPES, one-eyed giants. When he discovered Odysseus's men in his cave, the Cyclops immediately killed and ate two of them, then closed off the entrance to the cave with a huge rock. While the giant slept after his meal, Odysseus and his men devised a plan. They made a sharp spear from olive wood. When the giant awoke, they gave him some very sweet and potent wine that they had brought with them from Ismarus. When the giant had killed and eaten another two crewmen and fallen into a drunken stupor, Odysseus gouged out his one eye, leaving the

Cyclops blind. The men knew that they could never move the rock that closed the entrance. They waited anxiously for the giant to awaken. Meanwhile the cunning Odysseus helped his men to tie themselves under the bellies of the sheep. When the giant awoke, he moved the rock to let out the sheep to their pasture. He never suspected that Odysseus's men were leaving at the same time. It wasn't until the men were safe aboard their ship that they learned that POLYPHEMUS was the name of the monster. Polyphemus hurled rocks after the ship and vowed that his protector, POSEIDON, the sea-god, would avenge him, and that the sea would always be the enemy of Odysseus.

Odysseus Returns to Ithaca After the TROJAN WAR it took ODYSSEUS and his men 10 long years and many adventures before they got back to their kingdom of ITHACA (see above). By this time Odysseus, who had been shipwrecked many times, looked like a poor old man rather than a king. Only his old dog, ARGUS (3), and his loving old nurse, Eurycleia, recognized him. Odysseus chose to remain silent as he observed what was happening at his court. His wife, PENELOPE, who had waited for him faithfully for 20 years (10 years for the war, and 10 years for the return), was besieged by a host of aggressive suitors who wanted to usurp Odysseus's kingdom. The son of Odysseus and Penelope, TELEMACHUS, guided by the goddess ATHENE, had gone off in search of his father and come back to Ithaca convinced that he was still alive and was nearby. At last Penelope, in desperation, put her suitors to the test by asking them to string the magnificent bow of Odysseus and shoot an arrow straight through a double row of axes. The suitors failed; then the old man (Odysseus) took up the challenge. He strung the bow with ease and shot it straight and true. After that, with the help of his son, Telemachus, Odysseus slew all the greedy suitors and reclaimed his wife and his throne.

OEDIPUS (Swollen Foot) In Greek mythology, son of Laius, king of THEBES, and of JOCASTA. Father of Polynices, Eteocles, ANTIGONE and Ismene.

King Laius had been warned by an ORACLE that he would be killed by his own son, so he abandoned Oedipus on a hillside (a fate common to many unwanted children in mythology), having first pierced the child's feet and bound them together (hence the name Oedipus, meaning "Swollen Foot," or, some say, "Clubfoot").

Oedipus was rescued by a shepherd and brought up by the king of CORINTH. Years later another oracle told the young man Oedipus that he would kill his father and marry his mother. Believing that his foster parents were his real parents, Oedipus fled from them.

On his journey he met Laius, his real father. The two had a skirmish at a crossroads and Oedipus killed Laius. In Thebes, Oedipus correctly answered a riddle set by the SPHINX and in so doing won the hand of Jocasta, whom he married. Thus the oracles' prophecies were fulfilled.

When Oedipus eventually learned the truth about his parents and his relationships with them, he blinded himself in agony, and was either killed in battle or exiled to Colonus (in ATTICA), while his sons battled for the throne of Thebes (see SEVEN AGAINST THEBES, THE). He was guided in his wanderings by his loving daughter, Antigone.

SOPHOCLES, AESCHYLUS and EURIPIDES all wrote plays based on the story of Oedipus. The one by Sophocles, known as *Oedipus Rex*, has been called the greatest and most powerful of the Greek tragedies.

Psychiatrist Sigmund Freud (1856–1939) coined the phrase *Oedipus complex*, which refers to a psychological condition that may affect men who have unresolved problems in their relationships with their mothers.

OENEUS (or OENEOUS) (Vintner) In Greek mythology, king of CALYDON; husband of Althea, father of MELEAGER, Tydeus, Gorge and the beautiful DEIANIRA, who eventually married the hero HERACLES. Oeneus was deprived of his kingdom by his nephews, and though his grandson, DIOMEDES, avenged him, the old king was murdered by two remaining nephews in ARGOS when he went there with Diomedes.

OENOMAUS In Greek mythology, king of Pisa in ELIS (in the northeast PELOPONNESUS); father of HIPPODAEMIA. Many suitors contended for the hand of Hippodaemia in chariot races with Oenomaus. The penalty for losing was death, and Oenomaus made sure that they all lost. Thirteen suitors had been killed by the time PELOPS came along and won the race. (See *Pelops and the Charioteer*, under PELOPS.) Oenomaus died in a final chariot race with Pelops, who won his daughter and his kingdom.

OENONE In Greek mythology, a NYMPH, daughter of the river-god Cebren. She was loved by PARIS when he lived among the shepherds on Mount IDA (2). Paris deserted her when the goddess APHRODITE promised him the love of the most beautiful woman in the world, HELEN. (See *The Judgment of Paris*, under PARIS.) Oenone prophesied that his voyage to Greece (to claim Helen) would only bring ruin for him and his country, TROY. Her prophecy came true. (See TROJAN WAR.)

OLYMPIAN GODS In Greek mythology, the 12 (sometimes 13*) major deities who lived atop Mount OLYMPUS. Here they are listed in alphabetical order, with their attributes, and their Roman names opposite.

GREEK NAMES	ROMAN NAMES
Aphrodite (Love and beauty)	Venus
Apollo (Music; poetry)	Apollo
Ares (War)	Mars
Artemis (Moon and hunting)	Diana
Athene (Wisdom)	Minerva
Demeter (Fertility; corn-goddess)	Ceres
*Hades (Underworld)	Pluto
Hephaestus (Fire; blacksmith)	Vulcan
Hera (Marriage; women)	Juno
Hermes (Messenger; commerce; travelers; rogues)	Mercury
Hestia (Hearth)	Vesta
Poseidon (Ocean; earthquakes)	Neptune
Zeus (Light; the heavens)	Jupiter

* Since HADES (PLUTO) didn't live on Mount Olympus, he isn't always counted as an Olympian.

OLYMPIC GAMES The principal athletic meeting of the ancient Greeks. In mythology, it is said to have been instituted by PELOPS to honor the god ZEUS. According to tradition, the first games were held in 776 B.C.

The games were held every four years. Only Greek men were allowed to compete and the rivalry was ferocious, for while no gold medals were awarded, the winners received great honor and prestige.

The site of the games, on a flat plain at the meeting of two rivers, is in the northwest PELOPONNESUS, part of the territory of ELIS.

OLYMPUS A mountain range in northern Greece. Its highest peak is Mount Olympus (about 9,600 feet, or 2,920 meters, high). The Olympic range stretches along the border between THESSALY and Macedonia, near the Aegean coast. It overlooks the Vale of TEMPE, a valley in northern Thessaly famous for its beauty. In mythology, Mount Olympus was regarded as the home of the gods (the OLYMPIAN GODS). Within its mysterious heights (higher even than the visible mountain) were the abodes of the gods; there they lived, feasting on ambrosia and nectar and listening to sweet music. No harsh winds or rain or snow disturbed their heavenly peace.

OMPHALE In Greek mythology, the queen of LYDIA who took the hero HERACLES as her slave after he had desecrated the temple of APOLLO. Heracles performed many services for the queen, including ridding her kingdom of the two mischievous CERCOPES.

OMPHALOS (Navel) In Greek mythology, the stone swallowed by CRONUS, one of the TITANS, thinking that it was his son ZEUS (see *Zeus*

Rescues His Siblings, under ZEUS). The stone was set up at DELPHI (see *The Origins of Delphi,* under DELPHI) and became worshiped as the center (or navel) of the earth.

OPS (Abundance) Goddess of the harvest in Roman religion; personification of the earth's riches—plenty and fertility—later identified with RHEA and CYBELE, both Greek earth goddesses. Ops was the cult-partner of the Roman SATURN.

ORACLE In Greek mythology and early history, the medium or spokesperson of the ruling deity of a shrine. The oracle gave responses to inquiries about the future or the past. These utterances were regarded as profoundly wise and authoritative, since they were supposed to come from the gods. The answers of the oracles were often obscure, ambiguous and misleading, yet eagerly sought after by kings and peasants alike. The oracles and shrines were attended by priests, who were paid for their services; therefore it was in their interests to make sure that the words of the oracle were vague. In this way, the priests would not be blamed for disastrous events that occurred from following the advice of the oracles.

There were many oracles in ancient Greece. The most famous was the oracle at DELPHI, who spoke the words of the god APOLLO through the mouth of PYTHON. The oracle at DODONA spoke the words of ZEUS.

Other oracles includes those of ARTEMIS at Colchis; ASCLEPIUS at EPIDAURUS; HERACLES at ATHENS; ARES in THRACE; ATHENE at MYCENAE; PAN in ARCADIA; and APHRODITE at Paphos, in CRETE.

ORCUS Ancient Roman god of the UNDER-world, identified with the Roman god PLUTO and the Greek god HADES. Orcus was the bringer of death, rather than a king of the dead. He is sometimes depicted as a reaper, cutting down the corn with his scythe.

ORESTES In Greek mythology, the only son of AGAMEMNON and CLYTEMNESTRA of MY-CENAE; brother of ELECTRA, IPHIGENIA and Chrysothemis. Orestes killed his mother, who had killed her husband, Agamemnon. According to some accounts, Orestes was driven mad and pursued by the ERINYES (the FURIES) for the unforgivable crime of matricide. He took refuge in ATHENS. He was tried and acquitted at the court of Areopagus, a tribunal of Athenian judges. He then took possession of his dead father's kingdom and married Hermione, the daughter of MENELAUS and HELEN. Orestes's great friend was Pylades. The friendship between the two young men became proverbial.

The myth of Orestes is crucial in that it shows the invalidation of the supremacy of the mother (of the household or of the kingdom) over that of the father (that is, the old religion of pre-Hellenic Greece, a Mother Earth religion, succumbed to the supremacy of the new religions, which were male-dominated). Matricide had always been regarded as a terrible crime. But in this myth the son, Orestes, gets away with it after a court trial, championed by ZEUS, APOLLO and ATHENE, the warlike goddess who had sprung from the forehead of Zeus. Orestes's absolution represents the final triumph of patriarchy over the old, pre-Hellenic religions and customs.

ORION In Greek mythology, best known as a mighty hunter and as a constellation of stars. Orion was the son of POSEIDON and Euryale. He was a Boeotian Giant, with the power to walk on the seas. Orion loved MEROPE, daughter of King Oenopion of Chios (an island off the coast of ASIA MINOR). In a fit of anger the king made Orion blind and left him to die on the seashore. But Orion found a boy, Cedalion, to guide him east toward the sun, and he regained his sight. Orion was loved by many, including the goddess of the hunt, ARTEMIS, and the dawn-goddess, EOS. There are many lost myths about Orion, seemingly impossible to connect into a coherent story. It isn't known exactly how and why he was transported into the heavens, although Artemis is sometimes said to have placed him there (see below).

One story has it that Apollo, brother of Artemis, was jealous of his sister's affection for Orion. He sent a giant scorpion to sting Orion to death. In another variation, Apollo had a fight with Orion and flung him into the sea. Orion swam away. Apollo asked Artemis to shoot the bobbing "thing" in the sea with her arrow. This Artemis did and thus unknowingly killed her lover. She set the constellation Orion in the heavens, with the scorpion (Scorpio) at its feet. His faithful hunting dog, Sirius, also can be seen in the constellation.

ORPHEUS In Greek legend, a famous poet and singer, son of Oeagrus, king of Thrace, and of CALLIOPE, the MUSE; husband of EURYDICE.

The god APOLLO (some say he was the father of Orpheus) gave Orpheus a lyre, which he played so beautifully that even the rocks were moved to tears, trees bent to listen, flowers bloomed and rivers changed their courses.

As the ARGONAUT, Orpheus was able to distract the crewmen from the sweet singing of the SIRENS (see *Jason and the Argonauts*, under JASON).

When Eurydice died from a serpent bite, Orpheus charmed his way into the UNDERWORLD and persuaded HADES to release her. Hades did so, on the condition that Orpheus would not look back until he had reached earth. Orpheus failed in his promise and Eurydice disappeared instantly, never to be seen again.

The tragic story of Orpheus and Eurydice has been retold many times, in many ways, in many countries. In modern times French playwright Jean Cocteau (1889–1963) wrote *Orphée (Orpheus in the Underworld)*, a memorable play and film.

OSSA A mountain peak in THESSALY, adjoining PELION. (See also ALOEIDS.)

P

PALAMEDES Son of Nauplius and Clymene. One of the Greek heroes who fought against TROY in the TROJAN WAR. Palamedes was reputed to be both intelligent and ingenious. When ODYSSEUS feigned idiocy, in his attempt to avoid joining the Greek army on its way to Troy, it was Palamedes who put TELEMACHUS, son of Odysseus, in the path of his father's plow. Odysseus of course avoided running down his infant son, showing that he was sane, and was forced to join the army. In revenge Odysseus concocted a mean plot against Palamedes, accusing him of treachery against the Greeks. Palamedes was stoned to death by the army.

Palamedes is described as a sage, and credited with inventing certain letters of the Greek alphabet, and of inventing dice, measures and scales, lighthouses, and the discus. In literature, a "Palamedes" is an ingenious person.

PALES In Roman religion the rustic, ancient spirits of the earth, male and female. Their festival was celebrated on April 21, the date on which Rome was supposed to have been founded in 753 B.C.

The Pales gave their name to the Palatine Hill, one of the seven hills on which ancient Rome was founded.

PALLADIUM In Greek legend, the sacred statue of PALLAS ATHENE that was said to have fallen from heaven and was kept in the temple of ATHENE in TROY. According to legend, the image was sent by ZEUS to DARDANUS, the founder of Troy. The preservation of the city was believed to depend on possession of the Palladium. Thus, during the TROJAN WAR, two Greeks, DIOMEDES (1) and ODYSSEUS, stole it, and Troy fell to the Greeks. In another legend AJAX The Lesser carried it off. The Romans said that AENEAS took the statue to Italy. In fact, many cities claimed to own the statue (ATHENS, ARGOS, Luceria).

The word *palladium* is now figuratively applied to anything on which safety depends; for instance, "The liberty of the press is the palladium of all the civil, political, and religious rights of an Englishman" (from *Letters of Junius: Dedication*, a series of anonymous letters published in London in the 18th century).

A rare metallic element is also called palladium, named after an asteroid, Pallas, discovered in 1803 at about the same time the element was found.

PALLAS ATHENE In Greek mythology, one of the many names taken by the goddess ATHENE. In some traditions, Pallas was the name of a youthful playmate of the goddess.

PAN An ancient deity from the mountainous region of ARCADIA, in Greece. Pan was a deity of herds and flocks, fertility, forests and wildlife. He is usually depicted as half-man, half-goat. The Romans called him FAUNUS.

Pan was a notable musician, playing the SYRINX (Pan-pipes, or Pipes of Pan), a seven-reed flute still played by Arcadian shepherds. In one myth Pan challenged the god APOLLO to a musical contest (see *Midas and the Donkey's Ears*, under MIDAS). Pan is said by some to be the son of the god HERMES and of the NYMPH Penelope.

Pan was worshiped as a fertility symbol and was generally thought of as lusty and playful, though at times a little sinister. He was thought to be the cause of a sudden, terrifying, unreasoning fear in men and beasts, a feeling given the name *panic*, from Pan.

Almost every region in Greece, and perhaps in all the ancient world, had its own Pan, a primitive, ancient deity. (See ARISTAEUS and PRIAPUS.)

PANDORA (All-Giving) The first woman to appear on earth, according to Greek mythology. She was created by the gods and sent down to man to release upon the world all the misfortunes that could occur. Pandora had been created, at the command of the great god ZEUS, by the smith-god HEPHAESTUS. The other gods and goddesses breathed into her surpassing beauty, charm, graciousness and cunning. They also gave her a vase to bring with her to earth and told her never to open it.

PROMETHEUS ("Forethought") was able to resist the beauty of Pandora; but his brother, EPIMETHEUS ("Afterthought") at once took the beautiful creature to be his bride. After the marriage Pandora opened up the sacred vase (sometimes called Pandora's Box) and released upon the world all the ailments that it contained. Only Hope remained inside the vase, and it was Hope that enabled humankind to go on living despite all adversity.

PANDORA WAS THE BEAUTIFUL WOMAN SENT BY ZEUS TO UNLEASH ALL THE TROUBLES OF MANKIND UPON THE WORLD. (NEW YORK PUBLIC LIBRARY PICTURE COLLECTION)

Some legends say that Zeus released Pandora upon the earth because he was angry with Prometheus, champion of mankind. Pandora was to be man's punishment for having learned the use of fire from Prometheus.

In modern English usage, "Pandora's box" has come to mean a gift that at first seems valuable but turns out to be a prolific source of troubles.

PARIS In Greek mythology, son of PRIAM, the king of TROY, and of HECUBA. Before he was born soothsayers prophesied that Paris would cause death and destruction. Accordingly, his parents placed him upon a mountainside (Mount IDA [2]) and left the infant to die. Paris was rescued by shepherds and brought up by them. He fell in love with OENONE, but was later to abandon the NYMPH in favor of HELEN. He became a fine athlete and a very handsome man. Paris competed at the games at Troy and won many prizes, gaining the attention of King Priam, who recognized him as his son. In spite of the soothsayers' warnings, Priam brought Paris back into the household. The prophecies came true, for Paris (and his abduction of Helen) was one of the leading causes of the TROJAN WAR. (See *The Judgment of Paris*, below.)

In some versions of the story, Paris kills the hero ACHILLES, and is himself killed by PHILOCTETES.

The Judgment of Paris Paris was the son of PRIAM, the king of TROY, and one of the leading causes of the TROJAN WAR and the fall of Troy. He abducted HELEN, said to be the most beautiful woman in the world, wife of King MENELAUS. This is how the abduction came about:

ERIS (Discord) was present at the wedding of PELEUS and THETIS, the parents of ACHILLES. She made the goddesses quarrel among themselves by throwing a golden apple ("the apple of discord") among the guests. The apple was inscribed, "To the fairest."

HERA, the chief goddess and wife of ZEUS, ARTEMIS, goddess of the hunt, and APHRODITE, goddess of love, each claimed the apple. Asked to make the choice among the three goddesses, Zeus wisely declined and sent his messenger, HERMES, to ask Paris, the most handsome of

PARIS GAVE AN APPLE TO APHRODITE, THE FAIREST GOD-
DESS OF ALL. (NEW YORK PUBLIC LIBRARY PICTURE COL-
LECTION)

men, to make the decision. Each of the goddesses offered Paris bribes. Aphrodite offered
him love of the most beautiful woman in the
world: Helen of SPARTA. Paris awarded the apple to Aphrodite. Hera and Artemis became
enemies of Paris and of Troy on that day.

PARNASSUS A mountain in south-central
Greece, a few miles north of the Gulf of COR-
INTH (which separates mainland Greece from
the PELOPONNESUS). At the foot of the mountain
is DELPHI, the shrine sacred to APOLLO, whose
seer, the PYTHON, was renowned throughout
the ancient world. Mount Parnassus was sacred
to Apollo, DIONYSUS and the nine MUSES. Bac-
chanalian rites took place in its caves and gorges,
where, it was said, the pipes of PAN could be

heard. In the myth of DEUCALION it was on the
slopes of Mount Parnassus that the Ark landed
after the Flood.

PASIPHAË In Greek mythology, daughter of
HELIOS (the Sun); wife of MINOS, king of CRETE;
mother with Minos of ARIADNE, ANDROGEUS
and PHAEDRA. From her strange union with a
bull (sometimes called the Cretan Bull), Pasiphaë brought forth the MINOTAUR, a monster
that was half-human, half-bull. (See *Minos and
the Minotaur*, under MINOS.)

PATROCLUS The close friend of the Greek
hero ACHILLES. When Achilles withdrew from
the TROJAN WAR, Patroclus assumed command
of the MYRMIDONS, the troops of Achilles. Patroclus was slain in battle by HECTOR. Determined to avenge the death of his friend, Achilles
went back into the war, killed Hector and
dragged his body around the tomb of Patroclus.

PEGASUS The famous winged horse of Greek
mythology. He was born from the blood of the
GORGON, MEDUSA, when the hero PERSEUS cut
off her head. Pegasus carried Perseus to the
rescue of ANDROMEDA. He carried BELLEROPHON
to the triumphant fight with the monster CHI-
MERA. When Bellerophon decided to ride his
magical steed up to the home of the gods,
OLYMPUS, the god ZEUS sent down a gadfly to
annoy Pegasus, who threw off his master. Bellerophon fell to earth. Pegasus went on to
Olympus, where he helped Zeus launch his
thunderbolts.

Pegasus is said to have brought forth the
fountain of Hippocrene on Mount HELICON with
a stroke of his hoof.

Winged animals were common in Near Eastern mythology. It is thought that the myth of
Pegasus came to Greece in very ancient times
through the Greeks living in ASIA MINOR.

PELEUS Son of King Aecus; brother of TELA-
mon; husband of THETIS; father, with Thetis,
of the hero ACHILLES.

Peleus and Telamon murdered their younger
half-brother, Phocus, the king's favorite. Peleus
fled from the kingdom of AEGINA to Phthia.
There, he accidentally killed the king's son in
the CALYDONIAN BOAR HUNT and had to flee

once again. He came to IOLCUS in THESSALY, but bad luck followed him. There, the wife of King Acatus, Astydaemia, fell in love with him. When Peleus spurned her love, she accused him before the king of molesting her. King Acatus took Peleus hunting on Mount PELION. He stole Peleus's sword while the young man slept and left him to die on the mountain, which was famous for its savage CENTAURS. However, CHIRON, their wise leader, took pity on Peleus. He found his sword for him and sent him back to Iolcus, where he killed the treacherous Astydaemia.

Eventually Peleus married Thetis. All the gods attended their wedding, for Thetis was a favorite of ZEUS. However, the couple neglected to invite ERIS, the goddess of strife, and this oversight was one of the causes of the TROJAN WAR, in which Achilles, son of Thetis and Peleus, was a leading figure and hero. (See also *The Judgment of Paris*, under PARIS.)

PELIAS In Greek mythology, son of Tyro and POSEIDON. Half-brother of AESON, from whom Pelias usurped the throne of IOLCUS (in THESSALY). When his nephew, JASON, son of Aeson, reached manhood and demanded his share of the kingdon, Pelias sent him on what was thought to be a hopeless quest—to find and bring back the GOLDEN FLEECE. (See *Jason and the Argonauts*, under JASON.) Jason returned, triumphant, bringing with him MEDEA, the sorceress-queen. Meanwhile, Pelias had put Aeson to death. To avenge his father, Jason urged Medea to use her magic powers. Medea persuaded the daughters of the aging Pelias to slay their father and cook him in a stew, promising that he would arise, rejuvenated. Of course Pelias didn't survive. He was succeeded by his son, Acastus.

PELION A mountain in the north of THESSALY, connected with Mount OSSA on the northwest. In Greek mythology, the giant brothers, Ephialtes and Otus, known as the ALOEIDS, "piled Pelion upon Ossa" in an attempt to reach the heavens (OLYMPUS). The phrase has come to mean adding difficulty upon difficulty. Mount Pelion was the home of CHIRON, the gentle CENTAUR.

PELOPONNESUS (or PELOPONNESE) The peninsula that lies south of the Greek mainland, connected to it by the Isthmus of CORINTH. It is named after PELOPS, in Greek mythology the son of TANTALUS and the founder of the Atreid dynasty. In the ancient world the chief divisions of the Peloponnesus were ELIS, Achaea, ARGOS and CORINTH in the north; and LACONIA and Messenia in the south. SPARTA, CORINTH, ARGOS and Megalopolis were the chief cities.

PELOPS In Greek mythology, son of DIONE and TANTALUS; brother of NIOBE. He married HIPPODAEMIA and became the father of ATREUS and THYESTES.

Pelops's first appearance in mythology was an unfortunate one: He was served up in a stew made by his wicked father Tantalus to test the gods. All the gods and goddesses realized what was happening, except for DEMETER (who was distracted with grief from losing her daughter, PERSEPHONE). She ate a shoulder of the infant, but it was later restored when the gods brought the child back to life. The gods had to remake the missing shoulder from ivory. The "ivory shoulder" of anyone denotes a distinctive trait.

Though Pelops became a rich and successful king (of Pisa in ELIS), he and his descendants were forever followed by the dreadful curse of the charioteer MYRTILUS (see *Pelops and the Charioteer*, below). Pelops's descendants were called the ATREIDS after his son, Atreus.

Pelops and the Charioteer When Pelops, son of the wicked TANTALUS, grew up, he set off to look for a kingdom of his own. On his way he met the sea-god, POSEIDON, who befriended the youth and presented him with a fine chariot and a marvelous team of horses. These gifts led Pelops to challenge OENOMAUS, king of Pisa in ELIS, in a chariot race.

King Oenomaus had a passion not only for fine horses, but for his daughter, HIPPODAEMIA. Whenever a suitor sought his daughter's hand, Oenomaus challenged him to a chariot race, which the suitor invariably lost. The penalty for losing the race was death. When Pelops arrived on the scene, 13 suitors of Hippodaemia had died. Their heads were hung around the gates of the palace of Oenomaus.

Pelops bribed the king's charioteer, MYRTI-LUS, asking him to loosen the wheels of Oenomaus's chariot (for the king always drove his own chariot in the competitions for his daughter's hand). This Myrtilus did, on the condition that Pelops would allow him to spend one night with Hippodaemia, whom he loved.

Pelops won the race; Oenomaus was killed; and then Pelops killed Myrtilus. With his dying breath the charioteer cursed Pelops and all his descendants. The curse took hold, for Myrtilus was the son of the god HERMES, and the gods knew how to make curses work. (See ATREUS AND THYESTES for the continuation of this story, and also AGAMEMNON and MENELAUS, the descendants of Atreus and grandchildren of Pelops.)

PENELOPE In Greek mythology, the daughter of Icarius and Periboea; the wife of the hero ODYSSEUS; mother of TELEMACHUS. During the long absence of Odysseus during the TROJAN WAR and his long voyage home to ITHACA (see ODYSSEY, THE), Penelope was considered a wealthy and desirable widow. She was besieged by suitors whom she was obliged to entertain at great cost. Penelope held them off by claiming that she had to finish weaving a shroud for her father-in-law, LAERTES, before she could choose a husband. She wove all day and secretly undid her work by night. Her secret was disclosed by one of her servants, but Odysseus arrived in time to kill the suitors and reclaim his bride. (See *Odysseus Returns to Ithaca*, under ODYSSEY, THE.) Penelope's name has come to personify wifely virtues such as patience and faithfulness.

PENTHESALIA In Greek mythology, Amazon queen who led her female warriors to TROY to help the Trojans (see TROJAN WAR). Penthesalia fought bravely against both AJAX and ACHILLES, the Greek heroes. She was finally slain by Achilles. It is said that she was so brave and beautiful that Achilles fell in love with her even as he killed her. King PRIAM of Troy gave her a magnificent funeral.

In some accounts Penthesalia inadvertently killed her sister, HIPPOLYTA, and was forever after pursued by the FURIES.

PERSEPHONE In Greek mythology, daughter of DEMETER and ZEUS; called PROSERPINA by the Romans. She was worshiped as Kore (Maiden) in ancient Greece. Persephone is considered by many scholars to be the same person as Demeter. Ancient Greek artists pictured them as being identical.

Persephone was stolen away by HADES, god of the UNDERWORLD. Her mother, Demeter, went mad with grief and caused drought and famine on earth while she searched in vain for her daughter. At last Zeus sent HERMES to bring Persephone back to her mother, but Persephone was obliged to spend one-third of the year underground. Persephone personified the corn seed that lies underground in winter and springs up in the warm months. (See *Demeter and Persephone*, under DEMETER.)

PERSEUS In Greek mythology, son of the god ZEUS and DANAE; husband of ANDROMEDA (see *Perseus and Andromeda*, below); father of Perses; slayer of the GORGON, MEDUSA (see *Perseus and Medusa*, below). After many exploits Perseus may have become king of ARGOS; but legends differ about what actually came about. Some say that Perseus, Andromeda and their son, Perses, went to Asia and founded the land of Persia; others say that Perseus accepted the throne of TIRYNS and founded the city of MYCENAE.

The Childhood of Perseus The mother of Perseus (see *Perseus and Medusa*, below) was DANAE, daughter of King Acrisius of ARGOS. It had been predicted by an ORACLE that Acrisius would be killed by a son of Danae. Acrisius locked Danae in a bronze tower or chamber. But this didn't deter the great god ZEUS from entering the tower and covering Danae with a shower of gold, after which she bore the son that she named Perseus. Acrisius put mother and son into a wooden chest and cast them upon the sea, hoping thus to avoid the fate that had been foreseen. (See *Perseus and Acrisius*, below.)

The wooden chest was spotted by the fisherman DICTYS; he rescued the pair and brought them to the court of King POLYDECTES on the island of SERIPHOS. (See *Perseus and Polydectes*, below.)

PERSEUS HOLDS UP THE HEAD OF THE GORGON ME-
DUSA. (NEW YORK PUBLIC LIBRARY PICTURE COLLECTION)

Some years later Polydectes fell in love with
Danae and wanted to marry her. Perseus, now
a robust young warrior, knew that his mother
did not want the attentions of the king. To get
the young man out of the way, Polydectes contrived to send him on a dangerous and impossible quest: He asked him to bring back the
head of the GORGON, MEDUSA. (See *Perseus and
Medusa*, below.)

Perseus and Medusa   Perseus and his mother
had been cast away from ARGOS by King Acrisius, the father of Danae. (See *The Childhood of
Perseus*, above.) They found shelter at the court
of King POLYDECTES on the island of SERIPHOS.
When Perseus became a young man, Polydectes
sent him on a quest: to bring back the head of
the GORGON, MEDUSA, the sight of whom turned
men to stone.

Fortunately, Perseus had allies among the
gods. The goddess ATHENE, who had turned
Medusa from a beautiful maiden into a hideous
monster with snakes for hair, still hated Medusa for defiling one of her temples. Athene
warned Perseus never to look directly at Medusa lest he be turned to stone, and gave him
a burnished shield to use as a mirror. HERMES
gave him a sickle, a leather bag in which to
carry the severed head and a pair of winged
sandals so that he could fly. He also told him
where to find the GRAEA and how to borrow
the cap of HADES, which would allow him to
become invisible.

The Graea (Gray Women) were the sisters of
the Gorgons. They had only one eye and one
tooth among the three of them, which they
used in turn. Perseus snatched away the eye
and gave it back only when the Graea told him
where to find Medusa.

Now well protected by the weapons of the
gods, Perseus slew Medusa and cut off her head,
which he carefully stowed in his leather bag.
From the blood of Medusa sprang the winged
horse, PEGASUS, Chrysaor, children of Medusa
and the sea-god, POSEIDON.

Perseus and Andromeda   Perseus was the
Greek hero who slew the GORGON, MEDUSA.
(See *Perseus and Medusa*, above.) With Medu-
sa's head in his leather bag, Perseus set off on
his winged sandals to bring the head to King
POLYDECTES of SERIPHOS.

As he flew along the coast he saw a beautiful
woman chained to a rock and weeping. She was
ANDROMEDA, daughter of King CEPHEUS of
ETHIOPIA (in northeast Africa) and of CASSIO-
PEIA. Perseus saved Andromeda from being devoured by a sea-monster by uncovering the
head of Medusa and turning the monster to
stone.

Perseus and Andromeda fell in love and decided to marry. At the wedding feast, Perseus
defeated another suitor of Andromeda, PHI-
NEUS, by using the Gorgon's head to turn Phineus and his soldiers into an army of stone.

Perseus and Polydectes   Perseus, one of the
great heroes of Greek mythology, was the son
of DANAE. When Danae and her infant son were
cast adrift in a wooden box on the Aegean Sea,
they were rescued by a fisherman, DICTYS, and

brought to the court of King POLYDECTES, on the small island of SERIPHOS. (See *The Childhood of Perseus*, above.)

Polydectes and Dictys (who may have been the brother of the king) took good care of the mother and child. As the years went by, Polydectes became enamored of Danae. Perseus, now a strong young man, knew that his mother didn't welcome the advances of the king. Polydectes contrived to send the youth on what he thought was an impossible quest: to bring him back the head of the GORGON, MEDUSA, whose sight turned men to stone. (See *Perseus and Medusa*, above.)

While Pereseus was away, Danae was protected from the amorous king by Dictys; they took refuge in a temple. Polydectes amassed an army and went after them. Perseus came to the rescue and turned the king and his soldiers into stone, again with the head of the Medusa.

Dictys became the new king of Seriphos. Perseus, Danae and ANDROMEDA returned to ARGOS, the birthplace of Perseus.

Perseus and Acrisius

Perseus was the great Greek hero most famous for killing the GORGON, MEDUSA.

Before Perseus was born, Acrisius, his father, had been warned by an ORACLE that he would be killed by a son of Danae. Acrisius emprisoned Danae in a tower or chamber of bronze and thought her safe from all men. But nothing could deter the amorous god ZEUS. He appeared to Danae as a shower of gold and impregnated her. She bore a son, which she named Perseus.

Fearful for his life, Acrisius placed Danae and Perseus in a wooden chest and cast them adrift on the Aegean Sea. Danae and Perseus were rescued by DICTYS and brought to the kingdom of POLYDECTES, on the island of SERIPHOS. (See *The Childhood of Perseus*, above.)

After Perseus had killed Medusa (see *Perseus and Medusa*, above) and turned Polydectes to stone (see *Perseus and Polydectes*, above), he and his wife ANDROMEDA and Danae returned to Argos.

The now aging Acrisius fled the arrival of Perseus, the young hero, remembering the ancient prophecy. But he could not escape his fate. He went to Larissa, where games were being held. Perseus also attended the games.

He threw a discus that went awry and hit Acrisius, who died from the blow. Thus the prophecy that Acrisius would be killed by a son of Danae was fulfilled.

PHAEDRA In Greek mythology, daughter of MINOS of CRETE and of PASIPHAË; sister of ARIADNE and ANDROGEUS; wife of THESEUS, king of ATHENS. Love-goddess APHRODITE caused Phaedra to fall in love with her chaste young stepson, HIPPOLYTUS. The youth fled from her in horror and Phaedra killed herself, leaving a letter to her husband accusing Hippolytus of trying to violate her. Theseus then caused the death of his son. (See a summary of the tragedy, *Hippolytus*, under HIPPOLYTUS.) This episode, where Theseus lost both his wife and his son, seemed to mark the end of his heroic life.

The play *Phèdre* (Phaedra), by Jean Racine (1639–1699), is considered a masterpiece of French classical theater.

PHAETON In Greek mythology, son of HELIOS, the sun-god, and the NYMPH Clymene. The companions of Phaeton wouldn't believe that he was the son of Helios. Phaeton went to his father and demanded that he should be allowed to drive the sun's chariot across the skies. With great misgivings, Helios agreed. The high-spirited horses couldn't be controlled by young Phaeton, and plunged the chariot to earth (causing the devastation of the land now called LIBYA, in North Africa). The destruction was stopped by the god ZEUS, who hurled a thunderbolt at Phaeton. Phaeton was instantly turned into a swan and lived out his life on the legendary river Eridanus, surrounded by his sisters, the Heliades, who had been transformed into weeping willow trees forever mourning the death of their brother.

The most complete version of this story is told by OVID in *Metamorphoses*.

PHILOCTETES In Greek mythology, the most famous archer in the TROJAN WAR. The hero HERACLES had bequeathed his poisoned arrows to the archer. On the voyage to TROY, Philoctetes was bitten by a venomous snake (or, some say, wounded by one of the poisoned arrows) and left on the island of Lemnos to die. But it had been prophesied by an ORACLE that Troy could not be taken without Philoctetes. In the 10th year of the siege of Troy, ODYSSEUS commanded that Philoctetes should be sent for. Philoctetes was brought to Troy, where his arrows slew PARIS, and Troy thereafter fell to the Greeks.

PHINEUS In Greek mythology, brother of CEpheus, the king of ETHIOPIA in North Africa; uncle of ANDROMEDA, whom he wished to marry. But the hero PERSEUS rescued Andromeda (see *Perseus and Andromeda*, under PERSEUS), and claimed her as his bride. Phineus and his soldiers appeared at the wedding feast but were transformed into stone by the sight of the head of the GORGON, MEDUSA, wielded by Perseus.

PHOEBE In Greek mythology, a TITAN, one of the daughters of URANUS and GAIA. She was the wife of Coeus and the mother of LETO and Asteria. Her name, which means "bright" or "shining," was sometimes given to the moon and was associated with ARTEMIS and DIANA.

PHOENICIA (Purple) An ancient kingdom on the eastern Mediterranean, in the region of modern Syria, Lebanon and Israel. It was a major trade center of the ancient world. In HOMER and in the Old Testament its people were known as Canaanites. In the 9th century B.C. the Greeks gave the name Phoenician to those Canaanites who lived on the seacoast and traded with the Greeks. It is said that the name came from PHOENIX, brother of CADMUS and EUROPA.

The Phoenicians were famous as traders, navigators and artisans; they obtained a purple dye ("Tyre purple") from shellfish. However, their greatest contribution to Western civilization is thought to be the invention of the alphabet, an idea later taken over by the Greeks. The use of symbols for sounds in place of more cumbersome cuneiform and hieroglyphic images was a tremendous advance to learning.

Tyre was the best known seaport of Phoenicia, lying between Sidon (to the north) and Acre (to the south), approximately on the site of modern Sur.

PHOENIX In Greek mythology, son of AGEnor, brother of CADMUS, CILIX and EUROPA. When Europa was stolen away by the god ZEUS, King Agenor sent his three sons to search for her. (See *Europa and the Bull*, under EUROPA.) The brothers could not find her, and not daring to return to the king, they settled down elsewhere. Some accounts say that Phoenix traveled westward, beyond LIBYA, to what is now CARTHAGE, in North Africa. After Agenor's death he returned to Canaan, since renamed PHOENICIA in his honor.

PHRIXUS In Greek mythology, son of ATHAmas and NEPHELE; brother of HELLE. His stepmother, INO, demanded that Phrixus be sacrificed to the corn-goddess to ensure good crops. Phrixus and his sister, Helle, escaped on the back of a winged ram who had a fleece of gold. When Phrixus reached Colchis, he sacrificed the ram to the god ZEUS and gave the fleece to AETES, king of Colchis. The flight of Phrixus and Helle on the winged ram was important in the myth of the GOLDEN FLEECE (see *Jason and the Argonauts*, under JASON).

PHRYGIA An ancient region of central ASIA MINOR (now central Turkey). The goddess CYBELE was worshiped here (as well as, later, in Greece and Rome). With GORDIUS, legendary king of Phrygia, Cybele bore a son, MIDAS, who became king of Phrygia after Gordius.

PINDAR The great lyric poet of ancient Greece (518–438 B.C.). He was born near THEBES into a distinguished family. When he was 20 years old another noble family commissioned him to write a poem in honor of one of their sons, who won the footrace at the PYTHIAN GAMES (held at DELPHI). Pindar's fame dates from then. He was asked to write more poems to celebrate similar events. In all of them he alluded to the mythology of Greece and is therefore a most valuable source of knowledge, as well as a fine poet.

PIRITHOÜS In Greek mythology, son of ZEUS and Dia (the wife of IXION; king of the LAPITHS, a mythical people inhabiting the mountains of THESSALY; friend of the hero THESEUS. Pirithoüs married Hippodaemia. At the wedding feast, to which the CENTAURS had been invited, a great fight broke out between the Lapiths and the

Centaurs, wild creatures that were half-man and half-horse. The Lapiths (and Theseus, who was among the guests) defeated the Centaurs and drove them from their home on Mount PELION.

Theseus accompanied his friend to the UNDERWORLD, where the two attempted to steal away PERSEPHONE, the reluctant bride of HADES, god of the Underworld. Hades trapped both Theseus and Pirithoüs in deep chairs from which they couldn't arise. Theseus was rescued by the hero HERACLES, but Pirithoüs was trapped in his chair for all eternity.

PLEIADES (Sailing Ones) In Greek mythology, seven daughters of ATLAS and Pleione; sisters of the Hyades. Their names were Alcyone, Asterope, Celaene, ELECTRA, MAIA, MEROPE and Taygete. They were placed among the stars to save them from being pursued by ORION. They are sometimes called "The Seven Sisters."

Astronomically, the Pleiades is a cluster of stars easily seen in the Taurus constellation. One of the stars is invisible to the naked eye. Some say that the "Lost Pleiad" is Merope, who married a mortal and hides herself in shame. Others say that the lost star is Electra, who fades away from grief at the fall of TROY.

The ancients believed that when they could see the cluster of stars ("the Sailing Ones") the weather was auspicious for sailing.

PLUTO Roman name for the UNDERWORLD god HADES. He was also known as DIS. He was the son of SATURN and the brother of JUPITER and NEPTUNE. He was married to PROSERPINA, whom he kidnapped and dragged down into the Underworld.

PLUTUS In Greek mythology, son of DEMETER and Iasion (or Iason); god of wealth and of the earth's abundant harvests. (He is not to be confused with PLUTO, god of the UNDERWORLD.) Plutus was believed to be blind because he distributed wealth to good and bad alike. Plutus appears in HESIOD's *Theogony*, Aristophanes' *Plutus* and the *Divine Comedy* of Italian poet Dante (1265–1321).

In modern English, a plutocrat is an immensely rich person, usually the ruler of a country where the wealthy have power over the less wealthy.

POLLUX The Roman name for Polydeuces, brother of Castor. (See DIOSCURI and CASTOR AND POLLUX.)

POLYDECTES In Greek mythology, king of the island of SERIPHOS, protector of DANAE and her son, PERSEUS. Polydectes sent Perseus on a dangerous mission, asking him to bring back the head of the GORGON, MEDUSA, which turned men to stone. While Perseus was away, Polydectes pursued Danae, trying to win her love. Danae was protected by DICTYS, who was possibly the brother of Polydectes. Perseus returned with the head of Medusa and turned Polydectes into stone. Dictys then became king of Seriphos. (See *Perseus and Polydectes*, under PERSEUS.)

POLYPHEMUS In Greek mythology, the savage, one-eyed giant of HOMER's ODYSSEY. Polyphemus entraps the hero, ODYSSEUS, and his companions, and devours six of them. Odysseus blinds Polyphemus's one eye and with great cunning escapes. (See *Odysseus and the Cyclops*, under ODYSSEY, THE.) Homer's Polyphemus is identified with the CYCLOPES, master smiths and craftsmen, who were supposed to have one eye in the middle of their foreheads and live on the island of Sicily. Polyphemus appears also in VIRGIL's AENEID as a threat to the hero AENEAS and his crew.

POMONA The Roman goddess of fruit and fruitbearing trees. The poet OVID told the story of how she was loved by VERTUMNUS. Vertumnus disguised himself first as harvester, then as an old woman, and finally won her love.

POSEIDON In Greek mythology, sea-god and one of the OLYMPIAN GODS; son of CRONUS and RHEA; brother of ZEUS, HADES, DEMETER, HERA and HESTIA; husband of AMPHITRITE. The Romans identified Poseidon with NEPTUNE, an Italian water-god. Although Poseidon is best known as a sea-god, in ancient times among migrating people he had been a god of fertility and of herdsmen; thus he even pre-dates Zeus.

His emblem, the three-pronged trident, was a symbol for the thunderbolt, which would make Poseidon a sky-god of very ancient times. It was said that Poseidon could cause earthquakes; even in later times it was felt that he, as a god of earthquakes, needed to be propitiated.

Like all his siblings except Zeus, Poseidon was swallowed by his father, Cronus, and then, thanks to Zeus, later disgorged. (See *Zeus Rescues His Siblings*, under ZEUS.) In other legends, to save Poseidon, Rhea hides him in a flock of lambs near Mantinea, in ARCADIA, in the care of a nurse called Arne. In yet another story, Rhea puts Poseidon in the care of Capheira, a daughter of OCEANUS, who brought up the child in RHODES.

Poseidon and Amphitrite Amphitrite, a nereid (sea-nymph), was wooed and won for Poseidon, god of the sea, by Delphinus. In gratitude, Poseidon set the image of Delphinus among the stars as the Dolphin.

Amphitrite bore Poseidon three children: TRITON, Rhode and Benthescyme. They lived in an underwater cave in Eubol, off Aegae. In its spacious stables Poseidon kept white chariot horses with golden manes. When large, white-capped waves are seen in the ocean, they may be called "white horses" in memory of Poseidon's horses.

Poseidon and Athene Poseidon, god of the sea, was greedy for earthly kingdoms. He tried to claim the city of ATHENS from the goddess ATHENE, saying that he could do more good for the city than she could. The two appeared before a court of gods and goddesses. Poseidon struck his trident into a rock, and water immediately gushed forth; but it was seawater, salty, and therefore not very useful. Athene planted the first olive tree, which gave fruit, oil and wood. The court decreed that Athene's gift was the more beneficial and that she thus had more right to the land. The olive branch became a symbol of peace. (See also *Athene and Poseidon*, under ATHENE.)

Poseidon and Horses Poseidon, god of the sea, is said by some to have created the horse with a blow of his trident and also to have invented the bridle, which controls a horse. It seems certain that horse-racing was instituted by him and that the horse was sacred to him. One myth has it that Poseidon changed himself into a horse in order to capture the love of the goddess DEMETER, who had at one time transformed herself into a mare.

PRIAM In Greek mythology, king of TROY during the TROJAN WAR, though too old to take an active part in the war. He was the son of LAOMEDON and, some say, the father of 50 children, some of them with his second wife, HECUBA. Among them were the Trojan heroes, HECTOR and PARIS.

The death of Hector and the lack of respect paid to his body were severe blows to King Priam. Alone, he went to the Achaean (Greek) camp to bargain with the hero ACHILLES for his son's body. There, Priam was killed by NEOPTOLEMUS, one of Achilles' sons.

PRIAPUS An ancient god of fertility, protector of herds, bees, fish and the vine, he was a latecomer to Greek mythology. In most accounts Priapus was the son of DIONYSUS and APHRODITE; in others his mother was CHIONE and his father Dionysus, ADONIS, HERMES or PAN. Though his parentage may be in doubt, it is certain that Priapus was associated with the ancient Greek worship of Dionysus, the wine-god. Many scholars think that Priapus was another name for Pan, an ancient pastoral deity.

PROMETHEUS (Forethought) In Greek mythology, one of the TITANS, descended from the Earth Mother (GAIA) and the Sky Father (URANUS); son of Iapetus and one of the daughters of OCEANUS, possibly Clymene; brother of ATLAS and of EPIMETHEUS; father of DEUCALION.

Prometheus was a remarkable figure in Greek mythology. Some stories say that he was the creator of man; he was certainly the main champion of humankind, bringing the gift of fire and teaching people how to use it. He also taught humans astronomy, medicine, navigation, metalworking, architecture and writing (see *Prometheus, Fire-bringer and Champion of Man*, below).

ZEUS was angry with Prometheus for stealing fire and bringing it to men. He had Prometheus chained to a rock on Mount Caucasus, where an eagle or a vulture plucked at his liver all day; but Prometheus healed every night, so that his suffering seemed destined to go on for all eternity (see *Prometheus Bound and Unbound*, below). He was eventually rescued by HERACLES and given immortality by CHIRON, the CENTAUR.

To revenge himself on mankind Zeus sent PANDORA into the world and with her all the troubles and sicknesses of humankind (see *Prometheus and Pandora*, below).

References to Prometheus are found in most of the classical poets, such as HESIOD and AESCHYLUS *(Prometheus Bound)*. In the 18th century, German poet and scholar Goethe saw Prometheus as a symbol of man's creative striving and his rebellion against the restraints of society (Prometheus being a symbol of man chained to a rock but eventually escaping). The 19th-century English poet Percy Bysshe Shelley, in *Prometheus Unbound*, glorified the Titan who dared to revolt against the gods and triumph over tyranny.

Some scholars say that in earlier mythologies Prometheus remained chained to his rock through all eternity; but to the fair-minded ancient Greek poets who recorded the myths, it was unthinkable that the champion of humankind should be so punished; hence the story of Heracles, the hero who broke the bonds of Prometheus (see *Prometheus Bound and Unbound*, below), and of Chiron, the gentle Centaur who conferred his immortality on Prometheus to end his own suffering.

The story of the enmity between Zeus and Prometheus may represent the antagonism between an ancient god (Prometheus) and the invading OLYMPIAN GODS, personified by Zeus, who tried to overthrow the older religions.

Prometheus, Fire-bringer and Champion of Man

Prometheus, a TITAN, was a remarkable figure in Greek mythology. It is said that on one occasion Prometheus made two bundles out of the remains of an ox that had been sacrificed: One bundle contained the meat, the other, the bones. He wrapped the bones in succulent-looking fat; the meat he placed inside the stomach sac of the ox.

Asked to choose which package he preferred, the god ZEUS chose the package that looked succulent but contained nothing but bones. In his anger at being tricked (although some say that the great god surely knew he was being tricked) Zeus decided to forbid the knowledge of fire-making to mankind.

Prometheus, undaunted, stole fire from heaven, or from the forge of the smith-god, HEPHAESTUS, and brought it down to earth hidden in the hollow stalk of the fennel plant. He then began to teach people all the uses of fire—how to make tools and fashion metal, how to build, how to cook; and also how to sow and reap, and how to use herbs for healing.

Prometheus, Bound and Unbound

Prometheus, the champion of humankind (see *Prometheus, Fire-bringer and Champion of Man*, above), had thwarted the great god ZEUS in his attempt to conceal knowledge of fire from humans. He had to be punished. Zeus had Prometheus chained to a rock on Mount Caucasus, where he was tormented by an eagle or a vulture that plucked at his liver all through the day. Since Prometheus was healed every night, this torture would go on through all eternity.

Eventually Prometheus was released from this dilemma by the hero HERACLES, who slew the bird and unbound Prometheus. The gentle CENTAUR, CHIRON, then conferred his own immortality upon Prometheus, so that he would die but Prometheus would live.

As well as being punished for bringing fire to men, Zeus was holding Prometheus captive because he knew a secret to which Zeus wanted an answer: The sea-nymph THETIS was soon to bear a child that would be greater than its father. The father could be either Zeus or POSEIDON; the child could cause chaos among the OLYMPIAN GODS. Prometheus would not reveal his secret as long as he was held captive.

Prometheus and Pandora

Prometheus, the champion of humankind (see *Prometheus, Fire-bringer and Champion of Man*, above), was a cause of great anger to the great god ZEUS. Prometheus had tricked Zeus in the matter of sacrifices made by man and he had eventually escaped from the terrible torture inflicted by Zeus as punishment. Zeus decided that mankind must be punished for having received the forbidden gift of fire, one of the many bounties bestowed by Prometheus against the wishes of Zeus.

Zeus ordered HEPHAESTUS, the smith-god, to make a woman out of clay. The gods breathed life into her and made her irresistibly beautiful. She was named PANDORA (All-Giving) and sent to earth, bearing a sealed vase, of which she was forbidden to know the contents. In spite of warnings from Prometheus, EPIMETHEUS, his brother, immediately took Pandora to be his wife. Then Pandora opened the vase (sometimes called Pandora's Box), and every disaster that humans were ever to know was released upon the world. Only Hope remained in the vase, giving humankind the will to go on living.

PROSERPINA The Roman equivalent of PERsephone, queen of the UNDERWORLD; wife of PLUTO; sometimes identified with Hecate.

PROTESILAUS In Greek mythology, a Thessalian hero, son of Iphicles; husband of Laodamia. He was the first of the Greeks to spring ashore at TROY (see TROJAN WAR), and the first to die. Laodamia begged the gods to allow Protesilaus to return to earth so that they might spend three more hours together. The gods granted her wish and the lovers were reunited. Then Laodamia committed suicide and went to the UNDERWORLD with her husband.

PROTEUS In Greek mythology, a minor, but very ancient sea-god who served POSEIDON. Proteus had enormous knowledge and the ability to change his shape at will if he didn't want to stay around to answer questions. When finally cornered, he advised MENELAUS, who was becalmed off the coast of Egypt, that to escape he should pay proper honor to the god ZEUS. Menelaus listened to the advice of the sea-god and was eventually able to sail home to SPARTA. In another story, Aristaeus, the son of APOLLO, sought the advice of Proteus, who advised him to sacrifice cattle to the gods. This Aristaeus did, and was rewarded by seeing swarms of bees emerging from the corpses of the slain cattle.

(Aristaeus was an expert in the art of beekeeping.)

PSYCHE (Soul) In Greek mythology, a mortal woman so beautiful that the goddess APHRODITE was jealous of her and ordered EROS to punish her. (The tale of Eros and Psyche is told under EROS, who is known as CUPID by the Romans.)

PYGMALION In Greek mythology, son of Belus, a sculptor from Cyprus who despised women but adored the goddess APHRODITE. He made an ivory statue of her of such extraordinary beauty that he fell in love with it. As he embraced the statue, Aphrodite answered his prayers and made the statue come to life, giving it the name Galatea. This story, from OVID's *Metamorphoses*, enhances the legendary power of Aphrodite over all creation. It has been told many times, most recently in the play *Pygmalion*, by George Bernard Shaw (1856–1950), which has been made into motion pictures and the musical *My Fair Lady*.

PYRRHA In Greek mythology, daughter of EPImetheus; wife of DEUCALION. Together Pyrrha and Deucalion repeopled the earth after the great rain sent by ZEUS (see under DEUCALION).

PYTHIAN GAMES A sacred rite enacted in ancient Greece to honor the ancient serpent-monster, PYTHON, slain by the god APOLLO. It was one of the great Hellenic festivals celebrated in DELPHI, second only to the OLYMPIC GAMES in importance.

PYTHON In Greek mythology, a female serpent born of the Earth. The goddess HERA sent Python to torment her rival LETO, one of the many loves of ZEUS, and the mother of APOLLO. Python was slain by the young Apollo, who bid the serpent rot where it had fallen. The spot where this encounter took place was called Pytho, from the Greek word *pytho*, to rot. The name was later changed to DELPHI. The site became the most venerated shrine in ancient Greece, sacred to Apollo. The PYTHIAN GAMES were held every four years in honor of the ancient Python and were next in importance to the famous OLYMPIC GAMES.

Q

QUIRINUS According to some Roman mythologies, Quirinus was the Sabine name for
the god MARS. Others say that Quirinus was
the name taken by Romulus (of ROMULUS AND
REMUS), the son of Mars and the co-founder of
the city of Rome, after he was taken up to the
heavens and became deified. Not much is known
about Quirinus. His name was given to one of
the seven hills of ancient Rome.

R

RHADAMANTHUS (or RHADAMANTHYS) In Greek mythology, son of EUROPA and the god ZEUS; brother of MINOS and SARPEDON. According to HOMER (in the ODYSSEY), Rhadamanthus was the ruler of the Elysian Fields (where fortunate shades, or spirits, of mortals went). Later legends say that he was one of the judges of the UNDERWORLD.

RHEA (Earth ?) In Greek mythology, a TITAN, the mother of the great ruling gods of OLYMPUS. She was the daughter of GAIA and URANUS (Heaven); she was the sister-wife of CRONUS; the mother of DEMETER, HADES, HERA, HESTIA, POSEIDON and ZEUS.

The story of Rhea is a near-repetition of that of her mother Gaia: the father, Uranus, jealous of Gaia's children, had them confined under the earth; but with his mother's help the bravest son, Cronus, overcame his father and banished him. (See *Cronus Overthrows Uranus,* under CRONUS.) When Cronus became the husband of his sister Rhea, they had many children, of whom Cronus was so jealous that he swallowed them. Rhea managed to save Zeus, who rescued his siblings and went to war with Cronus. (See *The Childhood of Zeus, Zeus Rescues His Siblings,* and *The War with the Titans* under ZEUS.)

Rhea was identified with the Great Mother and goddess of fertility. Her cult was strongest in CRETE, which some say was the birthplace of Zeus. She was identified with CYBELE and also known as AGDISTIS; in Roman mythology she was identified with OPS, goddess of the harvest. Rhea, though a shadowy figure herself, was widely worshiped under various names as an earth-goddess.

RHODES The easternmost island of the Aegean. In Greek mythology, it was the favored abode of the sun-god HELIOS, whose wife was the NYMPH Rhodos. Their children were the first inhabitants of Rhodes.

ROMULUS AND REMUS In Roman mythology, the twin sons of the god MARS and Rhea Silvia. They were the legendary founders of Rome, the greatest city of the ancient world. Their mother, Rhea Silvia, was a VESTAL VIRGIN. She was condemned to death for losing her virginity. Her two infants were thrown into the river Tiber. Romulus and Remus were rescued by a shepherd, Faustulas, and suckled by a she-wolf. When they grew up they founded the city of Rome on the Palatine Hill. They quarreled over the plans for the city, and Romulus slew Remus. He became king of Rome and ruled for 40 years. He provided wives for the new settlers of Rome by capturing SABINE women. Romulus was at last taken up to the heavens in a mysterious whirlwind, said to be sent by his father, Mars. Some say that Romulus was then worshiped by the Romans under the name QUIRINUS.

The best-known artistic representation of Romulus and Remus is the bronze sculpture of a she-wolf nursing the two infants (now in the Capitoline Museum, Rome).

RUTULI (or RUTULIANS) A people of ancient Italy inhabiting Ardea and the land surrounding LATIUM. Their king was Turnus, who was killed in battle with the Trojans.

S

SABINES or SABINI One of the oldest peoples of central Italy. In a famous Roman legend, the women of the Sabines were captured by the new Roman settlers, subjects of ROMULUS, for they needed wives. War immediately broke out between the Sabine men and the Romans. The Sabine women helped to make peace by placing themselves and their infants between the warring tribes. The Sabines and the Romans became united as one people.

The seizure, or rape, of the Sabine women is frequently depicted in art. One of the most famous is the painting by the Flemish artist Peter Paul Rubens (1577–1640) in the National Gallery, London.

SAGITTARIUS (The Archer) A constellation between Scorpius and CAPRICORN; the ninth sign of the zodiac. In the zodiac, the archer is represented as the benign CENTAUR, CHIRON, of Greek mythology, who was wise in the ways of hunting and archery, as well as in the arts of medicine and healing.

SARPEDON In Greek mythology, a son of ZEUS and Laodemia or EUROPA. In the TROJAN WAR Sarpedon was a hero, the ally of King PRIAM. His particular friend was GLAUCUS (1), who mourned his death (in HOMER'S ILIAD) at the hands of PATROCLUS. The god Zeus had APOLLO carry the body of Sarpedon from the battlefield to be buried in LYDIA, his homeland.

In earlier legend, Sarpedon was the son of Zeus and Europa, and the brother of MINOS and RHADAMANTHUS. He became king of Lydia. Zeus granted him the privilege of living for three generations.

SATURN (Seed-Sower) God of agriculture, sowing and seed corn in Roman mythology. His symbol was the scythe. Saturn was a Roman adaptation of the Greek CRONUS. He was the father of JUPITER, NEPTUNE, PLUTO and JUNO.

SATURN'S SYMBOL WAS THE SCYTHE. (NEW YORK PUBLIC LIBRARY PICTURE COLLECTION)

His wife was RHEA, though earlier myths say that she was Lua or OPS.

In legends, Saturn was a king of Italy whose reign was celebrated as a golden age.

His feast, called the Saturnalia, was held in mid-December, the time of the winter sowing. It was a time of riotous feasting and debauchery, merrymaking and the exchange of gifts; it became incorporated eventually into Christian Christmas festivities after the pagan era ended.

SATYRS In Greek mythology, one of a class of woodland and mountain spirits attendant on DIONYSUS. They are usually represented as part-human and part-goat or -monkey. They were noted for riotousness and mischief, terrifying herdsmen and shepherds and chasing after NYMPHS. One legend relates that the satyrs were originally men, sons of HERMES and Iphthima; the goddess HERA turned them into half-human beasts to punish them for neglecting to keep watch over Dionysus. They were ever after faithful to the god and accompanied him to all his festivals. Medieval Christian art used the satyrs as images of the devil.

SCYLLA In Greek mythology, daughter of Nisus. She was cruelly treated by MINOS. (See *Minos and Scylla*, under MINOS.) This Scylla has no connection with the monster named Scylla (see SCYLLA AND CHARYBDIS).

SCYLLA AND CHARYBDIS In Greek mythology, two mythical characters who inhabited the Straits of Messina (between the south of mainland Italy and the island of Sicily). On the Italian side lived the monster Scylla, who had six long necks and jaws armed with three rows of teeth and who emitted ferocious and terrifying barks. On the Sicilian side lived Charybdis, who dwelled under a great fig tree. Thrice daily Charybdis swallowed up the sea and then spat it out again in a boiling whirlpool.

Although the witch CIRCE had warned the hero ODYSSEUS of the dangers of Scylla and Charybdis, Scylla managed to devour six of Odysseus's crewmen. (These monsters appear also in VIRGIL's AENEID.) The legend represents the dangers of navigation faced by early mariners in those waters, where there are treacherous currents akin to whirlpools.

The expression "to fall between Scylla and Charybdis," similar to the more modern "to jump from the frying pan into the fire," means to be caught in a dilemma—that is, to have to choose between two unsatisfactory alternatives.

SELENE (Moon) In Greek mythology, an ancient moon-goddess. Daughter of the TITANS Theia and HYPERION; sister of HELIOS (the Sun) and EOS (the Dawn). Selene is also called PHOEBE; she is Luna in Roman mythology; and some-times identified with ARTEMIS (DIANA in Roman mythology).

Selene was a beautiful woman, usually depicted with long wings and a golden crown that shed a gentle light in the darkness of night. She was carried across the skies in a chariot drawn by white horses. She was the mother of three daughters by ZEUS: Pandia, Erse (the Dew) and Nemea. It is said that the Nemean Lion was born to Selene and Zeus, and that it fell from the moon to the earth (see under HERACLES). Selene was also loved by PAN. The best-known legend of Selene was that of her love for the youth ENDYMION.

SEMELE (Moon) In Greek mythology, daughter of CADMUS and HARMONIA, lover of ZEUS, mother of DIONYSUS (see *The Birth of Dionysus*, under DIONYSUS). After her death in the flames created by Zeus, Semele was conducted from the UNDERWORLD to OLYMPUS, home of the gods, where she became immortal under the name Thyone. Semele was worshiped in Athens during the Leneitai (Festival of Wild Women), when every year a bull representing Dionysus was sacrificed to her.

Some say that Semele is a form of SELENE, an ancient moon goddess.

SERIPHOS (or SERIFOS) An island in the Western Cyclades group, in the Aegean Sea. In Greek mythology, this was the island where the infant PERSEUS and his mother, DANAE, came to rest, after escaping from Acrisius.

SEVEN AGAINST THEBES, THE In Greek mythology, the name given to the conflict between the rulers of the kingdom of THEBES and the rebels who wanted to usurp the throne. It was the subject of a tragedy by AESCHYLUS.

At the death of their father, OEDIPUS, his two sons, Eteocles and Polynices (who were probably twins), had made a pact to rule the kingdom of Thebes jointly, each one taking over the kingdom for a year at a time. But Eteocles refused to give up his kingship at the end of his year. Polynices appealed to King ADRASTUS of ARGOS and the war began. The "seven" were the champions brought together by Adrastus to help Polynices gain the throne. The city of

Thebes had seven gates. Eteocles set a champion to guard each one. Adrastus delegated a champion to capture each gate. It was fated that, at the end of the battle, the two brothers, Eteocles and Polynices, should meet in one-to-one combat and kill each other.

Creon, the new king of Thebes, ordered that Eteocles be left to lie on the battlefield rather than be buried. He was opposed by ANTIGONE, the sister of Eteocles and Polynices, who herself performed the forbidden burial service.

The war was continued years later by the EPIGONI, sons of the Seven.

SIBYL In Greek and Roman mythology, a name given to women who were able to foretell the future; a prophetess or seeress. The most famous was the Sibyl of Cumae, in Italy.

SILENI See SILENUS.

SILENUS In Greek mythology, son of HERMES or of PAN; an immensely wise old man, he knew both past and future and was the tutor of DIONYSUS. He is often depicted as a hairy, plump old man with the ears and legs of a horse, seated astride a wine cask or a donkey.

In its plural form, the Sileni denoted a category of rural divinities, personifying the genii

SILENUS WAS A WISE OLD MAN, TUTOR OF DIONYSUS. (NEW YORK PUBLIC LIBRARY PICTURE COLLECTION)

of springs and rivers. As such they were associated with the SATYRS who followed Dionysus in his revels.

SILVANUS Ancient Roman god of uncultivated lands and especially of forests. He was sometimes identified with PAN, FAUNUS and the SATYRS. The word *silvan* or *sylvan* has come to mean forested, or of the woods.

SIRENS In Greek mythology, the NYMPHS whose sweet song lured sailors to destruction by making them go mad and therefore become shipwrecked on the coast where the Sirens lived. In HOMER'S ODYSSEY, the hero, ODYSSEUS, is warned about the Sirens by CIRCE. He plugs the ears of his crewmen with wax, then has himself tied to the mast of the ship, while the crew row out of danger. In the myth of the ARGONAUTS (see *Jason and the Argonauts*, under JASON), the sailors were able to sail safely by the nymphs because the poet ORPHEUS was on board and sang more sweetly than the Sirens.

Homer never said that the Sirens were birds with the faces of beautiful women, as they are often depicted. However, the idea of the women as winged creatures became firmly rooted. It is thought that they form part of the universal association of winged creatures with death. The soul itself was believed to leave the body in the form of a bird.

In modern times the word *siren* is applied to any woman who is dangerously attractive.

SISYPHUS In Greek mythology, son of AEOLUS, brother of ATHAMAS, husband of MEROPE. Although Sisyphus is described as a cunning rogue in HOMER'S ODYSSEY, he is most famous for a terrible punishment visited on him by ZEUS: He was condemned to push an enormous boulder to the top of a hill; once at the top the boulder would come crashing down again of its own weight, and Sisyphus had to begin his task all over again. (Thus, Sisyphus has become the symbol for a fruitless task.) It is not known for what crime Sisyphus was being punished in this manner.

Another story about Sisyphus tells how he outwitted Death (THANATOS). The god Zeus had

ODYSSEUS HAD HIMSELF TIED TO THE MAST OF HIS SHIP SO THAT HE COULD RESIST THE SINGING OF THE SIRENS. (GIRAUDON/ART RESOURCE)

sent Thanatos to seize Sisyphus. Sisyphus asked Thanatos to demonstrate how the manacles that he carried worked. During the demonstration Sisyphus managed to lock up Thanatos. Zeus had to send ARES from OLYMPUS to release Death upon the earth again, for now nobody was dying.

Meanwhile Sisyphus asked his wife, Merope, to leave his body unburied when he died—for he knew that Thanatos would come for him a second time. When Sisyphus died, he went straight to HADES, god of the UNDERWORLD, and complained that his corpse hadn't received a proper burial. Hades, a just god, sent Sisyphus back to earth to arrange a decent burial. Sisyphus had a joyous reunion with his wife, broke his word to Hades to return and lived to a ripe old age.

SPARTA (or LACEDAEMON) Greek city and capital of LACONIA in the southern PELOPONNESUS. The ancient Spartans were famous for their cruelty to slaves and for their rigorous military training.

SPHINX In Greek mythology, a monster, half-woman, half-beast, the offspring of ECHIDNA and Orthos. She lived near THEBES and was supposed to set impossible riddles, one of which went something like this:

What goes on four feet, on two feet, and three,
But the more feet it goes on, the weaker it be?

The answer is a human being, who as an infant crawls on all fours, as an adult walks on two feet and in old age supports both legs with a stick. It is said that OEDIPUS solved this riddle and thus delivered the Thebans from the curse of the Sphinx.

The Greek Sphinx has nothing to do with the Egyptian Sphinx, except that both creatures were half-beast, half-human.

SOPHOCLES Along with AESCHYLUS and EUripides, one of the great tragic poets of ancient Greece. Not much is known about his life. He was born at Colonus, near ATHENS, in 496 B.C. He died at the age of 90, in 406 B.C., having written more than a hundred plays, only seven of which survive. These include *Ajax, Antigone, Oedipus* and *Electra*, all of which are concerned with Greek mythology and are important sources of our knowledge of that subject. Surviving scraps of evidence from the 5th century B.C. show that Sophocles was himself an actor and a dancer. Drama took a great stride forward when he increased the number of actors from two to three, and made the Chorus a more integral part of the play. Sophocles was active as an Athenian citizen, serving in the army, in the treasury and as a priest. He seems to have possessed serenity and lived a long life.

STYX (River of Hate) In Greek mythology, a river leading to the UNDERWORLD; personified as a NYMPH, the daughter of OCEANUS and TETHYS. The souls of the dead were ferried across the river Styx by CHARON, and upon Styx the gods swore their most solemn oaths.

In some accounts the nymph Styx was loved by the TITAN Pallas, and by him she had four children: Zelos (jealousy), NIKE (victory), Kratos (force) and Bia (violence).

As a reward for the help Styx gave to the OLYMPIAN GODS in their war with the Titans, it was decreed that vows made in her name would be eternally sacred.

SYRINX In Greek mythology, a NYMPH, daughter of the river-god Ladon. When she was being pursued by PAN, Syrinx called upon her father for help. He turned her into a reed. Pan consoled himself for her loss by fashioning the syrinx reeds into a seven-reed pipe. The syrinx, or Pan-pipes, is an instrument still played by shepherds in Greece.

T

TALUS (or TALOS) In Greek mythology, the nephew and apprentice of the great inventor, DAEDALUS. Talus, who is said to have invented the saw and also the compass, both vitally important tools, incurred the jealousy of Daedalus, who murdered him. Some stories say that Daedalus threw the boy from the top of the Acropolis and that the gods changed him into a partridge ("perdix"); Perdix was a nickname for either Talus or his mother, Polycaste, or both.

TANTALUS In Greek mythology, a king of LYDIA (in ASIA MINOR); father of PELOPS and NIOBE. One modern scholar (Michael Stapleton) calls him "a fittingly evil ancestor for the Pelopid house." Tantalus stole food from the gods and served it to mortals; he even attempted to serve up his son, Pelops, in a stew at a banquet for the gods (Pelops was rescued). Tantalus was punished for his misdeeds by the downfall of his kingdom and eternal hunger and thirst. It is said that he stands in a pool of water, but whenever he bends down to drink, the water recedes; and that over his head hang branches laden with fruit, but they are just out of reach. Hence the verb "to tantalize," which means to excite a hope and then disappoint it.

TARTARUS In Greek mythology, the lowest section of the UNDERWORLD, a sunless abyss below HADES. Here the most evil were punished. ZEUS imprisoned the TITANS here. In the *Divine Comedy* by the Italian poet Dante (1265–1321), it is called Hell. A savage-tempered, bullying person may be called a tartar, perhaps after the dreaded place of the Underworld.

TELAMON (or TELEMON) In Greek mythology, son of King Aecus of AEGINA; brother of PELEUS; father, with HESIONE, of TEUCER, the great archer.

Telamon and Peleus killed their half-brother, Phocus, after which Telamon fled the country. He lived a heroic life, taking part in the CALYDONIAN BOAR HUNT, sailing with the ARGONAUTS and accompanying HERACLES on his expedition against LAOMEDON of TROY.

TELEGONUS In some accounts in Greek mythology (but not in HOMER), the son of hero ODYSSEUS and the witch CIRCE. Circe sent her son to find Odysseus in his kingdom of ITHACA. Telegonus killed his father (the two were unknown to each other) with a poisoned spear given to him by Circe. Later he married PENELOPE, the widow of Odysseus.

TELEMACHUS In Greek mythology, son of ODYSSEUS and PENELOPE. As an infant he was placed in the path of his father's plow as a test of the father's pretended madness. When the TROJAN WAR ended Telemachus searched unsuccessfully for his father, returned to Ithaca and recognized Odysseus; together he and Odysseus slew all the would-be usurpers to the throne who had been imposing upon Penelope to choose a husband from among them. (See *Odysseus Returns to Ithaca*, under ODYSSEY, THE.)

TELEPHUS In Greek mythology, the son of HERACLES and Auge, the Tegean princess. Telephus became the king of Mysia, in ASIA MINOR, where the Greeks landed on their way to TROY (see the TROJAN WAR). Telephus was wounded by the Greek hero ACHILLES in an ensuing scuffle. He was told by an ORACLE that his wound could be cured only by the one who had inflicted it. Telephus went to the Greek camp and sought out Achilles. Since another oracle had told Achilles that only Telephus could show him the way to Troy, Achilles obligingly scraped some rust from his spear into the wound of Telephus, curing him. Telephus showed the Greeks the way to Troy, where they were victorious.

TELLUS (or TELLUS MATER) Roman goddess of fecundity. She dated back as a popular fertility deity to long before the formalized religion of the Roman state. At her festival on April 15, a pregnant cow was sacrificed to her.

TEMPE A valley in THESSALY, famous for its beautiful scenery. There are many references to the Vale of Tempe in Greek mythology. It was the scene of APOLLO's purification after the slaying of PYTHON; it was the scene of the metamorphosis of DAPHNE (from NYMPH pursued by Apollo into laurel tree); it was here that CYCNUS, son of ARES, killed unwary travelers and used their bones to build a temple to his father.

TERMINUS Roman god of boundaries and frontiers. The stones that marked the boundaries of property were consecrated to the god JUPITER, to whom yearly sacrifices were made.

TETHYS In Greek mythology, the daughter of two TITANS, URANUS and GAIA; sister-wife of OCEANUS. With him she bore the Oceanids (sea-NYMPHS). She was also the mother of STYX, and some say the mentor of the goddess HERA.

TEUCER In Greek mythology, the son of TELAMON and HESIONE; half-brother of the great AJAX. He was the best archer among the Greeks and played an important part in the TROJAN WAR, fighting alongside Ajax. Teucer founded the town of Salamis in CYPRUS.

THANATOS (Death) In Greek mythology, the personification of death (Mors in Latin). The son of Nox (Night), with no father (says HESIOD); twin brother of Hypnos (Sleep). The only mortal who managed to outwit Thanatos (at least for a while) was SISYPHUS.

THEBES A city of ancient Greece, in BOEOTIA, reputedly founded by CADMUS (see *Cadmus Builds the Citadel*, under CADMUS). Thebes was also associated with other Greek myths, such as those of OEDIPUS, the SEVEN AGAINST THEBES, the EPIGONI and others.

THEMIS In Greek mythology, a TITAN, daughter of GAIA and URANUS. Wife of Iapetus and later of ZEUS. Mother of the HORAE (Seasons), the Morae (Fates), Astrea and, some say, of PROMETHEUS. Themis presided over law and order, justice, hospitality and prophecy. One legend has it that Themis communicated with the ORACLE at DELPHI before Delphi became the favored shrine of the god APOLLO. Another says that she appeared before DEUCALION and told him to repeople the earth after the great destruction of the Deluge.

THESEUS In Greek mythology, chief hero of ATHENS, the major city of ATTICA. Son of AEGEUS, king of Athens, and Aethra, daughter of King Pittheus of Troezen. Theseus was brought up under the protection of Pittheus and Aethra until he was 16. Then he set off to Athens to claim his birthright. On his way and afterward, he had countless adventures, of which the most famous was the slaying of the MINOTAUR (see *Theseus, Ariadne and the Minotaur*, below). Upon the death of Aegeus, Theseus became king of Athens and was the hero of many a battle. At the end he retired to Skyros, an island in the Aegean, where he was murdered by Lycomedes.

Scholars believe that the character of Theseus may have been based on a real person, a hero of ancient times, similar in many ways to the demigod HERACLES. Mythologists may have adapted the character of Theseus to make him a suitable hero for their city of Athens.

Some Adventures of Theseus Theseus, the great hero of ancient ATHENS, had countless adventures. Among them were some showing that he let "the punishment fit the crime":

Periphates was a mean cripple who used a huge bronze club to kill wayfarers; Theseus, on his way to Athens, killed Periphates with the club, which he carried ever afterward as one of his weapons.

Sinis, "The Pinebender," was so strong and monstrously cruel that he bent young pine trees down to the ground, then lashed his victim (a hapless traveler) to the trees so that the victim would be killed by having his limbs torn apart. Theseus inflicted the same punishment on Sinis.

THE HERO THESEUS KILLED THE MINOTAUR WITH HIS CLUB. (THE BETTMANN ARCHIVE)

Procrustes, also called Polypemon, was the father of Sinis. He was another scourge of travelers. He would invite them into his house, where he had an iron bed. If the victim didn't fit the bed, Procrustes would either lop off the victim's overhanging parts or stretch his limbs to fit the bed. Theseus forced Procrustes to lie in his own bed, where he slew him. The word *Procrustean* has come to denote any cruel attempt to reduce men or ideas to fit one arbitrary standard.

In ELEUSIS, a city northwest of Athens, Theseus defeated the king in a wrestling match. Theseus is said to have perfected the art of wrestling. Eleusis had no king from that day on and came under the leadership of Athens.

Theseus and Aegeus   Theseus, the great hero of ATHENS, was the son of King AEGEUS, king of Athens. His mother was Princess Aethra, the daughter of King Pittheus of Troezen. Before he left Troezen Aegeus lifted a heavy rock and hid his sword and sandals beneath it. He instructed Aethra to bring his son to this rock when he became a young man and to remove the sword and sandals; if Theseus succeeded in doing this, he was to bring the items to Athens to claim his birthright from his father, the king.

Aethra brought her son, when he was 16, to the rock, which the lad lifted easily, and sent him on his way to Athens.

Theseus had many adventures on his journey (see *Some Adventures of Theseus*, above) and entered Athens as a hero. Warmly welcomed by his father (but not by MEDEA [see *Theseus and Medea*, below]), Theseus then went on to his greatest adventure, the slaying of the MINOTAUR, the dreaded bull-monster of King MINOS of CRETE. Every year Minos demanded seven men and seven maids to be sacrificed to the Minotaur, thus bringing great sorrow to the people of Athens. Theseus determined to put an end to this tragedy. In spite of his father's protests, he went aboard the fateful ship that brought the victims to Crete. Theseus promised Aegeus that if he succeeded in killing the monster, he would bring the ship back flying white sails in place of the black sails it had left with. Theseus did indeed defeat the beast, but he forgot to hoist the white sails. Aegeus, watching anxiously from the top of a cliff, saw the black sails and cast himself into the sea in despair. That sea—the Aegean—today bears his name. (See also *Theseus, Ariadne and the Minotaur*, below.)

Theseus, Ariadne and the Minotaur
Theseus was the great hero of ancient ATHENS. The slaying of the MINOTAUR was his greatest and most famous deed, in which he was helped by ARIADNE, daughter of King MINOS of CRETE. Minos demanded a yearly tribute from Athens because of the murder of his son, ANDROGEUS, by the Athenians: Each year, seven Athenian men and seven maidens were sent to Crete to feed the dreaded bull-monster, Minotaur.

Theseus determined to end the yearly tragedy suffered by the Athenians. He boarded the ship that bore the victims to Crete. When she saw him, Ariadne, daughter of King Minos, fell in love with the hero. She gave him a ball of string that would help him find his way out of the dreaded LABYRINTH where the bull lived. Theseus unwound the string as he followed the tortuous mazes that led him to the Minotaur. He slew the bull after a ferocious battle and then made his way triumphantly back to the entrance of the labyrinthine palace. When he went back to Athens, Theseus took the lovely Ariadne with him; but he abandoned her on the island of NAXOS and went on his way. Many explanations have been offered for the seemingly churlish behavior of the hero toward Ariadne (see under ARIADNE). (See also *Theseus and Aegeus*, above.)

Theseus and Medea Theseus, hero of ATHENS, was the son of AEGEUS, king of Athens. (See *Theseus and Aegeus*, above.) When he was a young man, Theseus set forth to claim his birthright from Aegeus. Aegeus had married the sorceress MEDEA, who knew at once that Theseus was the king's son. She tried to poison the lad; just in time, Theseus revealed the sacred sword that his father had left behind in Troezen. Aegeus dashed the poisoned cup from the boy's hand and embraced his son. Medea fled from Athens with her son, Medus.

Theseus and Pirithous Theseus was the greatest hero of ancient ATHENS, well known for his many exploits and especially for killing the dreaded MINOTAUR. (See *Theseus, Ariadne and the Minotaur*, above.) Theseus was also famous for having a deep and enduring friendship with PIRITHOÜS, king of the LAPITHS, a mythical people of THESSALY. The friendship originated when Pirithoüs mischievously stole some of Theseus's cattle. Theseus went in pursuit, but the two young men were so filled with admiration for each other that they forgot their quarrel and swore eternal brotherhood. The young heroes had many adventures together.

In a fight that started at the wedding feast of Pirithoüs and HIPPODAEMIA, Theseus helped his friend to drive the CENTAURS, wild creatures that were half-man, half-horse, out of Thessaly.

Pirithoüs later helped Theseus carry off HELEN. In return Theseus then descended to the UNDERWORLD to help his friend in his attempt to abduct PERSEPHONE, reluctant bride of HADES.

The two friends were caught by Hades (see under PIRITHOÜS) and had to remain in the Underworld until the hero HERACLES came to attempt their rescue. Theseus was freed, but Pirithoüs had to remain a captive for all eternity.

Theseus and the Amazons Theseus, great hero of ATHENS, accompanied the demigod HERACLES on his Ninth Labor, which was to capture the girdle of HIPPOLYTA, queen of the AMAZONS. Heracles captured the girdle (see *The Twelve Labors of Heracles*, 9. The Girdle of the Amazon, under HERACLES), whereupon Hippolyta made war upon Athens. Theseus vanquished Hippolyta and made her his wife. She bore him a son, HIPPOLYTUS.

After the death of Hippolyta, Theseus married PHAEDRA, with disastrous consequences: Phaedra fell in love with her young stepson, Hippolytus, and killed herself in despair; whereupon Theseus invoked the help of the sea-god, POSEIDON, in causing his son's death. (See under HIPPOLYTUS for a summary of the tragedy *Hippolytus*, by Greek poet EURIPIDES.)

The Death of Theseus Theseus, king and hero of ATHENS, led a life full of triumphant adventures; his most famous exploit was the killing of the dreaded MINOTAUR (see *Theseus, Ariadne and the Minotaur*, above). But his end was a sad one. He lost both his wife, PHAEDRA and his son, HIPPOLYTUS (see under *Theseus and the Amazons*, above), and finally was driven out of Athens by Menesthius, of the ancient line of Erectheus.

Theseus set sail for CRETE, now ruled by Phaedra's brother, DEUCALION, who had promised him refuge. Theseus's ship was blown off course and he took shelter on the island of Skyros, where he had a small estate. King Lycomedes of Skyros seemed to welcome the sad and aging king, but he treacherously pushed him off a cliff. Thus the great Theseus died. Later his bones were brought back to Athens and enshrined there.

THESSALY The largest division of Greece, located in the eastern mainland, encircled by mountains except for the valley (vale) of TEMPE in the northeast corner. Thessaly's mythical inhabitants were the LAPITHS, whose king, IXION, had fathered the CENTAURS, creatures that were half-man and half-horse. It was also the home of the mythical MYRMIDONS, created by ZEUS to increase Thessaly's population.

THETIS In Greek mythology, one of the nereids, sea-NYMPH daughter of NEREUS; wife of PELEUS; mother of ACHILLES. Thetis had been pursued by both ZEUS and POSEIDON, but on being told by seeress THEMIS that a son borne by Thetis would overthrow the OLYMPIAN GODS, Zeus persuaded Thetis to marry Peleus. When her son, Achilles, was born Thetis wanted to make him invulnerable. She dipped the baby into the river STYX, holding him by one heel. Since that heel didn't touch the magical water, it remained vulnerable. It was this heel that later caused Achilles's death in the TROJAN WAR.

THYESTES In Greek mythology, son of PELOPS and HIPPODAEMIA; brother of ATREUS; father of AEGISTHUS by his own daughter, Pelopia.

Thyestes and Atreus, rivals since childhood, were the victims of the curse made upon their house by the actions of their father, PELOPS. (See under PELOPS and ATREUS AND THYESTES.)

Thyestes ruled for a short time as king of MYCENAE (one of the most important cities of ancient Greece), with Aegisthus as his heir, but he was eventually driven out by AGAMEMNON and Aegisthus was deposed.

TIBERINUS In Roman mythology, the god of the river Tiber, upon which the city of Rome was founded. The river was vitally important to the fortunes of Rome; numerous festivals were held in honor of its god. Some say that Rhea Silvia, the mother of the twins ROMULUS AND REMUS, was thrown into the river and became its spouse. In VIRGIL'S AENEID, Tiberinus visits AENEAS, who is asleep on the banks of the river, and tells him in a dream that his destiny is to found a city on the banks of the river.

TIRESIUS The blind seer of THEBES, a figure who appears several times in Greek mythology.

According to some legends Tiresius was struck blind by the goddess ATHENE because he saw her bathing.

Another legend says that it was HERA who struck Tiresias blind.

Some scholars think that the figure of Tiresius as a wise man is a mythological embodiment of the person who is out of the ordinary (blind, lame or otherwise afflicted), endowed with special gifts such as those of Tiresius and HEPHAESTUS, the lame smith-god.

TIRYNS A town in the ARGOS region of the northern PELOPONNESUS. In Greek mythology it was founded by Proetus, brother of Acrisius, who built massive walls with the help of the CYCLOPES.

TITANS In Greek mythology, the first race on earth. They were the offspring of GAIA (Earth) and URANUS (Heaven or Sky). According to most sources, there were 12 of them, 6 males and 6 females. The males were Coeus, Crius, CRONUS, HYPERION, Iapetus and OCEANUS. The females were MNEMOSYNE, PHOEBE, RHEA, TETHYS, Theia and THEMIS.

The Titans were pre-Hellenic deities who held sway long before the ascendancy of the OLYMPIAN GODS. They were consigned to oblivion when the new gods, headed by ZEUS (the son of Cronus and Rhea), became the rulers of the earth. It is generally believed that the protracted war that the Titans fought with Zeus reflects the prolonged conflict between the ancient Pelasgian inhabitants of Greece and their Hellenic conquerors.

TITHONUS In Greek mythology, the son of LAOMEDON, king of TROY, and brother of PRIAM. He was loved by EOS, goddess of the dawn. She bore him a son, Memnon, one of the heroes of the TROJAN WAR. Eos begged ZEUS to make her husband immortal. Zeus granted her wish and Tithonus lived for a very long time; however, eternal youth was not given to him, and the young man became a shriveled old thing with little more than a strident voice. At last the gods took pity on him and turned him into a cicada.

TRIPTOLEMUS WAS INSTRUCTED IN THE ARTS OF AGRICULTURE BY THE GODDESS DEMETER. (NEW YORK PUBLIC LIBRARY PICTURE COLLECTION)

TRIPTOLEMUS In Greek mythology, son of CELEUS and Metaneira, brother of DEMOPHON. A favorite of the goddess DEMETER, Triptolemus received from her the secrets of corn and of agriculture. It is said that he invented the plough and the science of agriculture and was thus a pioneer of civilization. He was a central figure in the Eleusinian Mysteries. (See *Demeter and the Eleusinian Mysteries*, under DEMETER.)

TRITON In Greek mythology, a water-god; the son of POSEIDON and AMPHITRITE; father of Pallas. He was often represented as a merman, with the head and body of a man and a fishtail instead of legs.

It is said that he blew on a conch-shell trumpet to calm the waves for Poseidon. Sometimes Poseidon is depicted as being escorted by many Tritons.

Triton was a benevolent, helpful deity. During the Olympian war with the TITANS, Triton used his conch shell to terrify the giants. In

HOMER'S ODYSSEY Triton saves the ARGONAUTS from a storm and helps them find the Mediterranean Sea.

In astronomy, Triton is one of the satellites of the planet Neptune.

TROJAN WAR, THE A legendary war fought between Achaean (Greek) invaders and the defenders of TROY, a seaport at the northwestern tip of ASIA MINOR, around 1200–1300 B.C. (See TROY and *The Trojan War: Fact or Fiction?* below, for an account of recent archaeological discoveries that make it certain that such a war, or series of wars, took place.) The events of this war and the return to their homes of some of the Greek generals engendered a body of myth that was recounted over the centuries and eventually reshaped and written down by the great poet HOMER in two epics: the ILIAD (which describes the latter end of the Trojan War) and the ODYSSEY (the journeyings of one of the Greek heroes, ODYSSEUS).

The story of the 10-year struggle between the Greeks and Trojans is a complex one. The cause of the war, according to Greek mythology, was said to be this: The silver-footed sea-NYMPH, THETIS, and the king of AEGINA, PELEUS, neglected to invite ERIS (goddess of strife) to their wedding. In her anger, Eris threw an apple ("the apple of discord") into the midst of the wedding throng. The apple was inscribed, "To the Fairest."

Three goddesses immediately claimed the apple: HERA, the chief goddess and wife of ZEUS; ATHENE, goddess of war; and APHRODITE, goddess of love and beauty. When asked to make a choice between the three goddesses, Zeus wisely declined and gave the task to a young Trojan prince, PARIS, who was said to be exceedingly handsome.

The three goddesses wooed young Paris, tempting him with bribes. Paris succumbed to the offer of Aphrodite, who promised him the love of the most beautiful woman in the world in return for the apple. (See *The Judgment of Paris*, under PARIS.)

At that time, the most beautiful woman in the world was HELEN, the young queen of King MENELAUS of SPARTA. Paris went to the court of Menelaus, won Helen and carried her away to Troy.

King Menelaus immediately rallied around him all the former lovelorn suitors of Helen, who had promised to fight any who might try to steal Helen away from Greece. Menelaus chose his brother, AGAMEMNON, king of MYCENAE, as leader of the army. Agamemnon soon had a fleet of a thousand ships ready to sail for Troy. (Hence, in later literature, Helen's face was described as "the face that launched a thousand ships.") Among the first victims of the war was one of Agamemnon's own daughters, IPHIGENIA, sacrificed in order to gain fair winds to Troy.

ACHILLES was the principal hero of the Greeks who took part in the Trojan War. His contingent numbered about 50 ships and he led his own army, unlike the other Greeks who acknowledged the leadership of Agamemnon and his huge fleet. Achilles captured a number of towns on the coast near Troy. Among his prizes was the beautiful slave-girl BRISEIS. Agamemnon stole Briseis away from Achilles. Furious, Achilles withdrew from the war, causing a serious setback to the Greeks. The quarrel between Achilles and Agamemnon was one of the starting points of the events of the latter part of the Trojan War described by Homer in *The Iliad*. Later, Achilles would rejoin the war and help bring the Greeks to victory, this time under the leadership of his dear friend PATROCLUS. Patroclus was killed by the Greek hero HECTOR. Achilles then slew Hector and dragged his dead body around the ruins of Troy. (See *Achilles at War*, under ACHILLES.)

Led by the hero Hector, the Trojans were successful in many major engagements, especially when Achilles temporarily left the conflict after the quarrel with Agamemnon (see above, and *Achilles at War*, under ACHILLES). Eventually the Trojans lost the war when the Greek hero ODYSSEUS had the cunning idea of hiding troops within a huge wooden horse that was delivered as a gift within the walls of Troy. The selected troops broke out of their hiding place in the dead of night, slew the Trojans, and looted and set fire to their city. (See *The Wooden Horse of Troy*, below.)

The gods themselves took sides in the Trojan War and played an active part in the hostilities. APOLLO and the war-god ARES supported the Trojans, as did of course Aphrodite, the champion of Paris. Athene, Hera and POSEIDON backed the Greeks, and HEPHAESTUS, the smith-god, made armor for Achilles, the hero of the Greeks.

The Trojan War was the last great communal enterprise of the Greek heroes. Although it succeeded in its aim (to rescue Helen), the difficulties were great and long-drawn-out, and an air of failure and defeat seemed to hang over the enterprise. Few of the heroes returned to find their homes secure, and few dynasties survived for more than a few generations.

The Trojan War: Fact or Fiction?

The Trojan War of Greek mythology was a long-drawn-out battle between the Achaeans (Greeks) and the Trojans. The war lasted for 10 years, ending in the sack of TROY and a victory for the Greeks.

Scholars now think that the war did indeed take place, around 1200–1300 B.C. Recent archaeological finds confirm that there was a city of Troy: Extensive Bronze-Age burial grounds and many crematory urns, perhaps some of slain heroes, have been excavated; in addition, caches of food have been found buried beneath the walls of the city, very likely by people from the countryside who were taking refuge within the city walls during a lengthy siege by marauding tribes.

Difficult as it is to separate fantasy from truth, it seems certain that there were numerous trade routes common to the Greeks and the Trojans. Troy, at the northwestern tip of ASIA MINOR, controlled the seaway between the Aegean and the Black Sea, through the narrow inlet called, in ancient times, the HELLESPONT, now known as the DARDANELLES. This strait led to the Sea of Marmara, which in turn led to the Black Sea via the passageway known as the Bosporus.

Once Troy had fallen, the Greeks were able to establish colonies along the coast of Asia Minor. They dealt in gold, silver, iron, cinnabar, timber, linen, hemp, dried fish, oil and Chinese jade. So, in fact, the return of Helen to the Greeks may have symbolized the resto-

THIS ANCIENT DEPICTION OF THE TROJAN HORSE SHOWS THE WHEELS THAT MOVED IT AND THE GREEK SOLDIERS HIDING INSIDE WITH THEIR WEAPONS. (NEW YORK PUBLIC LIBRARY PICTURE COLLECTION)

ration of Greek rights to enter the Hellespont. The epic story of the ILIAD may be an assemblage of folk memories of a series of raids by the Greeks against the shores of Anatolia (Asia Minor)—and, in particular, Troy, the guardian of the Dardanelles—to ensure vital passage to the Black Sea and its valuable trade.

The Wooden Horse of Troy

The Trojan War, a 10-year battle between the Greeks and the Trojans, came to an end when the Greek hero ODYSSEUS had the idea of building a huge wooden horse, inside which would be hidden hundreds of Greek soldiers. The horse was given as a gift to the Trojans and dragged within their walls. At dark of night the Greek soldiers burst forth from their clever hiding place, fought the unprepared soldiers and citizens of TROY and destroyed the city, thus winning the war.

Many explanations of the Trojan horse have been put forth. The most likely is that it was a battering ram, a device used to knock down walls since ancient times. The massive walls of Troy, with their sloping bases, presented an almost unsolvable problem to enemy forces. It seems likely that the Greeks constructed a towering "ram" that would be capable of attacking the more vulnerable upper structure of the walls. The "legs" raised the battering ram up to the level of the superstructure. The machine would be moved up to the wall on rollers. To the soldiers, the battering machine may have looked somewhat like a gigantic horse. In the ancient world it was common for soldiers to give animal nicknames to pieces of equipment. For example, the Romans called their catapults scorpions; the very word *ram* comes from the name for a male sheep or goat, which has a solid, sturdy shape.

TROY One of the most famous cities in Western literature; the site of the 10-year-long siege and battle of Troy (see TROJAN WAR). Excavations during the 19th and 20th centuries prove that there were no fewer than nine cities built—one after and on top of the other—on the mound of Hissarlik, a strategic position overlooking the DARDANELLES, the strait that leads to the Black Sea. Troy commanded the trade routes between the Mediterranean and the Black Sea—it was in fact at the crossroads between east and west. In mythology the Trojan War was caused by the abduction of HELEN, wife of the king of SPARTA, by the Trojan prince PARIS. Many scholars think the abduction was a metaphor for the rivalry between the Greeks and Trojans over the lucrative trade route to the Black Sea.

The founder of Troy was DARDANUS, a son of ZEUS. PRIAM, king of Troy, was a descendant of Dardanus.

The city discovered by the archaeologists was in fact only about 200 yards across, more of a citadel than a city. Excavations in 1984 and 1985 have revealed many burial urns—possibly the resting places of the slain heroes of Troy and Greece. They have also revealed caches of food buried beneath the walls of the citadel, perhaps the supplies of the people from the neighboring countryside who came inside the walls of the citadel for refuge from the marauding tribes. (See *The Trojan War: Fact or Fiction?* under TROJAN WAR.)

TYPHON (or Typhoeus) A hundred-headed monster whose parents were GAIA (Earth) and TARTARUS. Although the largest monster ever born (according to Greek mythology) with coiled serpents for legs, the monster was defeated by ZEUS and thrown into HADES.

Another version of the Typhon myth was that Typhon did mighty battle with Zeus, hurling rocks and mountains against the thunderbolts of the god and eventually capturing Zeus. He cut the sinews from the hands and feet of Zeus, thus rendering him powerless. He thrust Zeus into a mountain cave, and stuffed the precious sinews into a bearskin sack, or leather bag. HERMES and PAN found Zeus and managed to steal back the sinews and restore them to Zeus's appendages.

The struggle between Typhon and Zeus continued. Typhon was weakened by delicious food given to him by the FATES. He made a final stand on Mount Haemus (Blood Mountain) in Thrace, where Zeus injured him so severely that his blood made the streams run red, giving the mountain its name. He was able to flee to Sicily, but Zeus caught up with him and finally crushed him into the earth under a volcano, Mount Etna, which still erupts from time to time with his struggles to escape.

Before he was imprisoned Typhon fathered with ECHIDNA a host of monsters, among them CERBERUS, the CHIMERA, the Lernaean HYDRA, the Nemean Lion, Orthos and the SPHINX.

The word *typhoon*, meaning a tremendous storm in the South Pacific, may have its origin in the name of the Greek monster; or it may derive from the Cantonese or Mandarin languages.

Typhon is mentioned in works by AESCHYLUS, HESIOD, HOMER, OVID and VIRGIL.

U

ULYSSES Son of LAERTES, husband of PENELOPE, father of TELEMACHUS. See ODYSSEUS.

UNDERWORLD, THE In Greek mythology, the black abyss known as HADES where the dead had their abode. In Roman mythology the Underworld was identified with DIS and ORCUS. The lord of the Greek Underworld was Hades or, sometimes, PLUTO. The consort of Hades was PERSEPHONE, who lived in the Underworld for four months of the year. (See *Demeter and Persephone,* under DEMETER.)

In Greek mythology the location of the Underworld underwent changes. In ancient times, it was supposed to be in "the Far West," the place that lay beyond the sea that encircled the earth, which at that time was thought to be flat. The Far West was thought to be barren and uninhabited. However, as geographic knowledge progressed, it became evident that other lands lay beyond the ocean, and were fruitful and peopled. And so the Underworld was now placed under the earth, a region of dark shadows and mystery, where the dead were buried.

Travelers seeking access to the Underworld had first to cross the Grove of Persephone. At the gate to Hades waited the dog CERBERUS, who had at least three heads, in some accounts as many as 50. A monstrous watchdog, Cerberus had a roaring bark to terrify all, but he could be appeased by a "sop," a piece of honeyed bread.

Bounding Hades and leading to its subterranean depths were many rivers: ACHERON (River of Sadness), Cocytus (River of Lamentation), LETHE (River of Oblivion) and STYX (River of Hate).

To cross the Styx, it was necessary to pay old CHARON, the miserly ferryman. Once in Hades the souls of the dead drank from the Lethe to obtain forgetfulness of their former lives and thoughts.

The fortunate few who had won the favor of the gods went to ELYSIUM, a special section of the Underworld, or perhaps that magical place called "the Far West." Here the shades, or spirits, of the dead lived in great happiness until eternity.

Those who were truly evil were sent to TARTARUS, the deepest, darkest, vilest section of the Underworld.

URANUS (or OURANOS) (HEAVEN) In Greek mythology, the personification of heaven and the starlit sky; called Coelus by the Romans. He was the son of GAIA (Earth). The rain from heaven made Gaia fertile; she bore the TITANS, the CYCLOPES and the HECATONCHEIRES. Uranus did not care for his offspring and banished them to the UNDERWORLD. Gaia, mourning for her children, bade her son CRONUS to wound and mutilate Uranus. This he did, with a flint sickle made by Gaia. From the spilled blood of Uranus sprang the FURIES, the Gigantes (GIANTS) and the goddess APHRODITE. Uranus, defeated and wounded, left the earth to the Titans. Before he died he prophesied that Cronus, in his turn, would be overthrown by one of his sons. His prophecy came true when Cronus was deposed by the god ZEUS.

HESIOD tells the story of Uranus.

V

VENUS Roman goddess of love and beauty, identified with the Greek goddess APHRODITE. In some accounts she was the daughter of JUPITER and DIONE, a NYMPH. Wife of VULCAN; mother of CUPID, and, by ANCHISES, of AENEAS, the hero of the epic AENEID. She was regarded by the Romans as the founder of their race.

As the goddess of beauty, Venus was portrayed by many artists. The Venus de Milo, in the Louvre, Paris, is one of the most famous statues in the world, dating to the 2nd or 1st century B.C. It was found on the island of Melos in 1820. In *Birth of Venus*, by the Italian artist Sandro Botticelli (c. 1444–1510), she is shown rising from the sea on a half scallop shell (Uffizi, Florence, Italy).

VERTUMNUS An obscure Roman god of fruits and fruit trees. In a story by OVID, Vertumnus pursued and won the fruit goddess POMONA by appearing before her in various disguises—a laborer, a harvester, a vine-grower and finally, an old woman. The Latin verb *vertere* means "to change"; the name "Vertumnus" probably refers to the various disguises of the god, as well as to the changes of the seasons that help bring about the fruiting of plants.

VESTA Roman goddess of the hearth, worshiped in every household of ancient Rome. She was identified with the Greek goddess HESTIA, one of the OLYMPIAN GODS.

Primitive Roman religion was a domestic

THIS FAMOUS PAINTING BY BOTTICELLI SHOWS VENUS (GREEK: APHRODITE) EMERGING FROM THE SEA. (ARCHIVI ALINARI/ ART RESOURCE)

VERTUMNUS, MASTER OF DISGUISE, WON POMONA BY APPEARING BEFORE HER AS AN OLD WOMAN. (NEW YORK PUBLIC LIBRARY PICTURE COLLECTION)

affair, concerned with the welfare of the family, house and farm. The focus of the home was the hearth. (The Latin word *focus* means hearth.) The caretakers of the hearth were the young females of the family (the males of the family being out in the fields, the mother and older females working at the loom or in the kitchen). (The fairy tale of *Cinderella* is a good example of the youngest daughter being the person to tend the hearth.) As families became more extended, richer and more sophisticated, the caretakers of the hearth became young women (see VESTAL VIRGINS) who were designated to guard the fires of the goddess Vesta rather than their own familiar hearths.

VESTAL VIRGINS Priestesses who guarded the temple of Roman goddess VESTA. They were guardians of the hearth who kept the sacred fires of Vesta burning. They served for 30 years. If one was found to be unchaste, she was buried alive or otherwise punished. (See ROMULUS AND REMUS.) The word *vestal* is used in the English language to describe any woman who seems virginal.

VICTORIA (Victory) Roman goddess of victory, identified with the Greek NIKE. She was the daughter of the TITAN, Pallas and the NYMPH STYX. Victoria was usually portrayed with wings, crowned with laurel and holding a branch of palm. Once the protectress of fields, she later was said to be responsible for the success of Roman battalions in war.

VIRGIL (or VERGIL) Publius Vergilius Maro. Great Roman poet (70–19 B.C.); born near present-day Mantua (now Italy, then, Cisalpine Gaul). Virgil's education took him to Cremona, Milan and Rome.

Virgil's first works were the *Eclogues*, short pastoral poems. Later he wrote the *Georgics*, more poems about country life. His final work was the AENEID, a giant epic poem that took him the last 11 years of his life to write, and remained unfinished, as far as he was concerned (nevertheless considered to be one of the great literary works of the world).

Unlike most writers (or other artists), Virgil enjoyed admiration and a great reputation during his own lifetime. *The Aeneid* became a school textbook almost as soon as it appeared. It was known and quoted by people of all classes. The *Aeneid* had great influence on worldwide thought but particularly on Roman thought, since it was a uniquely Roman myth that glorified the city and inspired all with pride and patriotic fervor. Furthermore, Virgil's fame and popularity continued into the Christian era, for the Christians saw his poetic epic as having foretold the birth of Christ and the advent of Christianity (which occurred only 40 years after the Fourth *Eclogue* was written).

Virgil's influence on Roman thought derives more from the *The Aeneid* than the *Eclogues* or the *Georgics*, for it foretells the glory of Rome, expressing the feelings of the time and the country of Virgil; the writing is still a pleasure to read today.

VIRGO (Virgin) One of the constellations; sixth sign of the Zodiac. In Greek mythology the

IN THIS DETAIL OF A GREEK VASE PAINTING, DIONYSUS LEADS HEPHAESTUS (VULCAN) TO OLYMPUS. (NEW YORK PUBLIC LIBRARY PICTURE COLLECTION)

the heavens and transformed her into the constellation Virgo.

VULCAN Ancient god of fire, worshiped by the Romans throughout their history. He was associated with volcanoes and volcanic fire. Later, he was identified with the Greek god HEPHAESTUS and therefore supposed to have workshops under Mount Etna and other volcanoes, where he was assisted by the CYCLOPES in forging thunderbolts for the god JOVE (or JUPITER). However, while the Greek Hephaestus was "the divine artificer," a great craftsman, Vulcan was only a fire-god. He was also called Mulciber (Softener or Smelter).

Vulcan's parents were Jupiter and JUNO; his wife was VENUS, with whom he fathered CUPID. In Greek mythology, Hephaestus created PANDORA out of clay; in Roman mythology, it was Vulcan who created her.

The English word *volcano* comes from Vulcan, as does the verb *to vulcanize*, which means to subject to or undergo a chemical process for treating crude rubber.

maiden ERIGONE hanged herself from a tree after finding the grave of her murdered father, Icarius of ATTICA. The gods took Erigone up to

Z

ZAGREUS In Greek mythology, the son of ZEUS and his own daughter, PERSEPHONE. In order to save his child from the TITANS, Zeus repeats his own history by hiding Zagreus on Mount IDA (2) and setting the CURETES to clashing their armor and shouting, just as they did for the infant Zeus (see *The Childhood of Zeus*, under ZEUS). However, Zagreus slips away as the Curetes sleep and in spite of brave efforts to save himself by magical transformations into various animals, Zagreus is seized and eaten by the Titans. This myth represents the annual sacrifice of a boy, which took place in ancient CRETE in honor of MINOS, the bull-king.

ZEUS (Day, Bright Sky) Roman JUPITER or JOVE. Zeus was the chief god of Greek mythology. He was the son of CRONUS and RHEA, both TITANS; brother of HADES, HESTIA, DEMETER, POSEIDON and HERA, who was also his wife.

Zeus was a sky- and weather-god, having authority over the sky, the winds, the clouds, rain, thunder and lightning. His name has a close connection with the Latin word for day, *dies.* Zeus was also the god of battle, the patron of games and agriculture and protector of the state. He was called the father of both gods and men. After defeating his father, Cronus (see *The War with the Titans*, below), Zeus reigned supreme over the gods of OLYMPUS, the home of the gods. He was the father of many children by Titanesses, goddesses, NYMPHS and mortal women. Among his offspring were APOLLO, ARES, ARTEMIS, ATHENE and DIONYSUS. (See *The Loves of Zeus*, below.) His most famous sanctuary was at DODONA.

Zeus is often depicted as wearing a crown of oak leaves (the oak tree was sacred to him), and bearing a scepter in one hand and a thunderbolt in the other. Often he wore his shield, called an AEGIS, and had an eagle at his feet.

The Childhood of Zeus
CRONUS, the TITAN father of Zeus, learned that one of his children

ZEUS, THE GREAT GOD OF THE GREEKS.
(ARCHIVI ALINARI/ART RESOURCE)

would kill him, so he swallowed his children as soon as they were born. Thus HADES, HESTIA, DEMETER, HERA and POSEIDON disappeared into his maw. But RHEA, wife of Cronus and mother of Zeus, saved her last child by wrapping a stone in swaddling clothes and presenting it to Cronus, who promptly swallowed it. The stone was called the OMPHALOS, later set up at DELPHI as the "navel of the earth." Rhea hid Zeus in a cave on Mount IDA, in CRETE. There he was nursed by the she-goat AMALTHEA and the

NYMPHS ADRASTIA and IDA. Young warriors called the CURETES clashed their weapons together to disguise the infant's cries.

Zeus Rescues His Siblings

When the young god Zeus grew to manhood he left Mount IDA (2), where he had been sheltered by NYMPHS, and went to visit the Titaness METIS. Metis was very wise indeed. She advised Zeus how to get CRONUS, the TITAN father of Zeus, to disgorge his brothers and sisters, whom Cronus had swallowed. Zeus was to disguise himself as a cupbearer and offer Cronus a drink so vile that the Titan would immediately vomit and his offspring would reappear. This Zeus did and all went according to plan: His brothers and sisters, HESTIA, DEMETER, HERA, HADES and POSEIDON were expelled alive and well from the body of their father, Cronus. The stone (which Cronus had been made to believe was Zeus wrapped in baby clothes) was also expelled and later set up at DELPHI as the OMPHALOS, or navel, of the earth.

The War with the Titans

Once Zeus had persuaded his father CRONUS, the TITAN, to release his brothers and sisters—HESTIA, DEMETER, HERA, HADES and POSEIDON (see *Zeus Rescues His Siblings*, above)—the siblings decided to go to war against Cronus and the Titans. For 10 long years Zeus fought against the Titans, who were led by the mighty ATLAS, for Cronus was now old. Finally Zeus enlisted the help of GAIA (Earth), who advised him to release the CYCLOPES and the Hundred-Handed Ones (the HECATONCHEIRES), who had been imprisoned in the UNDERWORLD. This Zeus did, and in gratitude the Cyclopes gave Zeus the thunderbolt as a weapon; to Hades they gave a helmet of invisibility; and to Poseidon a trident. With these weapons and the help of the Hundred-Handed Ones, Cronus and all the Titans were overthrown, and never troubled Hellas (Greece) again. Atlas was ordered, as punishment, to carry the sky on his shoulders for evermore.

When the war was over, the three brothers, Zeus, Poseidon and Hades, drew lots to see who should rule the universe. To Poseidon fell the rule of the seas and rivers; to Hades, the Underworld; and to Zeus all the rest of the universe, except for OLYMPUS, which was to be the realm of all the gods and goddesses.

The war between the Titans and the OLYMPIAN GODS may have been a symbolic description of the invasion of the land, now called Greece, by the migrating tribes who became the first Greeks. They brought their gods with them, among them Zeus. The ancient gods (the Titans) were displaced or absorbed by those of the conquerors.

Zeus and Hera

The wife of the god Zeus was his sister, HERA. One of the most famous myths about their coming together was that Zeus took the form of a cuckoo, who appeared before her wet and shivering. Touched by pity, Hera took the bird to her bosom to warm it. Then Zeus resumed his usual form and persuaded Hera to become his wife. They were solemnly married on Mount OLYMPUS. Although Hera remained the official consort of Zeus, the god continued to court goddesses, NYMPHS and mortal women, so that Hera lived in constant anger and jealousy. (See *The Loves of Zeus*, below.) By Hera, Zeus had two sons, ARES and HEPHAESTUS, and one daughter, HEBE. Some versions of the myth say that Hera gave birth to Hephaestus, the smith-god, without any help from Zeus. Hera and Zeus were also the parents of EILEITHYA, according to some sources.

Zeus and Metis

According to the poet HESIOD, Zeus's first wife was not HERA, but METIS, the wise one. She conceived a child by Zeus. Warned by URANUS and GAIA that the child would pose a threat to him, Zeus swallowed Metis, thus absorbing wisdom into himself. But the child was born, nevertheless. It was the great goddess ATHENE, who sprang fully grown and clad in armor from the forehead of Zeus.

The Loves of Zeus

Zeus was a wise and just ruler but, in spite of the anger and jealousy of his wife, HERA, he was inclined to have numerous love affairs. The scholarly explanation for the amorous exploits of Zeus, which may strike us as frivolous and unbefitting a great god, is that Zeus represents the new and powerful religion taking over lesser religious traditions and merging with them, which is what happened in ancient Greece as various migrating tribes overcame and sometimes absorbed the ancient inhabitants and their cults. Or perhaps, more simply, the ancient Greeks were trying to create for themselves the noble ancestry that would have come from the union of the great god Zeus with their ancestors.

To make a conquest, Zeus sometimes assumed a different shape: He became a cuckoo for Hera (see *Zeus and Hera*, above), a swan for LEDA, a bull for EUROPA and a quail for LETO.

Among the Titanesses Zeus dallied with were:

Leto, who became the mother of APOLLO and ARTEMIS

MAIA, daughter of ATLAS and Pleione, mother of HERMES

ELECTRA (2), daughter of Atlas, mother of HARMONIA (though some say that Harmonia was the daughter of ARES and APHRODITE)

Taygete, daughter of Atlas, mother of Lacedaemon

Among mortal women Zeus mated with were:

NIOBE, daughter of Phoroneus and the NYMPH Laodice, who bore ARGOS, founder of the city of that name

IO, sister of Phoroneus, who bore EPAPHUS

DANAE, daughter of Acrisius, who bore PERSEUS

SEMELE, daughter of CADMUS, who bore DIONYSUS

EUROPA, daughter of AGENOR and Telephassa

LEDA, wife of Tyndareus, who bore POLLUX and HELEN by Zeus and Castor and CLYTEMNESTRA by Tyndareus

Among others were:

THEMIS (Law), who bore the HORAE (Seasons); Eunomia (Wise Legislation); Dike (Justice); Eirene (Peace); and the FATES or Moerae (who are the daughters of Nox [Night] in some legends)

MNEMOSYNE (Memory), who gave birth to nine daughters who were the MUSES

DEMETER, who bore PERSEPHONE

Eurynome, who bore the three GRACES.

Selected Bibliography

Barber, Richard A. *A Companion to World Mythology.* New York: Delacorte Press, 1979.

Bulfinch, Thomas. *Bulfinch's Mythology.* New York: Crowell, 1970.

Brewer, Ebenezer. *Brewer's Dictionary of Phrase and Fable.* Revised by Ivor H. Evans. New York: Harper & Row, 1981.

Campbell, Joseph. *The Hero With a Thousand Faces.* New York: Pantheon Books, 1949; paperback, Bollingen Series, Princeton, N.J.: Princeton Press, 1968.

———. *The Power of Myth,* with Bill Moyers. New York: Doubleday, 1988.

Cotterell, Arthur. *A Dictionary of World Mythology.* Oxford: Oxford University Press, 1979, 1986.

Eliot, Alexander, ed. *Myths.* New York: McGraw-Hill, 1976.

Frazer, James G. *The Golden Bough.* London: Macmillan, 1912; abridged edition, 1922; paperback, 1957.

Gaster, Theodore H., ed. *The New Golden Bough: A New Abridgement of the Classic Work by Sir James Frazer.* New York: Criterion Books, 1959.

Gayley, L. M. *The Classic Myths in English Literature and Art.* Boston: Ginn & Co., 1983.

Godolphin, F. R. B., ed. *Great Classical Myths.* New York: The Modern Library, 1964.

Grant, M. *Myths of the Greeks and Romans.* Cleveland: World Publishing, 1962.

———. *Roman Myths.* New York: Scribner, 1972.

Graves, Robert. *The Greek Myths.* Mt. Kisco, N.Y.: Moyer Bell, Ltd., 1988.

———. *Greek Gods and Heroes.* New York: Dell (Laurel Leaf Library), 1965.

Guthrie, W. K. C. *The Greeks and Their Gods.* Boston: Beacon Press, 1954.

Hamilton, Edith. *Mythology.* Paperback, Boston: Little, Brown, 1942.

Harvey, Sir Paul. *Oxford Classical Dictionary.* Oxford: Oxford University Press, 1948.

Hawkes, Jacquetta. *The Dawn of the Gods.* London: Chatto & Windus, 1968.

Heyden, A. Van Der, ed. *Atlas of the Classical World.* London: Nelson, 1963.

Horizon Book of Ancient Rome, by the editors of *Horizon Magazine.* New York: American Heritage Press, 1966.

Mercatante, Anthony S., *Facts On File Encyclopedia of World Mythology and Legend.* New York: Facts On File, 1988.

New Larousse Encyclopedia of Mythology. Translated by Richard Aldington and Delano Ames. London and New York: Paul Hamlyn, 1968.

Otto, Walter. *The Homeric Gods.* New York: Pantheon Books, 1954.

Perowne, Stewart. *The Archaeology of Greece and the Aegean.* London: Hamlyn Publishing Group, 1974.

———. *Roman Mythology.* New York: Peter Bedrick Books, 1974.

Pinsent, John. *Greek Mythology.* New York: Peter Bedrick Books, 1983.

Powell, Anton. *Ancient Greece, Cultural Atlas for Young People.* New York: Facts On File, 1989.

Rose, H. J. *Handbook of Greek Mythology.* London: Methuen & Co., 1964.

Schwab, Gustav. *Gods and Heroes: Myths and Epics of Ancient Greece.* New York: Pantheon Books, 1946.

Stapleton, Michael. *The Illustrated Dictionary of Greek and Roman Mythology.* Introduction by Stewart Perowne. New York: Peter Bedrick Books, 1986.

Time-Life. *Time Frame Books: Barbarian Tides, 1500–600 B.C.* Alexandria, Va.: Time-Life Books, 1987; *A Soaring Spirit, 600–400 B.C.* Alexandria, Va.: Time-Life Books, 1987; *Empires Ascendant, 400 B.C.–A.D. 200.* Alexandria, Va.: Time-Life Books, 1987.

Warrington, John. *Everyman's Classical Dictionary.* London: J. M. Dent & Sons, 1961.

Zimmerman, J. E. *Dictionary of Classical Myth.* New York: Harper & Row, 1964.

INDEX